|| W9-BZL-617

the series on school reform

Patricia A. Wasley	Ann Lieberman	Joseph P. McDonald
Coalition of	NCREST	Annenberg Institute
Essential Schools		for School Reform

SERIES EDITORS

This series also incorporates earlier titles in the
Professional Development and Practice Series

What's Happening in MATH CLASS?

Envisioning New Practices Through Teacher Narratives

VOLUME ONE

Deborah Schifter, EDITOR

FOREWORD BY SUZANNE WILSON

International Reading Association
800 Barksdale Road
Newark, DE 19714

Teachers College
Columbia University
New York and London

This work was supported by the National Science Foundation under Grant No. TPE–9050350. Any opinions, findings, conclusions, or recommendations expressed here are those of the authors and do not necessarily reflect the views of the National Science Foundation.

Published simultaneously by Teachers College Press, 1234 Amsterdam Avenue, New York, NY 10027 and The International Reading Association, 800 Barksdale Road, Newark, DE 19714

Library of Congress Cataloging-in-Publication Data

What's happening in math class? / Deborah Schifter, editor : foreword
  by Suzanne Wilson (v. 1); foreword by Patricia Wasley (v. 2).
      p.   cm. — (Series on school reform)
  Includes bibliographical references and indexes.
  Contents: v. 1. Envisioning new practices through teacher narratives —
v. 2. Reconstructing professional identities.
    ISBN 0-8077-3482-9 (v. 1 : cloth : acid-free paper). — ISBN
0-8077-3481-0 (v. 1 : paper : acid-free paper). — ISBN
0-8077-3484-5 (v. 2 : cloth : acid-free paper). — ISBN
0-8077-3483-7 (v. 2 : paper : acid-free paper)
    1. Mathematics—Study and teaching.   I. Schifter, Deborah.
II. Series.
QA11.W465   1996
510′.71′2—dc20   95-25216

ISBN 0-8077-3481-0 (paper)
ISBN 0-8077-3482-9 (cloth)
IRA ISBN 0-87207-143-X
IRA Inventory Number 143

Printed on acid-free paper
Manufactured in the United States of America

03 02 01 00 99 98 97 96   8 7 6 5 4 3 2 1

To Alan

Contents

Foreword

I love reading about cooking. When friends come to dinner, I spend hours pouring over recipes, searching for something new. I meander through the writing of Barbara Gruzzuti Harrison, M. F. K. Fisher, Laurie Colwin, finding small tips. Reading inspires me to experiment, and fills gaps in my scattered understandings. I like my cooking library and I like exploring it.

I wish I had the same kind of library for teaching. True, I've read many education books. I know the reform rhetoric that Schifter mentions. I gobble up stories of practice by the likes of Vivian Paley. But my bookshelf for teaching doesn't compete with my bookshelf for cooking. And when I went off to teach third graders a couple of years ago, such a library would have served me well. With a bookshelf on teaching, I could have pulled down a book, read stories about teaching and learning, shopped for new ideas, read for pleasure.

It was the details I missed most, the little things that make all the difference. So I was delighted to read this volume, chock-full of insight, detail, ideas, stories. The authors remind us of what we already know—but often forget: the toothy smiles, smudgy fingers, and damp curls of children engaged in learning. And then the authors teach us things we don't yet know: That students will at first guess that m is the number that precedes n, rather than $n - 1$. That youngsters might guess that the word "ruler" derives from some old king who dictated that we should all measure in inches. That it takes weeks of slow, often pedestrian labor to develop a room full of students who think they have something to say about mathematics. As any teacher knows, these details are what makes it possible to improve one's practice, for good teachers are a tad clairvoyant: learning to "read" children's minds, predicting what will intrigue them and what will not.

One of the things that I get from reading cookbooks are the less direction-oriented aspects of producing food. Sometimes I get a sense of texture, smell, taste, or temperature. Some authors seem to sense things about food and cooking that help me develop a similar set of senses. Moreover, learning these things about cooking makes even the experience of eating richer, deeper, more complex. The teachers who write these essays offer readers the same experience: Their stories communicate the texture and taste, thrill and fear, surprise and wonder of teaching. Although novices at crafting their stories, the teacher-authors here offer us images of students and teachers, ideas and lessons, schools and classrooms brimming with teaching's intangible side: the intuition and flexibility it demands, the knowledge of pupils and subject matter that teachers need if they are to hear the wisdom between the lines of students' talk. Good teaching—like fine cooking—is part art, part science. All too often in our writing we focus more on the skill and science, less on the sensory and art. These narratives help us redress that imbalance.

Schifter and the other teacher educators who write commentary in this volume are right: these windows onto teachers' experience are necessary. We need to see—through the eyes and words of teachers—what happens in classrooms when teachers try to teach mathematics in ways unfamiliar. But this volume is more than a window onto the realities of trying to change extant practices. It's also a book about teaching that anyone might read: elementary or secondary school teachers, policy makers or parents, teacher educators or administrators, teachers of mathematics or teachers of language. Teachers might come away with an idea to try; cognitive psychologists with a new inkling about children's minds; teacher educators with an insight about the contexts of teacher learning. And in savoring it, we'd all come away with a deeper appreciation of teaching.

Suzanne M. Wilson
East Lansing, Michigan
April 1995

Acknowledgments

When I received word four years ago that the National Science Foundation would fund the Mathematics Process Writing Project (MPWP), the project that produced this book, my first reaction was elation; my second, panic. After all, I had been teaching mathematics, or mathematics education, for 17 years. Could I suddenly become a writing teacher?

I turned to Rebecca Faery, the then new director of the writing program at Mount Holyoke College, for advice. "Of course you can teach writing," she reassured me. "After all, the principles of learning that guide the teaching of writing are the same as those for teaching mathematics." And she was—to some extent—right.

But I relied on other resources as well. Rebecca had organized a faculty writing group that met weekly to discuss members' work-in-progress. The feedback I received on a just-begun writing project of my own was to contribute significantly to its product. But the opportunity afforded me by that group also required that I think about such questions as: Which of my fellow participants' comments are helpful and which are confusing or irrelevant? Where was I being defensive and what allowed me to hear criticism? What did my own emotions—pride, satisfaction, anger, frustration, annoyance—indicate? I took this experience with me into the MPWP and it helped guide me as I responded to project participants.

I also frequently called upon what I had learned from Lesléa Newman and Michael Thelwell, teachers with whom I had studied fiction writing. For although the MPWP teachers were not writing short stories, they needed to develop the feel for the telling detail, the sensitivity to nuances of speech and gesture, that give this genre its truth-telling power.

However, the crucial learning came from building this project together with its participants. The first wave—Kathleen Bridgewater, Virginia Brown, Anne Hendry, Rita Horn, Nina Koch, Nancy Lawrence, Jill Lester, Barbara Anne Miller, Valerie Penniman, Margaret Riddle, Rosemary Rigoletti, Janice Szymaszek, Lisa Yaffee, Joyce Zippe—were willing to help me figure out which classroom structures worked, what assignments were useful, and what pace was reasonable to set. At the start I had only vague notions of what their papers could be; it was these teachers, pursuing their own visions, who showed me what was possible.

Thus, by the time I met with the next two groups, we had a base to work from. Their critiques of their predecessors' written work helped us come up with alternative topics and formats. And although I had learned much from that first wave about how to teach writing, their successors continued to give me valuable feedback. Many thanks to Christine Anderson, Marie Appleby, Kathy Baker, Virginia Bastable, Maria Buendia, Elizabeth Clark, Mary Flynn, Allen Gagnon, Catherine Ginsberg, Humilia Gougeon, Perrie Graveline, Vicky Gruneiro, Robin Gurdak-Foley, Virginia Hawley, Caryl Isenberg, Peter Kostek, Doris LeBlanc, Donald Lennon, Jill Lester, Michael Lipinski, Michelle Mather, Joanne Moynahan, Donna Natowich, Deborah O'Brien, Anne Marie O'Reilly, Jessica Redman, Sherry Sajdak, Donna Scanlon, Jan Schott, Karen Schweitzer, Alissa Sheinbach, Mary Signet, Geri Smith, Susan Smith, and Nora Toney.

I regret the space limitations that prevent inclusion of all the teachers' papers in this book and its companion volume, *What's Happening in Math Class?*, *Volume 2: Reconstructing Professional Identities*. Together, the two contain the words of fewer than half the project's participants, but all are represented in spirit—all 48 contributed to the discussions about teaching, learning, mathematics, and writing that formed the backdrop of this work; all offered thoughtful responses to their colleagues' writings; and each helped in the creation of a space safe enough to allow risk taking and encouraging enough to support serious, time-consuming effort.

Once the papers were completed, the feedback I received from pre- and in-service education students at other institutions helped me to see how these writings could be used in a variety of settings. Many thanks to Cathy Fosnot, Lynn Hart, Ron Narode, and their students.

Deborah Ball, Virginia Bastable, Lynn Goldsmith, and Marty Simon helped me think through the organization and presentation of this body of work. The essays written by Raffaella Borasi, Dan Chazan, Joan Ferrini-Mundy, Marty Simon, and Gini Stimpson add a significant dimension.

Thanks to Sarah Biondello, Brian Ellerbeck, and Karl Nyberg, editors at Teachers College Press.

And more than thanks to Alan Schiffmann, who has applied his heart and intelligence to the development of ideas presented in this book, as well as to the sustenance of its editor.

Constructing Meaning for the Rhetoric of Mathematics Education Reform

Deborah Schifter

> When I started teaching over twenty years ago, it was so simple. I took the book and went section by section to explain the concept(s) and skills needed to learn the material in that section. I prepared thoroughly and always reviewed the material before attempting to introduce it. I answered questions both on the material and on my presentation. I had strategies and alternative approaches ready to provide clarification if necessary. I thought if I presented a concept clearly and the students listened, then they should "get it." "Telling it right" was enough. I provided students with homework and testing situations to practice the skills they learned. Clearly, then, if they were not successful it must be because they were not doing their part or were just not cut out of the right stuff. In general, it seemed that most of my students were doing fine. I was, I felt, an effective teacher. My successes far outweighed my failures. (Gagnon, 1993, p. 1)

In this passage—likely to evoke a flood of memories in the reader—high school mathematics department chair, Allen Gagnon, looks back over a practice of 20 years, a practice for which he was regarded, and regarded himself, as a good, successful teacher. All of us have been students in such classes; indeed, many of us have taught such lessons. The images are familiar: This is what most conscientious mathematics teachers throughout the country still do, and what students, parents, school administrators, and policy makers expect of them.

Now, however, out of a convergence between changing social needs and two decades of research in cognitive psychology, a new practice of mathematics instruction is being proposed, one that does not match these familiar images. "Teaching for understanding," "facilitating the construction of mathematical concepts," "student-centered learning"—phrases like these dominate discussion at conferences and workshops, and constantly recur in policy statements and journal articles. Arguing that flawless memorization and computational proficiency are no longer enough, the new consensus urges instead that students engage in mathematical exploration—posing questions, formulating

1

conjectures, debating the validity of various solutions; and it reconceives the mathematics classroom, traditionally regarded as simply a gathering of individual learners brought together for reasons of economy, but now thought of as a "community of inquiry" (National Council of Teachers of Mathematics, 1989, 1991, 1995; National Research Council, 1989, 1990).

How are teachers, school administrators, or parents to attach meaning to the new rhetoric of mathematics education reform when their only experiences of learning or teaching mathematics have resembled those described by Gagnon? And how are those of us who think we *do* understand the meaning of these abstractions to know if we are attaching the *same* sense to them?

In fact, although codified in the *NCTM Standards* and embraced by influential segments of the education policy community, inventing the practice that will give substance to the vision animating the reform effort has only just begun, and it follows from the very nature of that vision that classroom teachers must be the primary agents of the process (Cohen & Ball, 1990).

The teachers' narratives included in this book offer content for the rhetoric of mathematics education reform—in effect, giving voice to the new pedagogy. As the authors worked to transform their practice along the lines mandated by the *Standards*, they were constructing possible meanings for its principles: Scenes drawn from the classroom present us with specific and detailed interpretations of such rhetorical motifs as "facilitating student construction of their own mathematical understandings," "students becoming powerful mathematical thinkers," "classrooms as communities of inquiry," and "teaching mathematics to *all* students."

With so much still to be learned about how the reform agenda translates into a day-to-day mathematics instruction, these efforts cannot be considered definitive. On the other hand, contributors to this volume, as well as its editor, agree that any serious interpretation must evidence deep and persistent rethinking of the mathematics students should be expected to learn, what learning it means, and how classrooms can be organized to support that learning. What is being claimed, then, for the teaching described in these chapters is not that it is exemplary, to be imitated by others (although some readers might find activities, instructional strategies, or classroom routines they would like to try), but rather that these narratives deserve attention because they provide rich and thoughtful images that can help us determine whether those of us who urge, say, that "teachers should be facilitating student construction of their own mathematical understandings" in fact share similar instructional goals: "You mean the sort of thing that happens in so-and-so's class when . . . ?" Thus, in telling us stories from their own experience, the narrators lend grounding for much needed discussion of possible meanings—enacted meanings—of such phrases. To help initiate just this kind of discussion, teacher educators have been invited to weigh these stories against their own understandings of the rhetoric of reform.

TEACHERS GIVE VOICE TO THE NEW PEDAGOGY

With increased authority—and responsibility—for shaping mathematics instruction in their classrooms, teachers also will need to invent new forms of collegiality, new opportunities for collective reflection. In some schools, and in some in-service programs, teachers meet together regularly to solve pedagogical problems and consider issues that arise as they work to transform their teaching. In general, however, what teachers are learning in their own classrooms is not being communicated to their colleagues or to others with an interest in mathematics education. The success of the movement for reform cannot rest on individual teachers constructing the new practice classroom by classroom, independently of one another and without engaging in many-sided exchanges about their efforts. And teacher educators, curriculum developers, and researchers must both encourage and attend to such exchanges if *they* hope to play a consequential role in the reform process. In the end, it is the teachers who must show one another, as well as the rest of us, what the new mathematics instruction can be like.

But once the urgency of the need for teacher dialogue has been understood, the absence of teacher voices from the ongoing national conversation about mathematics education reform becomes deafening (Cochran-Smith & Lytle, 1990; Duckworth, 1986; Lytle & Cochran-Smith, 1990; Miller, 1990). This silence has provoked some teacher educators, myself included, to wonder: What are the forms and the forums through which teachers might share what they are learning as they begin to transform their practice along the lines mandated by the *Standards*?

In recent years, the conviction has been growing that cases or stories may be more helpful than theoretical expositions to people who need to learn to think in new ways about complex, context-dependent domains like teaching (Barnett, 1991; Carter, 1993; Shulman, 1992; Shulman, 1986; Witherell & Noddings, 1991). Only through telling stories about their classrooms can teachers convey the richness, the interconnectedness and subtlety of what they have come to understand—about their students, schools, and communities; about subject matter; about both established classroom structures and experimental practices—as they face the challenge of constructing new ways of teaching/being teachers. The current mathematics education literature provides examples upon which such teacher narratives might be modeled: case studies of classroom teachers written by researchers (e.g., Fennema, Carpenter, Franke, & Carey, 1993; Schifter & Fosnot, 1993; Wilcox, Lanier, Schram, & Lappan, 1992); case studies conducted by university faculty who also teach mathematics kindergarten through twelfth grade and make their own teaching the object of their research (Ball, 1993a, 1993b; Borasi, 1992; Lampert, 1988, 1989); and cases written by full-time classroom teachers (Barnett, Goldenstein, & Jackson, 1994; Countryman, 1992). Studies like these provide rich accounts of classroom process, illustrating the kinds of dilemmas that arise in daily instruction and explicating how teachers experience, think about, and resolve them.

This book and its companion volume, *What's Happening in Math Class?, Volume 2: Reconstructing Professional Identities* (Schifter, 1996), are products of an experimental project designed to support teachers willing to write such narratives of classroom process and professional transformation.

AN EXPERIMENTAL PROJECT

The Mathematics Process Writing Project (MPWP) was conducted by SummerMath for Teachers, a K–12 in-service mathematics program based at Mount Holyoke College in South Hadley, Massachusetts. Since 1983, SummerMath for Teachers has offered summer institutes and academic-year courses based on constructivist perspectives on learning (Schifter, 1993; Schifter & Fosnot, 1993; Simon & Schifter, 1991).

Initially, the goal of MPWP was to produce detailed, reflective, first-person narratives exploring classroom process and instructional goals and decision making. The idea for the project came from the recognition that although a significant number of SummerMath for Teachers participants—having engaged in summer institutes, semester-long mathematics courses, and/or a year-round classroom supervision program—had made considerable progress in transforming their teaching, many others were unable to move forward. The reasons were varied, but the need for curricular materials was cited frequently.

In responding to these teachers' needs, the quandary of the staff was that there were so few good published materials available and traditional formats were of little use. For example, a powerful lesson often is launched by a single question. Yet, that same question, baldly stated and lacking context—as is usually the case with traditional materials—may yield no more than a mechanical exercise in computation. Clearly, the ability to strategically position such questions in the flow of a lesson would be of far greater value.

Thus, MPWP was originally designed to address this issue, taking advantage of the knowledge and experience of teachers who had been working to enact the new mathematics pedagogy. But as they began to write, it became clear that many participants would choose to explore how their professional identities were challenged in the process of constructing this new practice—adding a second emphasis to the work of the project.

Each year for 3 years (1990–1993), 14 to 19 teachers (a total of 44 women and 4 men) who previously had attended at least one SummerMath for Teachers offering were invited to become teacher-writers in a one-semester course that met weekly for 3 hours and additionally for two full-day workshops. Some participants had been working with SummerMath for Teachers for as long as 7 years; others had entered the program the previous summer and were just beginning to work through what it means to enact a practice based on a constructivist view of learning. (A fuller description of MPWP is found in Schifter, 1994, 1996.)

THIS BOOK

Of the 49 narratives produced by project participants, 13 are included here. Another nine, devoted to issues of changing professional identity, appear in a companion volume (Schifter, 1996), and others have been or will be published elsewhere, for example, Lester (1996) and Smith (1993).

The papers in this book are quite varied. Some explore particular grade-specific mathematical topics—third graders investigating multiplicative commutativity, sixth graders using Logo to discover properties of triangles, high school students constructing meaning for the concept of variable. In contrast to traditional presentations, these papers contextualize such activities in the life-process of particular classrooms. The reader learns about the teacher's goals for the lesson, about what was happening before a particular problem was posed, and what happened afterward; about the questions students asked, the ideas they suggested, and how they interacted with one another and with the teacher; about what students learned, what the teacher learned, and more.

Other papers address issues that classroom teachers are likely to face as they engage the new mathematics pedagogy: How does one teach students to listen to one another, work collaboratively, and participate in mathematical inquiry? How does one reach all students? What role can computer technology play in students' construction of mathematical concepts?

Through the papers, we come to know individual students, their strengths and weaknesses, their understandings and confusions. We also come to see how students of diverse abilities can be challenged and supported as they construct mathematical concepts.

The papers span grades 1 through 12. Some of the classes described have been grouped by ability; others are heterogeneous. All of the authors teach in public schools.

The papers reflect the demographics of western Massachusetts. Mount Holyoke College, the sponsor of the project, is located in South Hadley, a college town with a sizable working-class population. Close by are Amherst and Northampton, also homes to well-known colleges. Just south of South Hadley is Holyoke, a small city with many of the problems endemic to this country's depressed urban centers. Until mid-century, Holyoke was a thriving mill town, but it has since suffered continuing economic decline. The school population is about 70% Hispanic, mainly immigrants from Puerto Rico, and 30% Anglo. The surrounding hills are dotted with small towns, each containing only one or two elementary schools, often with just a single class per grade level.

Characteristic of the papers is their specificity. Most include detailed descriptions of classroom events, including dialogue. Teachers used various strategies to capture dialogue—some tape recorded their mathematics lessons; others took notes during class, transcribing them later; still others reconstructed discussions after the school day ended. Most writers tried to provide depictions as true to the events as possible; a few chose to create composite characters or classes in order to protect the anonymity of their students. All student names are pseudonyms.

The authors vividly narrate students' words and gestures, bringing readers into their classrooms to "see" and "hear" for themselves. But unlike videotape, this medium presents scenes from the teachers' perspective, complete with their thoughts, doubts, frustrations, and second thoughts. Thus, their audience comes to share the dilemmas they face, the decisions they make, and the satisfactions they experience.

In order to move the discussion forward another step, I have solicited essays from five teacher educators, each of whom was asked to read several narratives and comment on a theme of my choosing that the narratives exemplify in common. As the terms *teacher* and *teacher educator* are used here, they distinguish the kinds of contributions that make up this book. "Teachers" write about issues raised and addressed by their own instruction. "Teacher educators" write expository pieces in which they reflect—and invite the reader to reflect—on more general principles, issues, or concerns touched upon or illustrated by teachers' work. Thought of as categories that define the authors' professional status, the boundaries are blurred. Several of the "teachers" also work as teacher educators; and some "teacher educators" teach school mathematics.

Specifically, then, the book is organized by theme—each chapter contains two to four teacher narratives followed by an essay written by a teacher educator. The five chapters that comprise this volume address such issues of practice as implications for instruction of constructivist perspectives on learning; concerns about the way mathematics is engaged in the classroom; strategies for introducing students with traditional expectations for instruction to a new culture of mathematics learning; the difficulties and rewards of reaching all students; and the uses and limitations of computer technology as a support for mathematical inquiry.

A companion volume, *What's Happening in Math Class?, Volume 2: Reconstructing Professional Identities* (Schifter, 1996), organized in similar fashion, explores some of the challenges posed by the reforms for the multiple identities teachers enact professionally: as mathematical thinkers, acquiring the requisite understandings of disciplinary content and modes of thought; as managers of classroom process, redefining and resituating responsibilities for student learning; as monitors of student progress, learning to listen for the sense in students' mathematical constructions; as colleagues, creating contexts for addressing together issues arising out of their instruction; and, finally, as members of the wider mathematics education community, entering the national conversation about the process and goals of the reforms.

A note on chapter titles—while not knowingly drawn from any particular text, I treat them as if quoted. With the exception of the title of Chapter 5, each one announces a widely accepted principle of the reform agenda. New paradigms are as inseparable from their rhetorical as from their conceptual innovations.

REFERENCES

Ball, D. L. (1993a). With an eye on the mathematical horizon: Dilemmas of teaching elementary school mathematics. *Elementary School Journal, 93*(4), 373–397.

Ball, D. L. (1993b). Halves, pieces, and twoths: Constructing representational contexts in teaching fractions. In T. P. Carpenter, E. Fennema, & T. Romberg (Eds.), *Rational numbers: An integration of research* (pp. 157–196). Hillsdale, NJ: Lawrence Erlbaum.

Barnett, C. (1991). Building a case-based curriculum to enhance the pedagogical content knowledge of mathematics teachers. *Journal of Teacher Education, 42*(4), 263–272.

Barnett, C., Goldenstein, D., & Jackson, B. (1994). *Mathematics teaching cases: Fractions, decimals, ratios, & percents*. Portsmouth, NH: Heinemann.

Borasi, R. (1992). *Learning mathematics through inquiry*. Portsmouth, NH: Heinemann.

Carter, K. (1993). The place of story in the study of teaching and teacher education. *Educational Researcher, 22*(1), 5–12, 18.

Cochran-Smith, M., & Lytle, S. L. (1990). Research on teaching and teacher research: The issues that divide. *Educational Researcher, 12*(2), 2–11.

Cohen, D. K., & Ball, D. L. (1990). Policy and practice: An overview. In D. K. Cohen, P. L. Peterson, S. Wilson, D. L. Ball, R. Putnam, R. Prawat, R. Heaton, J. Remillard, & N. Wiemers (Eds.), *Effects of state-level reform of elementary school mathematics curriculum on classroom practice* (Research Report 90-14). East Lansing: National Center for Research on Teacher Education and Center for the Learning and Teaching of Elementary Subjects, Michigan State University, College of Education.

Countryman, J. (1992). *Writing to learn mathematics: Strategies that work, K–12*. Portsmouth, NH: Heinemann.

Duckworth, E. (1986). Teaching as research. *Harvard Educational Review, 56*(4), 481–495.

Fennema, L., Carpenter, T. P., Franke, M. L., & Carey, D. A. (1993). Using children's mathematical knowledge in instruction. *American Educational Research Journal, 30*(3), 555–583.

Gagnon, A. (1993). Struggling. Unpublished manuscript.

Lampert, M. (1988). The teacher's role in reinventing the meaning of mathematics knowing in the classroom. In M. J. Behr, C. B. Lacampagne, & M. M. Wheeler

(Eds.), *Proceedings of the tenth annual meeting of the North American Chapter of the International Group for the Psychology of Mathematics Education* (pp. 433–480). DeKalb: Northern Illinois University.

Lampert, M. (1989, March). Arithmetic as problem solving. *Arithmetic Teacher*, pp. 34–36.

Lester, J. (1996). Is the algorithm all there is? In C. T. Fosnot (Ed.), *Constructivism: Theory, perspectives, and practice.* New York: Teachers College Press.

Lytle, S. L., & Cochran-Smith, M. (1990). Learning from teacher research: A working typology. *Teachers College Record, 92*, 83–103.

Miller, J. (1990). *Creating spaces and finding voices: Teachers collaborating for empowerment.* Albany: State University of New York Press.

National Council of Teachers of Mathematics. (1989). *Curriculum and evaluation standards for school mathematics.* Reston, VA: Author.

National Council of Teachers of Mathematics. (1991). *Professional standards for teaching mathematics.* Reston, VA: Author.

National Council of Teachers of Mathematics. (1995). *Assessment standards for school mathematics.* Reston, VA: Author.

National Research Council. (1989). *Everybody counts: A report to the nation on the future of mathematics education.* Washington, DC: National Academy Press.

National Research Council. (1990). *Reshaping school mathematics: A framework for curriculum.* Washington, DC: National Academy Press.

Schifter, D. (1993). Mathematics process as mathematics content: A course for teachers. *Journal of Mathematical Behavior, 12*(3), 271–283.

Schifter, D. (1994). Voicing the new pedagogy: Teachers write about teaching and learning mathematics. *Center for the Development of Teaching Paper Series.* Newton, MA: Education Development Center.

Schifter, D. (Ed.). (1996). *What's happening in math class?, Volume 2: Reconstructing professional identities.* New York: Teachers College Press.

Schifter, D., & Fosnot, C. T. (1993). *Reconstructing mathematics education: Stories of teachers meeting the challenge of reform.* New York: Teachers College Press.

Shulman, J. (Ed.). (1992). *Case methods in teacher education.* New York: Teachers College Press.

Shulman, L. (1986). Those who understand: Knowledge growth in teaching. *Educational Researcher, 15*(2), 4–14.

Simon, M. A., & Schifter, D. (1991). Towards a constructivist perspective: An intervention study of mathematics teacher development. *Educational Studies in Mathematics, 22*(5), 309–331.

Smith, G. (1993). What do I teach next? *The Constructivist: Newsletter of the Association for Constructivist Teaching, 8*(1), 1–8.

Wilcox, S., Lanier, P., Schram, P., & Lappan, G. (1992). Influencing beginning teachers' practice in mathematics education: Confronting constraints of knowledge, beliefs, and context (Research Report 92-1). East Lansing: Michigan State University, National Center for Research on Teacher Learning.

Witherell, C., & Noddings, N. (1991). *Stories lives tell: Narrative and dialogue in education.* New York: Teachers College Press.

CHAPTER 1

"Facilitating Students' Construction of Their Own Mathematical Understandings"

The rhetoric of the current mathematics education reform effort—see, for example, the title of the editor's Introduction to this volume—is founded on the metaphor of construction, as in "facilitating students' construction of their own mathematical understandings." This cumbersome phrase is at once the assertion of a view of learning—"understandings" being the result of students "putting things together" for themselves—and, when addressed to teachers, an exhortation to reorient their practice. The four narratives that follow were chosen precisely in order to help us think about what "facilitating students' construction of their own mathematical understandings" might mean, not as an exercise in theoretical definition, but as enacted interpretation in the classroom.

The authors of these narratives teach in rural communities that are racially homogeneous but economically diverse. The schools Anne Hendry, Virginia Brown, and Joanne Moynahan work in contain just one class per grade. Three randomly grouped classes constitute second grade in Elizabeth Clark's school.

Martin Simon's concluding essay draws upon these narratives to illustrate his understanding of what constitutes significant mathematical sense-making and how teachers can help their students to achieve it.

$$+ \quad - \quad \times \quad \div$$

MATH IN THE SOCIAL STUDIES CURRICULUM

Anne M. Hendry

During the month of November, our focus in the first grade was to study the Pilgrims and their arrival in America. For several weeks we discussed this historical event. We constructed a large cutaway of the Mayflower. The children made costumes and prepared for a feast that we would share with the other primary grades. As part of our math experience at this time, we would also explore a unit on measurement.

Before school, moving desks and chairs and using masking tape, I outlined the shape of a boat 16 by 6 feet, on the classroom floor. This was to represent the Mayflower. I also prepared a scroll for a child to read to the class and then to post on the bulletin board with our initial problem involving measurement on it. I selected one child, instructing him that at math time he would be the messenger from the King bringing an "Edict" to the Pilgrims.

When math time arrived, I asked the children to put on their costumes and sit on the floor of the "ship," saying that we were leaving England to sail to America. However, they soon learned that the journey we were about to take did not cross the ocean as the Pilgrims did: We were beginning several days' journey into the concept of measurement.

With a knock on the door, Zeb, the child who was appointed to be the King's messenger, read the "Edict," which said, "This ship cannot sail until you tell me how big it is." The children were puzzled.

"Well, what should we do? Who has an idea?" I asked. Thus our discussion on measurement began . . . or I thought it would begin. But there was a period of silence—a long period of silence.

What do young children know about measurement? Is there anything already present in their life experiences to which they could relate this problem? I watched as they looked from one to another, and I could see that they had no idea where to begin. Surely, I thought, there must be something they could use as a point of reference to expand on. Someone always has an idea. But the silence was long as the children looked again from one to another, to Zeb, and to me.

I am never sure what knowledge my students already possess concerning topics I plan to teach. Sometimes, I will begin a new unit of study by asking, "What can you tell me about . . . ?" or "What do you already know about . . . ?" Frequently, from the bits and pieces of knowledge that children already have, we are able to construct an incredible amount of valuable information to use throughout the lesson.

However, as to whether there was anything already present in their life experiences to which they could relate this problem, I was not sure. I did not know what, if anything, they knew about measurement. My goal was to have them understand a need for a standard form of measurement, to understand the concepts of an inch and a foot, and to become familiar with the ruler and how to use it.

Because they were so fascinated with the cutaway of the Mayflower on the bulletin board, I decided that the ship would be an appealing, tangible vehicle for them to measure. It would be something I could easily outline on the classroom floor and I could leave it there for them to explore in their free time. I felt the ship would hold their interest, encourage discussion, and allow for several days of exploration. Rather than measuring a variety of small items, this would be more memorable and a problem they would have a vested interest in solving.

I was having second thoughts about the enormity of the problem for a first grader when, shyly, Ann raised her hand. "I think it's 3 feet long," she said. "Why?" I asked. "Because the letter from the King said so," she responded. "I don't understand," I said. "Can you tell me why you think the ship is 3 feet?" "Because the King's letter said so. See!" Ann said. "I'll show you."

When the letter was held up, the light, filtering through the paper, made the capital "E" I had written for the word "Edict" look like a 3 to some of the children. I clarified this point with her and the others who agreed that they also had seen a 3 on the King's paper. The King, they thought, already knew the answer.

I felt we were back to square one again with more silence, until Tom raised his hand and said, "Mrs. Hendry, I know it can't be 3 feet because the nurse just measured me last week and said that I was 4 feet, and this boat is much bigger than me!"

From Tom's initial observation, our discussion on measurement was basically off the ground. Hands immediately went up. The children now realized that they knew a little about measurement, especially in relationship to their own size and how tall they were.

"Let's see how many times Tom can fit in the boat," someone suggested. Tom got down and up several times along the length of the boat: The children decided that the boat was four "Tom's" long.

"How can we tell that to the King, since he does not know Tom?" I asked. "Send Tom to the King," was the easy solution of some, while others protested that they wanted Tom to stay on the boat for the trip. I was really hoping that they would relate to the information Tom had already given us about his size. I thought someone might add 4 feet, four times, presenting us with a quick solution to the problem. But this was not the route they decided to take.

Mark raised his hand and suggested that we could measure the boat with our hands like they do with horses. His neighbor had a horse that was 15 hands. "Then we could tell the King how many 'hands' long the boat was." The children agreed that this might be a better idea.

"All right," I said. "Since it was Mark's idea, he can measure the length of the boat with his hands." Mark was also the biggest child in the class.

At first, Mark randomly placed his hands on the tape from one end to the other, but when he double checked, he came out with a different answer. The children were puzzled for a while as to why this happened. It took several more tries and much discussion before they came to an important conclusion. The children decided that it was necessary for Mark to make sure that he began exactly at the beginning of the boat and did not leave any gaps in between his palms and his fingers as he placed them on the tape. Measuring this way, he discovered the boat was 36 hands long.

Great! We decided to tell the King this, but just to be sure, I suggested we have Sue, the smallest child in the class, measure the other side. She did and related to the class that her side was 44 hands long. Now there was confusion.

"Why are they different?" I asked. "Can we use hands to measure?" "No," the children decided. This would not work either, since everyone's hands were not the same size.

Al suggested using feet. We tried this, but, once again, when someone else double checked with her feet, we found two different measurements. The children at this time began to digress a little to compare each other's hands and feet to discover whose were the biggest and smallest.

Finally, our original discussion continued, while the children explored various concepts and ideas. Joan sat holding a ruler, but, for some reason, did not suggest using it. Perhaps, I thought, it might be that her experience with a ruler was limited, and she might not have been quite sure how to use it.

Our dilemma continued into the next day when the children assembled again to discuss the problem with some new insights. One child suggested that since Zeb knew the King, and everyone knew Zeb, we should use his foot. "Measure it out on a piece of paper and measure everything in 'Zeb's' foot." Using this form of measurement, the children related to the King that the boat was 24 "Zeb's foot" long and 9 "Zeb's foot" wide.

Curiosity began to get the best of the children and they continued to explore this form of measurement by deciding to measure each other, our classroom, their desks, and the rug using "Zeb's foot." I let them investigate this idea for the remainder of the math period.

On the third day of our exploration, I asked the children why they thought it was important to develop a standard form of measurement (or in words understandable to a first grader, a measurement that would always be the same size) such as using only "Zeb's foot" to measure everything. Through the discussions over the past several days, the children were able to internalize and verbalize the need or importance for everyone to measure using the same instrument. They saw the confusion of using different hands, bodies, or feet because of the inconsistency of size.

I held up the ruler that Joan had been holding a few days before and asked if anyone knew what it was or how to use it. Mark said it was called a ruler and that his dad used one to measure things.

Tom asked if it was called a ruler because a king was sometimes called a ruler and maybe a long time ago a king made it using his foot like we did with Zeb's. I thought this was an interesting analogy and intuitive on Tom's part.

Donna said that the numbers were for inches, and John wanted to know what the word inch meant. Their questions about the ruler and inches led us to the encyclopedia to learn more about the history of measurement. Borrowing a copy of the *World Book Encyclopedia* from the sixth-grade classroom, I quickly read the history of measurement and presented to the class a watered-down version, highlighting the important pieces of information pertinent to their questions.

For some reason, they became fascinated with the idea that inches came from the word "uncia" and that an "uncia" was comparable to the width of their thumb. They shortened the word to "uncas" and explored this idea for a while. Using their thumbs, they began to measure small things in "uncas." Eventually, they decided to record their own height in "Zeb's foot" and "uncas" because it was, they felt, something they had invented.

After exploring "Zeb's foot" and "uncas," we turned our thinking back to the ruler. The children had really constructed and experienced the necessity for a concrete form of measurement that was standard for everyone. They applied what they learned with "Zeb's foot" to using the ruler. Once again, they began to measure the boat, the classroom, and themselves, only this time using a ruler.

When we researched the real dimensions of the original Mayflower, we learned that it was 90 feet long but could not find records of its width. I suggested 25 feet only to help us in constructing it. We decided that on the last day of our exploration of measurement, we would make the outline of the ship out in the schoolyard using baling twine and sticks.

As we finished our project and we looked at how big the Mayflower probably was, I thought back to the long silence when the original question had been posed. I remembered my fears that we would go nowhere with this problem, and then I thought about how far we had come. Except to ask probing questions when the children were stymied and to act as resident researcher with the encyclopedia, my participation had been minimal. Their active participation, cooperation, and enthusiasm had carried them into an exploration of measurement far more involved than I had anticipated.

As I contemplated these first graders' enthusiasm for measuring a ship, a problem that at one point I thought was proving to be too overwhelming, I could see the importance of having them have a vested interest in its solution. They were not intimidated by its bigness, but challenged by it. I was proud of them!

$$+ \quad - \quad \times \quad \div$$

PATTERNS: PREDICTION AND PROBABILITY

Elizabeth Clark

For the past few weeks, my second-grade students have been working with dice. The idea was to make observations about what happened when two dice were rolled repeatedly. Each group of children wrote predictions on a small Post-it and then had a chance to test them in a small group by rolling dice and recording outcomes for 30 minutes. The children noticed that "seven kept winning" and they were surprised that this happened as each small group recorded their findings. There were many hypotheses. Many children made the observation that it was hard to roll a twelve or a two.

Next we met as a class and made predictions about what would happen when only one die was rolled. Which number would come up most often? Most children thought one number would predominate when one die was used, just as seven had predominated when they were using two dice. After the children had a chance to test their predictions with one die, we met as a class to compare the two charts and to share observations. I held up the two charts that had been used for recording (see Figure 1.1).

Teacher: Are there any comments or questions?
Ted: With one die it can only go up to 6. When you have two it can go up to 12.
Teacher: Why do you think that is true?

Many hands were waving. Even children that I had worried about at the beginning of the year were becoming more involved in our group processing sessions.

Laurie: You can only get up to 6 because there are only 6 numbers on the die.
Teacher: I'm confused. (I hold up two dice and turn them around.) They still only go up to 6.
Laurie: But when you roll two you can put the numbers together and get bigger numbers like 10 and 12.
Jennifer: That's right. With one, you can only go up to 6 because there's nothing to put with it. When you have two dice, you can get lots of different answers.
Ted: You can get 5 + 2 or 6 + 3 and lots of others.
Teacher: Did other people notice what Jennifer and Ted noticed?

FIGURE 1.1. Numbers Rolled Using Two Dice and One Die

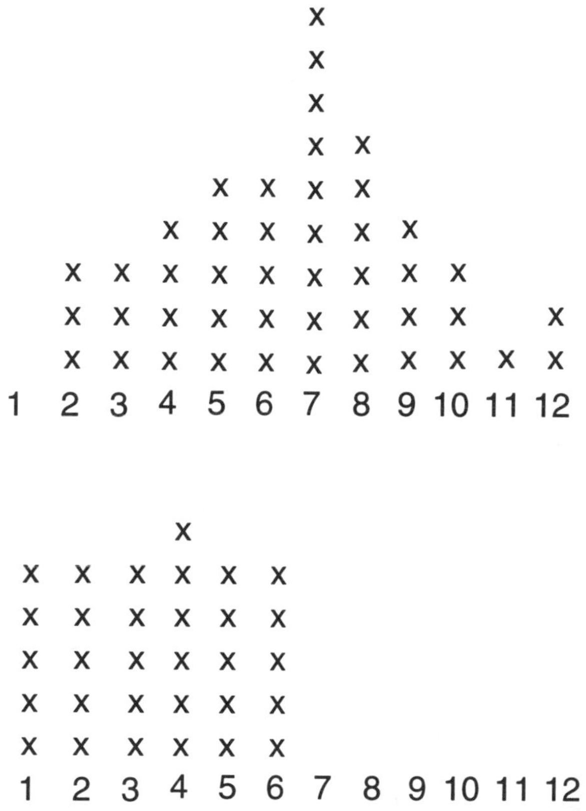

```
                        X
                        X
                        X
                        X  X
                  X  X  X  X
               X  X  X  X  X  X
            X  X  X  X  X  X  X  X  X
            X  X  X  X  X  X  X  X  X        X
            X  X  X  X  X  X  X  X  X  X  X
            1  2  3  4  5  6  7  8  9 10 11 12


               X
      X  X  X  X  X  X
      X  X  X  X  X  X
      X  X  X  X  X  X
      X  X  X  X  X  X
      X  X  X  X  X  X
      1  2  3  4  5  6  7  8  9 10 11 12
```

Other children agreed. Again I held up the two charts.

Teacher: Other comments and questions?

Alyssa: The numbers on the one-die chart came out almost the same with no number winning. On the two-dice chart, the 7 beat the other numbers.

Teacher: I'm confused. I just heard Ted and Jennifer say that there were more different answers with two dice. So I'm wondering why it happens that instead of getting more different answers, you often get the same answer. If there are more possible different answers, why do you think 7 came up so many times?

Again children made the observation that it was hard to roll a 12 or a 2. Many children thought it was because the 7 was a middle number, but the answers were vague. I very much wanted children to see that there is a pattern.

Teacher: When we made our predictions, many people thought 12
    would win. Why do you think 12 has only two checks?
Allison: You can only get 12 when you get two 6s and that's hard to
    get.
Teacher: Do other people agree with Allison that you can only get a 12
    one way?

I went to the board and made two dice showing 6s. I wrote the number 12 and wrote "1" and circled it.

Teacher: Does everyone agree that this is the only way to get a 12 us-
    ing two dice?

By now hands were waving and it was hard to keep up with everyone's observations. A few children weren't ready to agree and offered other combinations for 12 such as 10 + 2 or 7 + 5. Of course their classmates were happy to point out that there is no 7 or 10 on a die.

Shelley: There's only one way to get a 12 and there is only one way to
    get a 2.
Teacher: Are you sure? Do other people agree?

Then I made two dice showing 1s. I wrote the numeral 2 and wrote a "1" and circled it.

Teacher: Does everyone agree that this is the only way to get a two us-
    ing 2 dice?

There was agreement and since the time was getting short I wrote the other possible answers in between (see Figure 1.2).

Sam: You can get 11 with 6 and 5 when you have two dice.

I drew two dice showing 6 and 5.

Teacher: Are there other ways to get 11?
Carol: (Carol is a very thoughtful girl who waits before sharing an
    idea.) Well, the die that says 6 could roll a 5 next time and then

FIGURE 1.2. How Many Ways to Roll Each Sum?

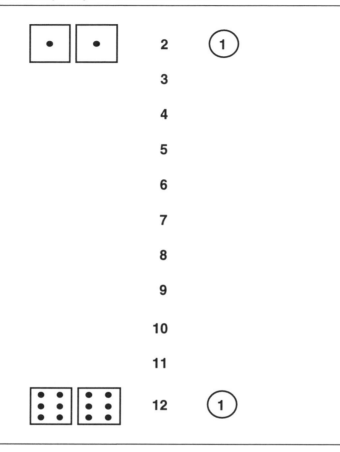

the other one could roll 6 so even though it's still 6 + 5 it would be another way to get 11.

I drew four dice showing Carol's observation and asked for comments.

Teacher: Do other people agree? Are there two ways to get 11?

By now there was great involvement as other possible combinations were offered. As I drew the dice for each combination offered, there was a bubbling excitement that was almost giggling. I could hear Bill's high-pitched voice above the others.

Bill: There's a pattern. See! It's one way, then two ways, then three.
Jonah: It's like a football field. The number of ways is the highest in
    the middle and it's smaller at each end.
Tanya: Can I tell the pattern?
Teacher: Do you want to tell us about the pattern, Tanya?
Tanya: There is only one way to get 12, two ways to get 11, three
    ways to get 10, four ways to get 9, five ways to get 8.

As Tanya spoke I filled in the remainder of the pattern.

So much enthusiasm. So many questions. So many ideas for future math lessons. So many connections to be made. There was never so much enthusiasm over a math page.

$$+ \quad - \quad \times \quad \div$$

THIRD GRADERS EXPLORE MULTIPLICATION

Virginia M. Brown

This past year I have been teaching a class of third graders—an average, heterogeneous group of children and the only third-grade class in this rural school. There are 13 boys and 7 girls.

DELVING INTO MULTIPLICATION: A FIRST EXPERIENCE

In early December I decided to introduce the concept of multiplication, using the strategy with which I introduce most of my mathematics lessons: I posed a problem and asked the students to see how many ways they could solve it mentally. I chose a problem that involved simple repeated addition, yet not so simple that it did not require some mental stretching. I decided to avoid regrouping so that the logistics of that maneuver would not interfere with their thinking at this beginning stage of concept development. The problem said: *Kevin has 3 pencil cases in his desk with 12 pencils in each case. How many pencils does Kevin have?*

After I posed the problem, I looked around the room at the pensive faces of the children and saw that much thinking was going on. Some looked down at their desks, others looked at the ceiling, a few stared straight ahead, but the process of mental problem solving was evident. I gave the children a considerable amount of time to think and then asked for solutions.

Peter offered 34 as his result; Cathy's answer was 24; Kevin's reply was 36; Mike's was 15. The rest agreed with one of these. I asked the class how they felt about these answers, and the following dialogue ensued:

Emily: I don't think 15 could be right.

Teacher: Why?

Emily: Well, the problem says 3 pencil cases with 12 pencils in each case. That means you have 12 here (pointing to an invisible case on her desk), 12 here, and 12 here. You have three 12s, so the answer couldn't be 15.

Mike (who had originally offered 15 as his answer): I don't like my answer anymore. I was adding 12 and 3, but now I don't think that makes sense.

Emily (smiling): It doesn't make sense because you would be adding 3 pencil cases and 12 pencils. You can't write with a pencil case.

Steve was waving his arm vigorously, anxious to speak. I asked him to tell us what he was thinking.

Steve: I don't think 24 could be right either, because I know 12 and 12 equals 24. That would only be two 12s, but there are three 12s because there are 3 pencil cases, so 24 can't be right.

As Steve spoke, other children were nodding in assent, including Mike who had initially arrived at 15 for his answer and Cathy whose answer was the one being challenged. She asked to have her answer erased, no longer agreeing with it.

The class agreed that the other two answers were within the realm of possibility, and I asked for volunteers to explain the solution with which they agreed.

Jon, anxious to be the one to demonstrate his problem-solving expertise, was kneeling on his chair, hoping this extra height would cause his waving hand to be the one most visible to my eyes. Although I often call on the less exuberant children, I was pleased with his enthusiasm and asked him to share his idea with us.

Jon: Well, I think the answer is 36 because—can I show you on the board? (Jon approaches the board and writes the expression shown in Figure 1.3(a) before he continues.) You have 2, 4, 6 in the ones place, and 1, 2, 3 in the tens place, so that's 36.

Peter: Oh, I guess I forgot one of the 2s, so I got 34, but I agree with 36.

Teacher: I see. Did anyone solve the problem a different way?

Zack: I said 10, 20, 30, plus I knew there were 6 more, so 36.

At this point I decided to tell the class that we were actually doing multiplication (most children were already familiar with the term) and showed them how to write "3 × 12 = 36." I then asked if there were any other methods

FIGURE 1.3. Children Take Apart and Rearrange Numbers to Find Factors of 36

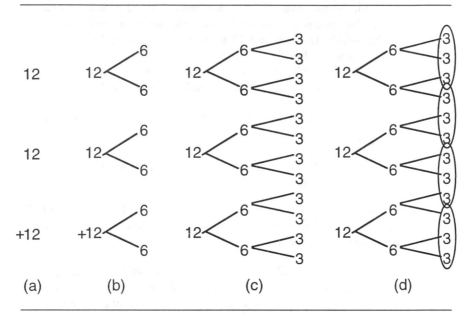

(a)   (b)   (c)   (d)

used to solve the problem. Jeff's hand went up, and his expression told me he thought he had made the discovery of a lifetime. I called on him.

> *Jeff:* I did it the same way Jon did, but I just figured out another way. Can I show it on the board? (Jeff goes to the board, fills in Figure 1.3(b), and then goes on.) Here are the three 12s. If you break each into two 6s, you have six 6s, and that equals 36.

The class was at first puzzled by this seemingly unrelated manipulation of numbers. Several children sat with furrowed brows and asked their neighbors where the 6s came from. However, I was excited about the flexibility in Jeff's thinking and saw that, although this had not been on my agenda for the day, he could lead the class into an exploration of different factors of 36.

Jeff explained once more what he had discovered, and as his explanation sank in, the confusion seemed to dissipate. I asked the class to write Jeff's idea in the form of an equation.

> *Marie:* Since you have the number 6 six times, you would write "6 × 6." (She demonstrates on the board.)

I had noticed Tom's eyes-upward thinking pose and was hoping he would be able to offer us his thoughts on the problem. Tom needs more time to think than most children, and I was really happy when his "ah-ha" look appeared on his face and his hand went up.

> *Tom:* If you broke each 6 up into 3 + 3, then you would have 3 + 3 and 3 + 3 and 3 + 3 and 3 + 3 and 3 + 3 and 3 + 3, and that would also equal 36. (Tom demonstrates on the board next to the 6s as Jeff had done next to the 12s [see Figure 1.3(c)]. He checks the class's reaction.)
>
> *Anna:* Yes, and you would write it "12 × 3 = 36" because you have 3 twelve times. Wow, we've found a lot of things that equal 36. Oh, look! This one is backwards of our first one, "3 × 12."

The original problem involving pencils and pencil cases had long been forgotten. Thanks to Jeff, the children were taking on the challenge of thinking about various ways to arrive at 36 with multiplication. I decided to continue with this line of thinking and asked if there are any more combinations that equal 36.

The children were quiet as mice for the next few minutes. Most were intently studying the board, foreheads in a frown, faces fixed in intense concentration. All at once several hands were raised. I called on Bill since he was one who had not yet had a chance to contribute.

> *Bill:* I was looking at Tommy's 3s and in my mind I circled his 3s in groups of 3. That would make 9 in each circle. I wound up with 4 circles. (See Figure 1.3(d).)

Bill went to the board to show his idea and proudly added his equation to the list: "4 × 9 = 36." I wanted to be sure that the rest of the class understood what he had done so I asked if someone could paraphrase. (Since I frequently use this strategy, the children had become familiar with the word at the beginning of the year.)

> *Emily:* Well, he circled three 3s, which equals 9, and he did this 4 times, so 4 × 9 = 36. And so we can add another one to the list because if 4 × 9 = 36 then 9 × 4 = 36, too.
>
> *Anna:* Does that always work? I mean, saying each one backwards will you always get the same answer?
>
> *Teacher:* Interesting question! What do you think?
>
> *Anna:* I'm not sure. It seems to, but I can't tell if it would *always* work—I mean for *all* numbers.

Again the class became quiet. At this initial stage of exploring multiplication, in the minds of the children this "backwards" property, Anna's description of commutativity, was just conjecture. Proof for them meant that it had to be true in *all* instances, and they had not yet been convinced that this was the case. Knowing that the recess bell was about to ring, and wanting to encourage their mathematical inquisitiveness, I told them to see if they could figure out a way to prove or disprove Anna's question overnight, and we'd start the next day's math lesson with it.

THE DILEMMA: DOES COMMUTATIVITY ALWAYS WORK?

The next day the question was again brought up as to whether in all cases the reverse of a multiplication equation always resulted in the same answer. Many of the children thought it did, but some were not sure. One pointed out that since it worked for addition, it must work for multiplication, but couldn't explain why he thought that way. Another child said she had thought about it in bed the previous night and had figured out a way to prove it. I asked her to show us her idea, and this is what followed:

Angela: Well, let's take 4×3. It really means this: $3 + 3 + 3 + 3$.
(She demonstrates with unit cubes as she speaks [see Figure 1.4(a)].)
If you take one of the 3s and break it up, giving one to each of the other 3s, you wind up with three 4s, like this. (See Figure 1.4(b).)

This seemed clear to Angela, and most of the other children accepted her demonstration, trying it out on other numbers. However, a few, including Anna, the girl who had originally raised the question, were not satisfied. "I'm still not sure it would work for *all* numbers."

At this point we temporarily left the issue of commutativity behind. They weren't coming up with new ideas to prove or disprove their conjecture, so we went ahead with my agenda. I showed them how to arrange their cubes as an array, and for the next week the class explored multiplication facts using arrays. Then I brought them back to commutativity. "Could anyone think of a way to use arrays to prove that the answer to a multiplication equation would be the same no matter which order the numbers are in?"

The class thought about this for some time as they worked with their arrays, some alone, some with partners. Then Lauren raised her hand.

Lauren: I think I can prove it. (She brings her cubes to the rug at the front of the room, and the class gathers around her.) See, in this array I have three 7s, and in this array I have seven 3s. (See Figure 1.5.) Now watch. I take this array (she picks up the three 7-sticks) and look, they fit exactly, so 3×7 equals 7×3 and

FIGURE 1.4. Student's Demonstration that 4 Groups of 3 Equals 3 Groups of 4

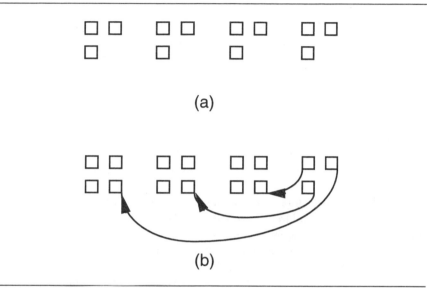

(a)

(b)

there's 21 in both. No matter which equation you did it for, it would always fit exactly.

At the end of Lauren's explanation, Jeremy, who had been listening intently, could hardly contain himself. He said that Lauren's demonstration had given him an idea for an even clearer way to prove it and took his place in the center of the circle with Lauren's cubes.

Jeremy: I'll use the same equation as Lauren but I'll only need one set of sticks. (He picks up the three 7-sticks.) When you look at it this

FIGURE 1.5. Student's Demonstration of Multiplicative Commutativity

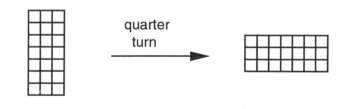

quarter
turn

way (he holds it up so that the 7s are vertical) you have three 7s. (He runs a finger down each stick of 7 and counts.) One 7, two 7s, three 7s. So this way you have 3×7. (He then turns the sticks sideways.) But this way, you have seven 3s. See? You have one 3, two 3s, three 3s, four 3s, five 3s, six 3s, seven 3s. (Again he runs his finger down the sticks as he speaks.) So, this one array shows both 7×3 and 3×7.

Anna (nodding her head in a contemplative manner): That's a really good way to show it, and so was Lauren's. It would *have* to work for all numbers.

Dale: Yes, if you don't add on any, and don't take any away, they have to equal the same amount. Jeremy's explanation made it really clear to me. Turning the array sideways really helps to see it.

No longer conjecture, the commutative property of multiplication was now reality to these children. It was theirs! They discovered it and now they proved it—beyond a shadow of a doubt!

The work with arrays not only yielded an understanding of the commutative property of multiplication ("backwards," as Anna liked to call it), but also enabled the children later to make discoveries relating to the distributive property as well. They could demonstrate that 4×7 is always the same as $2 \times 7 + 2 \times 7$ and that 6×8 is always the same as $5 \times 8 + 1 \times 8$. This proves very useful to the children when they are trying to learn multiplication facts, which I believe is important once they have come to understand the concept of multiplication.

$+ \quad - \quad \times \quad \div$

OF-ING FRACTIONS

Joanne Moynahan

I have found that sixth graders look forward to new horizons—even in math. They have explored whole numbers for years and think they have them under control. Although I know the students still have much to explore in whole numbers, starting the year with something they know is not firmly grounded grabs their attention. They are willing to take risks in new areas.

What did my students know about fractions? Did they know that the denominator is the number of equal parts in the whole? Did they know that the numerator represents part of the whole? Did they know the vocabulary connected to fractions? What was their previous experience with fractions? These were the questions I kept in mind during the initial fraction activities this class experienced in sixth grade. I discovered that they did know that the "bottom number" of a fraction was very important—"The bottom number tells you how many parts there are in the whole thing"—although most did not use the word "denominator" when talking about fractions. The same was true of the numerator; they talked about the "top number," which they understood as referring to part of the whole thing—it told them how many parts. They knew that all the parts had to be equal, that thirds meant three parts all the same size, not just three pieces. I was not concerned with the vocabulary. But I used the vocabulary myself, and they quickly followed suit. With these questions answered, I knew we were ready to begin working with fractions. The question was where to begin.

What real-life situations require working with fractions? When did I last use fractions outside of the classroom? It was in the kitchen. I wanted to make ½ of a recipe. In order to do that I had to find ½ of a few fractions and ½ of a few whole numbers. When I was clothes shopping, the sign said "⅓ off ticketed price." I had to know what ⅓ of the ticketed price was to determine my savings. I decided to begin with multiplying, or "of-ing," fractions.

I looked through my fraction folder and found the type of problem I thought would lead to a discussion of multiplication of fractions.

1. *The Davis family attended a picnic. Their family made up ⅓ of the 15 people at the picnic. How many Davises were at the picnic?*
2. *John ate ⅛ of the 16 hot dogs. How many hot dogs did John eat?*
3. *One-fourth of the hot dogs were served without relish. How many were served without relish?*

I wanted to keep it simple so I looked for problems that required multiplying a whole number by a fraction. I debated about adding a problem that would have something other than 1 for a numerator but decided that could wait. Unit fractions were a good beginning. Students could work through the three problems and we would be able to have a whole group discussion with the time remaining. I thought these problems would be solved easily with unifix cubes or diagrams. I did not first show the class how to solve this type of problem. It was up to them to use whatever means possible. Then they could figure out what operation—addition, subtraction, multiplication, or division—was involved.

Before I passed out the problems for the fraction explorations, I mentioned that they might find the unifix cubes helpful. The unifix cubes were in great demand. It was nice to see that so many trusted my judgment! A few needed only paper and pencil. As I traveled around getting a feel for the situation, I noticed many had recorded an answer without recording how they decided on the answer. Once students are in the working mode, I don't like to interrupt. However, papers with only an answer recorded would not be of any use to me. I did interrupt and reminded them to draw a picture or a diagram so I could follow their thinking when I was at home with their papers.

As I approached Jeff and Carl, they were working on "John and the hot dogs," but because of my recent announcement, they went back to the Davises to record their thinking.

> *Jeff:* We decided 5 Davises were at the picnic but we only wrote the answer. Now we're going back to show you how we got it.
>
> *Teacher:* Good idea. Why don't you talk to me about it while you're drawing a picture?
>
> *Carl:* Well, we took 15 unifix cubes to stand for the people. It said the Davises were ⅓ of the people so we put the cubes into 3 piles. One pile was the Davises so there were 5 Davises at the picnic.
>
> *Teacher:* So, ⅓ of 15 is 5?
>
> *Jeff:* Yeah. See, you can see it in our picture.

I saw that they had drawn 3 groups of 5 squares. I felt satisfied that they were working well and moved on to another group. Tim was searching through the box of unifix cubes. He pulled out 2 sticks of cubes, took 4 cubes off one stick and put them aside, then handed the rest to his partner. If the cubes were stored properly, there were 10 cubes to a stick. Tim trusted that there were, indeed, 10 cubes to a stick. Susan wasn't quite so sure.

> *Tim:* Here, Susan, these are the hot dogs. John ate ⅛.
>
> *Susan:* Are you sure there are 16? I'm going to count. (Susan picks up one stick, and counts as she pulls each cube off the stick. She does the same with the other stick.) Okay, there are 16. I guess we need 8 piles.

Susan dealt the cubes, 1 to each of 8 piles. When she saw that she had quite a few left, she dealt around again, ending up with 8 groups of 2 cubes.

> *Tim:* John ate 2 hot dogs.
>
> *Susan:* You record the picture this time. I did the first one.

Another group was in the process of counting out the 16 hot dogs. What they did with those hot dogs caught me off guard, however.

> *Lynn:* Here are the 16 hot dogs. Now what do we do?
>
> *Sally:* We need to put 8 together because it says he ate ⅛.

Sally saw the denominator as the number *in* a group rather than the number *of* groups. It looked like she was putting the hot dogs in half. Lynn screwed up her face, obviously not trusting Sally's grouping.

Lynn: Why are you putting them in half? He didn't eat half, he ate ⅛.
Sally: Because that means he ate 1 out of every 8.

Sally saw the fraction as a ratio, 1 out of 8. Lynn looked confused. I wanted to see how this would work out so I just continued to observe without making any comment.

Lynn: Huh?
Sally: See, he ate 1 of these (pointing to one group of 8) and 1 of these (pointing to the other group of 8), so he ate 2 hot dogs.
Lynn: I'm not sure about that. Let me try it my way. These are the hot dogs. It says he ate ⅛ so make 8 piles. (Lynn arranges the cubes as 8 groups of 2.) There. John ate 2. Hey, that's what *you* got. I guess your way works but I like my way better.

Neither Lynn nor Sally had confidence in their math ability. Clearly, their ability to solve problems was not lacking, only their confidence. I moved to another group, still thinking about Sally. I was really excited to see a strategy that I hadn't anticipated. I never would have thought about a ratio in this context. When I was a student I used ratios only in the chapter on ratios or the one on probability. My guess was that Sally would have given me a blank stare if I asked her about ratios.

As I looked at Mary and Ann's paper, it seemed they were working with pizzas instead of hot dogs. Mary drew a circle and then divided it into 4 parts by first dividing it in half and then dividing each half in half. Ann counted each section to be sure there were 4 parts. Mary counted out 16 unifix cubes and started dealing them around the circle. Ann looked a little perturbed.

Ann: Let me do the rest. You're doing everything. (Ann sweeps the blocks off the circle.) The problem told us ¼ of the hot dogs were served without relish and there were 16 hot dogs. I'm going to deal them around the circle.
Ann: Four hot dogs were served without relish, right?
Mary: Right. Now take off the cubes and draw them into the circle. Make sure you write the answer in a complete sentence.

Mary had given up some of her control here but she was going to be sure that Ann did it right. I have integrated math and writing by insisting that answers be written in complete sentences. Capitals, spelling, and punctuation are important in math, too. I have found that requiring complete sentences has helped students to check the reasonableness of their answers. It has helped me to assess their language skills as well.

Since it was early in the year and the children were still shy about sharing their ideas in front of the class, I thought it would be a good idea to line up some volunteers for sharing ahead of time. Each group I asked seemed pleased and eager. A quick check of the clock told me I could let them work for a few more minutes before processing as a whole class. If everyone hadn't finished all three problems, it wouldn't matter.

Getting everyone settled in the front of the room near the chalkboard was no easy task, but worth the effort. Some sat on the rug, some at desks. When we tallied answers there was complete agreement. Five Davises attended the picnic; John ate two hot dogs; four hot dogs were served without relish.

My "volunteers" shared their strategies. Jeff and Carl used unifix cubes to share their solution to the first problem. Sally shared her "1-out-of-8" thinking for the second problem. No one seemed particularly excited about her strategy. I was pretty sure I would see others using it in the days ahead, however. Mary and Ann showed their way of solving the problem.

As we discussed each problem I recorded a shortened version on the dry-erase board. I wanted to keep a running list for future use. Several days of saved work such as this can provide a good resource for finding patterns and generating rules. At the end of sharing the board looked like this:

$\frac{1}{3}$ of 15 = 5
$\frac{1}{8}$ of 16 = 2
$\frac{1}{4}$ of 16 = 4

We didn't have much time left before the recess bell, but I thought I would just give them something to think about and posed the following question:

Teacher: Does anyone know what they were doing with these numbers? (Long pause.) What operation did you use? Did you add, subtract, multiply, or divide? (Another long pause.) What symbol could we put in here instead of "of"?

I was answered with blank stares. I did not expect to resolve that question at this time but posed it for those who were ready for a challenge. This question came from me, however—not the students—and at that time they were not really invested in finding an answer to it. They felt satisfied that they had solved the problems. But then some of the students accepted my challenge.

Mary: I think we should put division in there.
Teacher: Why?
Mary: Well, the problem said $\frac{1}{3}$ of the people were Davises. I drew a circle and divided the circle into three parts—then I put the people in.

Jeff: I agree. We divided our cubes into three groups.

It really did *seem* like division. They took 15 people and divided them into three smaller groups, all the same size. However, that's dividing by 3, not 15. The number sentence $\frac{1}{3} \div 15 = 5$ does not represent what they did when they divided the 15 cubes (representing 15 people) into three equal groups. They did not divide by 15.

> *Teacher:* Does everyone agree? Should I erase the "of" and put in "divided by"? Think about what you know about division. (I erase the "of" and put in " $\div$.")

Children began discussing among themselves. I wondered if anyone would pick up on my clue about thinking about what they did know. After a few minutes I gave the signal (raising my hand) to "finish your thought and then stop talking so we can have a whole group discussion." It took a while for everyone to focus. Rebecca was the first to offer her thoughts on the question.

> *Rebecca:* I don't think divide is right.
> *Teacher:* Why do you think divide won't work?

Rebecca came to the board and wrote $\frac{1}{3} \div 15 = 5$.

> *Rebecca:* This (pointing to the 15) means how many 15s are in $\frac{1}{3}$. That (pointing to the 5) means five 15s are in $\frac{1}{3}$. I *know* that's not right. There aren't any!

Rebecca is one of the more able students in this class. She pays attention to detail, makes generalizations, and can think abstractly. If something doesn't make sense to her, she will work on it until it does.

Jeff had a puzzled look on his face and hesitantly raised his hand.

> *Jeff:* Why can't we take 15 and switch it with $\frac{1}{3}$? The big number should come first.
> *Teacher:* I'm not sure I understand. Why don't you come to the board and do the switching?

Jeff was thinking back to what he knew about division. One "truth" that most students come to sixth grade with is that in a number sentence the big number has to come first in division. When using the long division algorithm, the big number goes inside and the smaller one has to be the divisor. This is a generalization students make from the many division problems they've had up until now. It is a rule that has always worked for them. But switching the numbers around did not work here. Jeff did use what he knew about division, however.

Jeff came to the board and wrote $15 \div \frac{1}{3} = 5$. He seemed to be pretty sure division would work if he could only get the order of the numbers to make it work. I asked him what that sentence meant.

Jeff: Well, now it means how many $\frac{1}{3}$s are in 15.

Jeff managed to open a new problem for the class to ponder. So often students do this when they are allowed and encouraged to talk about their thinking. It is one of the ingredients of a math class where everyone learns— even the teacher. Jeff opened an avenue I hadn't anticipated exploring: how to divide by a fraction. I thought this was a lesson on multiplying fractions.

Mary was sitting close enough to me so that I could see her paper. She was furiously drawing circles and dividing them into thirds. Then she began thinking out loud.

Mary: It takes three to make one, so—there are (Mary stopped to count her thirds) 45?

Rebecca was very quick to pick up on the 45. She responded, trying very hard to be patient.

Rebecca: See. Divide won't work. There were 5 Davises, not 45.

Rebecca, as well as the rest of the class, was sure that the number of Davises at the picnic was 5. I was not sure everyone was at the same place as Mary in understanding that there are 45 thirds in 15. In order to help others understand what Mary was saying and to slow the pace a little, I asked Mary to come to the board and share her thinking. She agreed, drew 15 circles, and divided them into thirds. The whole class counted with her: One, two, three, . . . , forty-five. At this point most of them could see that divide didn't work even though it seemed they were dividing.

Teacher: What do you think it should be?
Rebecca: I think it's times.

I invited Rebecca to come to the board. She began writing a line of $\frac{1}{3}$s.

Rebecca: That's $\frac{1}{3}$ 15 times. Now add them up.

I could see that Rebecca had moved to the abstract. She was considering the number sentence without connecting it to the Davises. Where in her diagram were the Davises? Rebecca could see that she was not convincing her classmates. She offered this final defense:

> *Rebecca: I* didn't multiply. I'm just trying to prove that you can. I divided the 15 people. She (pointing to Mary) says divide and I'm trying to show that multiply works.

R-I-N-G! That marked the end of class.

> *Teacher:* We'll talk more about this tomorrow. Think about it overnight—a pillow problem.

Later that day I was discussing the lesson with a colleague. She asked me why I thought knowing "of" means multiply was important. That was a pillow problem for me. "Pillow problems" are problems to think about overnight. Sometimes an idea needs time to develop into something firm enough to talk about. Why *was* knowing "of" means multiply important? Any real-life situation that required finding part of something could be answered without knowing you multiplied. However, these students would face situations in the near future when knowing the "of" means multiply and vice versa would be helpful. The first situation would be the Stanford Achievement Test in the spring. They would be asked to compute examples like ⅓ × 15. Even if they forgot the rule they had constructed for multiplying fractions, they would be able to solve it by reading it as ⅓ of 15.

If the algorithm for multiplying fractions was to make sense, they needed to understand that "of" means multiply. My instinct was that understanding had to come first. Once they were sure multiplication was the operation they used in problems like " ¼ of the hot dogs," we could form a rule for multiplying fractions. They had a foundation in multiplication. I don't think they had a foundation in "of-ing."

As I thought about Rebecca's explanation I was bothered because I couldn't "see" the Davises either. I was sure many of the students felt the same way. Her explanation showed 15 thirds, not 15 people. Rebecca had taken the number sentence out of the picnic context and used the numbers to prove her point. The students needed more time manipulating cubes and making diagrams.

The next day I overheard Mary and Rebecca having a friendly argument as they walked down the hall. They are good friends and both share enthusiasm for a challenge. Rebecca stuck to her belief that it was multiplication and Mary to hers that it was division.

We began class with a discussion of the "pillow problem." Since I had asked them to think about something overnight, I wanted to check in with them. I anticipated a quick discussion. I asked if anyone had anything to add to yesterday's discussion about "of-ing." Mark had something to say in support of Rebecca's explanation.

Mark: The question is ⅓ of 15 = 5. You can't really do ⅓ × 5 because we need to pretend we don't know the answer yet. Like Rebecca did yesterday, add ⅓ 15 times. It would be 5. When you add the same thing a number of times, that's multiplying.

Mark was trying to say that you couldn't put the 5 in the number sentence except after the equal sign. Five Davises were at the picnic but something was done to the ⅓ and the 15 to equal 5. The only thing that seemed to work was Rebecca's adding the 15 thirds.

Jacob raised his hand and suggested trying a plus. I erased the "of" and put in a plus. That idea was quickly dismissed. Fifteen plus ⅓ didn't equal 5; it equaled 15⅓. Then he suggested subtract. Again, I did as he suggested. Disagreement was a little slower in coming, but subtraction was discarded, too.

Mary was busy writing furiously on a scrap of paper. She wrote with one hand and raised the other. After I called on her she talked to the class while she continued to write.

Mary: Division is the opposite of multiplication. Take 12 × 2 = 24. Then 24 ÷ 2 = 12. So . . .

Mary was able to make sense of things by writing them down. Most of the class was not ready to think in the abstract by listening to her words. In order to keep others involved, I stopped Mary before she finished her thought.

Teacher: Mary, I think you need to write that on the board. I'm having trouble following what you said.

Mary repeated what she had said while she wrote it on the board and then continued her thought.

Mary: 12 × 2 = 24 so 24 ÷ 2 = 12. If ⅓ × 15 = 5, then 5 ÷ 15 = ⅓. Does that work?

I like Mary's "if, then" strategy. She and many others were not sure what 5 divided by 15 was, but Mary was definitely trying to resolve this problem. She was using previously grounded concepts to make sense of a new situation.

Teacher: How many 15s are in 5?
Mark: There aren't any. You can't make any 15s if you only have 5. Wait. You could make a part of a 15.

Jeff: I got it! You would have ⅓ of 15! It does work. Rebecca was
right—it is multiply!

I didn't even ask for a show of hands. I could tell by the murmurs and
smiles on the faces before me that the vote would have been in favor of multiplication. I hadn't anticipated this turn of events. I thought we would have a
brief discussion, leaving the question of "of-ing" unresolved. Mary, who had
arrived at school still convinced that dividing was right, had managed to con-
vince others that multiplying was right.

That was a good beginning for the day's lesson. The problems were

1. *Thirty people attended a party. One-fifth were late. How many were
   late? Five people can sit at a table. How many tables do I need?*
2. *There were 20 problems on a test. One-fourth were bonus problems.
   How many were bonus problems? There were 4 problems on each
   page. How many pages?*
3. *I have 21 mice. One-seventh are blind. How many are blind? Seven
   mice can fit in a cage. How many cages are needed?*
4. *We read 36 stories. One-fourth were funny. How many were funny?
   Each book had 4 stories. How many books were read?*

Again, I made the decision to stay with unit fractions. The second part of
each problem is related to the first. For example, in the first problem, ⅕ of
30 yields the same answer as $30 \div 5$. Perhaps this connection will help to
clarify that "of" means multiply.

When students were settled with their partners to work on these problems, I reminded them to show their thinking by drawing a diagram. I also
added an extension for students like Jeff, Mary, and Rebecca.

Teacher: In addition to drawing a diagram, today while you are working, be thinking about our discussion—are you multiplying or dividing? When you finish the problems, the extension is to write a
number sentence for each problem.

I watched Lynn and Sally count out 30 unifix cubes for the first problem.
Sally made groups of 5 with the cubes. She was using the ratio concept again.
One-fifth means 1 out of 5 to Sally. Is this ratio concept always going to
work? How will she apply it to mixed numbers? How will she approach
½ × ¾?

Several students did not use the blocks on this assignment. Instead they
drew diagrams. Mary and Ann stayed with a circle diagram using "*x*"s to rep-

resent mice. Gale and Charlene were not using cubes either. Their diagram was unique (see Figure 1.6).

> *Teacher:* Interesting. Talk to me about problem 4. What are all those "S"s?
>
> *Charlene:* Those are stories: "S" for story. That was my idea. Do you know what "FS" is?
>
> *Teacher:* Freaky story?
>
> *Charlene:* No. Funny story. There were 36 stories and ¼ were funny.
>
> *Gale:* And each book had 4 stories. See—one row across is a book so there are 9 books. It just worked that way.

An array—now that's something worth exploring. Their diagrams for the other problems weren't arrays.

> *Teacher:* I wonder if you made a diagram like this for the mice, would the cages be there?

They started making a new diagram for the mice. They were really excited when they could "see" the cages. I was excited, too, and asked them if they would share this discovery during whole group share. They readily agreed.

We began sharing time with a poll of answers. Again, there was no disagreement. I called on Charlene and Gale first. They both came to the board with their paper and big grins.

FIGURE 1.6. ¼ of 36 Stories Were Funny

```
FS   S   S   S
FS   S   S   S
FS   S   S   S
FS   S   S   S
FS   S   S   S
FS   S   S   S
FS   S   S   S
FS   S   S   S
FS   S   S   S
```

FIGURE 1.7. ⅕ of the People Were Late

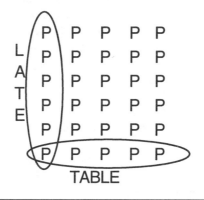

TABLE

Charlene: We found a way to make one diagram that got the answer for both parts. We didn't do it on the first one, but we can do it now.

Gale: Thirty people attended a party. One-fifth were late. How many were late?

Charlene: In our new way, we just used letters. For this one we would use a "P" for people. We would put the people in 5 rows. (See Figure 1.7.)

Gale: One row down shows the late people and one row across shows a table. It works like this for all the problems.

Lynn: That looks like the things we did in third grade. Remember when we did all that multiplying? Or was it division?

Carl: Well, I think we did that for both. First it was for multiplication, but we used it for division, too.

Teacher: What are we using it for today? (While I ask this question I add "⅕ of 30 = 6" to our list on the dry-erase board.)

Mark: I think it shows both. First it shows ⅕ × 30. We didn't take it any whole time, we only took it ⅕ of a time. That's the down row. Then it shows 30 ÷ 5. You can see that in the across row. There are 5 in each row and there are 6 rows. (I add "30 ÷ 5 = 6" to the dry-erase board.)

I wanted to check for understanding here so I asked for a volunteer to try this method for problem 2. I was very surprised when Sally raised her hand. I hadn't thought it through like Sally had, however.

Sally: It's sort of like the way I do it so I think I can. There were 20 problems on a test and ¼ were bonus. That means 1 out of 4 were bonus. So I would put 4 in a row like this: "P P P P." I'm using "P" too, but now it stands for problems, not people. Now 1 in each row is a bonus problem, that's a "BP." (Sally puts a "B" in front of the first "P" in each row.) If 4 problems are on a page, then each row across is a page. (See Figure 1.8.)

Rebecca: I think you should add "¼ × 20 = 5" and "20 ÷ 4 = 5" to the list on the dry-erase board. It looks like multiplying by ¼ is the same as dividing by 4. I guess that's why we were confused at first about what we were doing.

Teacher: Are you proposing a rule for multiplying fractions?

Rebecca: I don't think so, but maybe I can: To multiply a fraction, divide by the bottom number.

That rule wouldn't hold true for long, but it was a start. I wrote the rule on the dry-erase board. Should the next lesson introduce problems with a numerator other than one? Perhaps. I wanted to find some problems that would require repeated addition and help to clear up any fuzziness about the multiply-or-divide dilemma.

I looked through some textbooks for problems that could be solved by repeated addition and had a numerator other than one. I found just what I needed in a new sample copy of a sixth-grade text. *"One crank of the handle on Janet's well raises the bucket ⅔ of a foot."* We could do a lot of exploring here. . . .

FIGURE 1.8. ¼ of the Problems Were Bonus

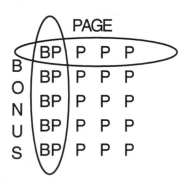

$$+ \quad - \quad \times \quad \div$$

FOCUSING ON LEARNING MATHEMATICS

Martin A. Simon

On what basis do teachers make instructional decisions? How do they decide what to teach and how and when to teach it? Traditionally, the content and organization of the textbook or the local curriculum guide has figured heavily in these decisions. In addition, teaching practice has been affected by both well-established images of how teachers teach mathematics and the latest technology (teaching machines, the Hunter Model, manipulatives, cooperative groups, computers), as well as by teachers' memories of how they learned the mathematical content involved. What is missing from this mix is an informed view of students' mathematical thinking and learning. It stands to reason that instruction that is sensitive to students' knowledge and their processes of learning is likely to be more effective.

All teachers are concerned about learning as an outcome. However, it is the minority of teachers who are prepared to consider the processes of learning. Indeed, many teachers have not had the opportunity in their teacher preparation or ongoing professional development to focus on students' mathematical learning. Although a traditional practice of teacher demonstration followed by student imitation can be analyzed in terms of its implicit views of learning and mathematics, it would be inappropriate to assume that teachers who engage in such a practice do so as a result of a consciously arrived at, explicit view of mathematics learning. (See Cobb, Wood, Yackel, & McNeal, 1992, for a discussion of traditional "school mathematics" versus "inquiry mathematics.")

The teachers in this book have had an uncommon professional development opportunity that encouraged them to reflect on the learning of mathematics in some rich contexts (described in Schifter & Fosnot, 1993, and Simon & Schifter, 1991). As a result, they not only have come to personally meaningful ways of thinking about mathematics learning, but also have come to make mathematics learning and students' mathematical knowledge central considerations in their mathematics instructional decision making.

Each of the teachers in this chapter has co-created with her students a context for learning mathematics in which the students are encouraged to think creatively, to question, to explore, and to communicate their ideas. There is very little teacher showing and telling. This is evidence of a trust in the students as learners and sense-makers. These teachers are confident that, given appropriate problems and teacher facilitation, students will seek to make sense of mathematics and will question and explore in ways that allow them to make connections and build more powerful mathematical ideas. Contrast this perspective with the notion that students need to be externally motivated and are capable of learning only what is given to them verbally or through demonstration. This contrast highlights a fundamental difference in teachers' expectations of learners. The powerful effects of the former orientation can be seen in the preceding episodes.

Anne Hendry's goal was to help her first graders learn about measurement. Instead of providing the conventional demonstration of how to measure, followed by practice of this skill, she engages her students in a fundamental question of measurement: How do we communicate to another how big something is? (Note that it is the social component of this problem, how to communicate with one's community about size, that creates the problematic situation.) The problem that Hendry poses allows for a range of responses yet creates a high probability that the students will wrestle with basic ideas such as how we measure to get replicable results (triggered by Mark's original haphazard measuring of the boat) and the need for a standard unit.

Virginia Brown's lesson on multiplication, Elizabeth Clark's lesson on probability, and Joanne Moynahan's lesson on multiplication of fractions are further examples of teachers creating problematic situations for students and supporting an atmosphere of exploration and risk taking as the students develop their unique ways of thinking about the situation. The teacher is continually challenging the students—in contrast to the traditional approach of leading them through tiny increments aimed at "foolproof" imitation and constant success. Clark's interaction with Laurie provides an example. Clark was asking students for their observations of the one-die chart versus the two-dice chart.

> *Ted:* With one die it can only go up to 6. When you have two it can go up to 12.
> *Teacher:* Why do you think that is true?
> *Laurie:* You can only get up to 6 because there are only 6 numbers on the die.
> *Teacher:* I'm confused. (I hold up two dice and turn them around.) They still only go up to 6.

Many teachers would have recognized Ted's answer as their "desired" answer, responding with a signal that the answer was correct. Such a response often comes from a view (perhaps unarticulated) that learning is a result of getting students to give a string of correct responses. Thus one does not want to disturb this string by questioning that might lead a student to retreat from the correct response. However, Clark's question challenges the answer. If the response was not based on a sound understanding, the student(s) might abandon that answer, at least temporarily. Here, the underlying view is that learning happens in response to challenges. It may be necessary for students to explore some alternative conceptions before returning to the more appropriate one, this time with a firmer understanding of why it is appropriate.

The view of learning that I have attributed to these teachers is consistent with *constructivism*. According to constructivism, each person has a unique web of knowledge that he or she brings to any situation. When a challenge arises for which prior concepts are inadequate, "disequilibrium" occurs. Learning, that is, the development of new or modified concepts, is an adaptive response to the problematic situation. This view of learning suggests that each learner will develop an idiosyncratic set of understandings. Although the understandings of two or more learners may "fit" (i.e., no conflict is perceived when intersubject communication occurs), one cannot assume an exact match among the understandings of the learners involved (von Glasersfeld, 1987, 1995). This also suggests that teachers (or students) cannot *give* their understandings to another person. This idea can be validated easily: Interview students who have all listened to the same lecture and you will hear quite discrepant ideas of what was discussed.

If learning is viewed not as the passive absorption of ideas from the teacher or textbook, but rather as active sense-making and construction of ideas by the individual, significant implications for teaching must follow. However, it is important to emphasize that from a constructivist perspective, students construct their own understandings regardless of the type of instruction or even whether instruction is involved. What is at issue is the *nature of students' constructions*. Current mathematics education reforms are the result of widespread dissatisfaction with what students have learned. Often they have learned isolated procedures and facts without conceptual understanding. They have developed ways of being effective in mathematics classes that have no mathematical value (e.g., solve the problems using proportions if the chapter is about proportions; if in a word problem one number is large and the other is small, divide, but if they don't divide evenly, multiply).

If we view learning through a constructivist lens, we are likely to question the assumption that students will learn what we tell them and what we show them. Our perspective shifts from, What are we teaching? to, What are they learning? We question what problems will challenge their current conceptions, promoting the development of more powerful ones. We search for learning contexts in which the students can use what they know (with the flexibility to accommodate individual differences) as they explore and problem solve.

In the lessons in this chapter, we see ongoing attempts by teachers to assess children's knowledge and to set tasks that will make problematic the mathematical ideas that they, the teachers, identify as important and potentially learnable by their students. Each demonstrates listening to children's ideas as opposed to carrying out a fixed plan of how to lead the students to a particular response.

These lessons provide an interesting example of a balance between teachers' anticipations and planning on one hand and the free flow of exploration and discussion (often in unanticipated ways) on the other. (I describe my own pursuit of such a balance in Simon, 1995.)

Brown reflects:

> I chose a problem that involved simple repeated addition, yet not so simple that it did not require some mental stretching. I decided to avoid regrouping so that the logistics of that maneuver would not interfere with their thinking at this beginning stage of concept development.

She is thinking about what the students know, what they can learn, and how they might engage with the problem. Later she decides to postpone further discussion of commutativity until her students have been introduced to arrays, a powerful tool for working with that idea. Balancing Brown's thoughtful anticipation is her openness to mathematical content generated spontaneously by the students (e.g., the factors of 36 and the question of commutativity). A similar openness is seen in Moynahan's response to Sally's "ratio" solution to the fraction problems.

This openness and responsiveness to students is more than just making use of the enrichment that comes from their ideas; it is *a way the students can help the teacher to help the students*. If each student has a unique web of understandings and if the teacher has an incomplete understanding of her students' knowledge, then it is impossible to give each student what he or she needs at the time it is needed. However, if a context is created in which students have the freedom to explore, reflect, and communicate their ideas, they will pursue much of the experience they need to make the connections appropriate for them. Once again, this involves trust in students as learners. Note, however, that each of these lessons provides structure for the students' explorations. My comments should not be construed as "leave students alone and they will construct all the big ideas of mathematics."

Having used the ideas of constructivism to think a bit about learning as an individual process, let us now take a social perspective on these examples of mathematics activity and learning. Increasingly significant in the mathematics education literature is social constructivism (Cobb, Yackel, & Wood, 1993; Ernest, 1991), which holds that concurrent with and interactive with the individual's construction of knowledge is the development of shared knowledge by the community. Mathematical knowledge is the construction of communities: both everyday users of mathematics (cf. Carraher, Carraher, & Schlieman's 1985 discussion of Brazilian street merchants) and communities of professional mathematicians (Ernest, 1991). Mathematical communities develop mathematical knowledge, rules for how mathematical knowledge is developed, and shared notions of what is important to the community. The view that mathematics is constructed by people, that it is not a series of absolute truths that we have only to uncover, is a potentially powerful idea. It shifts the role of the teacher from imparting a set of "truths" to that of helping connect the students' mathematics with the mathematics of the larger society.

A child is part of several communities that use mathematics. The episodes in this chapter give us the opportunity to consider the classroom as one mathematical community in which they engage. In this community, the knowledge and norms for mathematical behavior that come to be shared contribute to and constrain the mathematical constructions of individual community members. Likewise, the knowledge of individuals contributes to and constrains the knowledge and conventions developed by the mathematical community. Note that from the perspective of the observer (for the episodes described in this book, you and I are observers), knowledge is "taken-as-shared"; that is, community members experience the knowledge as shared, yet we are aware that there is no way to assess whether their knowledge *matches* that of other members. This point is consistent with the earlier discussion of *fit*.

Using this perspective, we can examine the episodes in terms of mathematics that is taken-as-shared and in terms of the norms or conventions for mathematical activity that are being established in these classrooms. In Hendry's classroom, the systematic procedure for measuring (no gaps and no overlap) is taken-as-shared; that is, after the original discussion, it is *assumed* that measurement reflects such a systematic approach. No further questioning of how the measuring was done is necessary. In Brown's lesson, the realization that one can take apart factors of 36 to find new factors of the same product became taken-as-shared; new solutions no longer required justification of the basic idea. These are examples of how mathematical knowledge is built in a community; as knowledge is taken-as-shared, it becomes an accepted building block for further knowledge.

Of great importance also are the norms that are established for mathematical activity. In all four of these classrooms, the students' role has been established as one that involves the exploration of mathematical systems, the development of mathematical ideas, the communication of ideas and questions, and validation of those ideas. Mathematics is seen as involving understanding and as related to real-world knowledge. (Each of the teachers focused students' work on problems with real-world contexts.) Doing mathematics is seen as generating ways to think about a problem, not just answers (for example, in Moynahan's class, the classroom discussion really began *after* the answers were agreed upon).

In several of the episodes, there seems to be an expectation established that learning can be derived from incorrect solutions. Consider Emily's critique (in Brown's lesson) of 15 as the number of pencils, which led to a discussion not only of the reasonableness of the magnitude of the answer, but also of consistency in the use of units. Note that students were not defensive about withdrawing answers that they subsequently believed were incorrect. Making a reasoned attempt at a problem and later revising one's thinking was considered to be effective mathematical behavior in this particular classroom community.

In Brown's lesson, ideas are seen as building on each other. For example, Anna asks the important question, "Does that always work?" and her question sets off a process in which the children begin to recognize the need for deductive proof. Lauren suggests a proof using arrays, which Jeremy then modifies. What is more, it was Anna and Dale who declared that the idea had been conclusively proven, not the teacher—validation was indeed an aspect of the students' role. (The issue of mathematical validation and justification is discussed in Balacheff, 1991; Lampert, 1990; Simon & Blume, in press.)

I refer to one final example that indicates how mathematical norms can be constituted. Tom (in Hendry's lesson) raises the question of whether "it was called a ruler because a king was sometimes called a ruler and maybe a long time ago a king made it using his foot like we did with Zeb's." Tom is spontaneously thinking about why things are the way they are—making connections. Then John wanted to know what "inch" means since he knows what a "foot" is. Hendry follows up these contributions with an unplanned investigation into the history of measurement, a response that undoubtedly contributed to a perception on the part of the students that the kinds of thinking demonstrated by Tom and John were appropriate and valued in this classroom community.

I have tried to communicate the importance of how these teachers think about mathematics learning and to convey the nature of their thinking by using a social constructivist perspective. In fact, I have given a very incomplete discussion of social constructivism. (For a more extensive treatment of the implications of social constructivism for teaching see Ball, 1993; Cobb, Yackel, & Wood, 1992; Simon, 1995.) These teachers can make powerful instructional decisions because they have learned to assess and consider students' current knowledge and learning processes and to use such information in their planning and spontaneous decision making.

I am *not* holding up these episodes as pure examples of a new paradigm or as ideal examples of mathematics teaching. Most of us are, and will be for a long time, teachers in transition. The reflectiveness of these teachers and their involvement in teacher-enhancement opportunities suggest that they are committed to continuing to improve their practice. These examples show us students enthusiastically involved in developing mathematical ideas, not for external rewards, but for the satisfaction of doing interesting mathematics in a community constituted for that purpose.

REFERENCES

Balacheff, N. (1991). Treatment of refutations: Aspects of the complexity of a constructivist approach to mathematics learning. In E. von Glasersfeld (Ed.), *Radical constructivism in mathematics education* (pp. 89–110). Dordrecht, The Netherlands: Kluwer Academic.

Ball, D. L. (1993). With an eye on the mathematical horizon: Dilemmas of teaching elementary school mathematics. *Elementary School Journal, 93*(4), 373–397.

Carraher, T. N., Carraher, D. W., & Schlieman, A. D. (1985). Mathematics in the streets and in the schools. *British Journal of Developmental Psychology, 3*, 21–29.

Cobb, P., Wood, T., Yackel, E., & McNeal, B. (1992). Characteristics of classroom mathematics traditions: An interactional analysis. *American Educational Research Journal, 29*(3), 573–604.

Cobb, P., Yackel, E., & Wood, T. (1992). A constructivist alternative to the representational view of mind in mathematics education. *Journal for Research in Mathematics Education, 23*, 2–33.

Cobb, P., Yackel, E., & Wood, T. (1993). Theoretical orientation. In T. Wood, P. Cobb, E. Yackel, & D. Dillon (Eds.), *Rethinking elementary school mathematics: Insights and issues. Journal for Research in Mathematics Education* (Monograph No. 6). Reston, VA: National Council of Teachers of Mathematics.

Ernest, P. (1991). *The philosophy of mathematics education.* London: Falmer.

Lampert, M. (1990). When the problem is not the question and the solution is not the answer: Mathematical knowing and teaching. *American Educational Research Journal, 27*(1), 29–63.

Schifter, D., & Fosnot, C. T. (1993). *Reconstructing mathematics education: Stories of teachers meeting the challenge of reform.* New York: Teachers College Press.

Simon, M. (1995). Reconstructing mathematics pedagogy from a constructivist perspective. *Journal for Research in Mathematics Education, 26*(2), 114–145.

Simon, M., & Blume, G. (in press). Mathematical justification: A classroom teaching experiment with prospective teachers. *Journal of Mathematical Behavior.*

Simon, M. A., & Schifter, D. (1991). Towards a constructivist perspective: An intervention study of mathematics teacher development. *Educational Studies in Mathematics, 22*(5), 309–331.

von Glasersfeld, E. (1987). Learning as a constructive activity. In C. Janvier (Ed.), *Problems of representation in the teaching and learning of mathematics* (pp. 3–17). Hillsdale, NJ: Lawrence Erlbaum.

von Glasersfeld, E. (1995). A constructivist approach to teaching. In L. Steffe & J. Gale (Eds.), *Constructivism in education* (pp. 3–16). Hillsdale, NJ: Lawrence Erlbaum.

CHAPTER 2

"Students Becoming Powerful Mathematical Thinkers"

To advocates of the current effort to reform mathematics education, the insights into learning on which it is based promise student understandings that are "deep," "rich," "conceptual." There is reproach in the rhetoric: "shallow," "impoverished," "mechanical" are by implication attributed to the outcomes of a practice designed, decades ago, to ensure a basic computational proficiency. To the extent that committing facts, definitions, and algorithms to memory by dint of drill-and-practice retains a place in the new mathematics classroom, that place is subordinated to a much more expansive vision that sees "students becoming powerful mathematical thinkers."

In the lexicon of reform, "thinking" is counterposed to "just following rules." It is usually "problem-generated," and is often characterized in terms suggestive of initiative—for example, "investigation," "exploration," "invention"—as well as an openness to unanticipated discovery. "Making connections" and "identifying and analyzing patterns" also are often invoked, as are "offering, testing, and revising conjectures," and "building mathematical arguments and assessing their validity."

In the narratives that follow, the contrast between "mathematical thinking" and "just following rules" is very much in play. Virginia Bastable is concerned because for her high school geometry students, " . . . operating with [irrational] numbers is a process of trying to remember what rule goes with what operation, rather than having a coherent sense of these operations." Donna Scanlon worries that, unless her algebra students succeed in connecting algebraic notation to other, more accessible modes of representation—for example, geometric shape—the language of variables will remain closed for them.

Bastable teaches in a regional high school in a college town; Scanlon, in a high school in a stressed urban system. In her essay, Joan Ferrini-Mundy explores the challenge of negotiating between thoughtful planning and moment-to-moment intellectual agility, a challenge that faces teachers who, like

Bastable and Scanlon, adopt the aspiration that their students become powerful mathematical thinkers.

+   −   ×   ÷

A DIALOGUE ABOUT TEACHING

Virginia Bastable

January 3

Dear Alice,

Hi. Hope you are doing well and still living up to those New Year's resolutions! Things around here are about the same. We've settled into a winter routine.

Right now my mind is on schoolwork, particularly my heterogeneously grouped geometry class where I'm about to tackle a unit based in area and the Pythagorean theorem. Every year I try to do something different from what I have done before, but I haven't ever been satisfied. I see a lot of problems in this unit. For one thing my students don't even think of irrationals as numbers! They did do some work with them last year in Algebra I, studying the rules about reducing, adding, and multiplying expressions with irrationals; but for most of my students, operating with these numbers is a process of trying to remember what rule goes with what operation, rather than having a coherent sense of these operations.

Also I realize I have strong emotions attached to this theorem by Pythagoras. It is such an elegant example of mathematics as both philosophy and practicality. It is about ideas and how humans can manipulate them to come up with something beautiful. Additionally, it has so many applications. I also like the way it embodies both the visual—remember Pythagoras was talking about actual squares—and the abstract, the algebraic notation we use now.

Writing to you has helped me see that I want to accomplish a lot during this work. I want my students to begin to form the kind of picture I have of this theorem. I want them to realize that square roots are numbers and want them to understand how to compute with them. I also want them to be able to apply this theorem in a variety of situations. No wonder I have been dissatisfied in the past. Now that I have a sense of what I want to accomplish perhaps I can find some ideas to work with. What is it you do in your classes? For now, I'm going to see what I can find in the pile of books I have on my desk.

Say hello to the rest of the family.

Write soon,

Meg

*   *   *

January 9

Dear Meg,

Yes, this is a dull time of year for those of us who don't ski. I'm doing okay with the resolutions. How about you, did you get that exercise program going? Everyone here says hello.

It's nice to know we are worrying about the same things. My students haven't studied irrationals, but they do have some experience with area. I've sent you some problems. (See Figure 2.1.) They aren't brilliant but you wanted to know what it is I do and this is some of it. All they need to know for this first sheet is how to find the areas of rectangles and right triangles. The problems are multistep, and I find it works best for students to work in groups.

You made me wonder about the Pythagorean theorem. I'm looking through my files to see what ideas I can come up with. Since my students haven't studied square roots, I need to include that, too. I'll let you know what I find.

Take care,

Alice

*   *   *

January 15

Dear Alice,

Yes, surprisingly I am keeping up my exercise routine. I swim three days a week and walk three others. I find having one day off each week helps me stick to this regimen.

Today I feel really excited. I just had to write to describe one of my classes. It was wonderful, even though it didn't go the way I had planned. Here's what happened.

Yesterday I passed out the worksheet you sent. The students began by working in their problem-solving groups and then were to finish the problems for homework. My purpose was for them to practice the area formulas I knew they were familiar with. When they came in today, I asked them to compare their work with each other. As is our routine, while they did this, I wandered around the room to check that homework was done. After a few minutes, I began the whole group discussion by asking, "What problem do you want to start with?"

FIGURE 2.1. Alice's Problem Sheet

Use diagrams to calculate the areas requested in each problem.
Hand in the diagrams along with explanations of how you got your answers.

1. A is a square with area 64. B is a square with area 25.
    The entire figure is a square. Find the area of the unshaded region.

2. The area of the whole figure is 121. The whole figure is a square.
    The area of square A is 64. Find the <u>perimeter</u> of square B.

3. A square and a rectangle have equal perimeters. One side of the square is 12
    cm. One side of the rectangle is 18 cm. Which figure has the larger area?

4. The whole figure is a square. Find the area of the shaded region.

5. How many square tiles 3 inches on a side will it take to cover a floor
    that is 10 feet by 8 feet?

Julie raised her hand. "Let's talk about the one with the square inside the square. Jake and I did it different ways."

I wasn't surprised that these two would have different approaches. Within this heterogeneous group of geometry students, Julie and Jake are on opposite ends of the spectrum in almost every aspect of learning style. Julie is very concrete; Jake, abstract. Julie draws out each problem in detail; Jake has flashes of ideas that just "come" to him. Diagrams are Julie's favorite method of solution; Jake enjoys manipulating formulas. Yet they often choose to work together, I guess because they happen to be good friends out of school.

Julie drew the problem on the board (problem 4 in Figure 2.1) and asked Jake to show his method. Jake explained: "I saw that the sides of the large

square are 12, so the area is 144. Each of the right triangles is ½ of base ×
height or 16. There are four of them. So 144 − 64 = 80.''

There were murmurs of agreement. Then Julie said, ''Now watch my
way.''

''Did you get the same answer as Jake?'' asked Bill.

''Yes, but I wanted to see the rectangles—the ones that the triangles are
half of—so I drew the lines across and down like this (as in Figure 2.2). Then
I saw the tilted square was made up of four triangles and an even smaller
square. The triangles are 16, ½ of 32, and the little square is 4 by 4 so it is
16, too—5 × 16, for the four triangles and the little square, makes 80.''

Harry wanted to know how Julie knew the little square was 4 by 4. She
explained she counted on the graph paper.

This is interesting, I thought; one method uses subtraction as its basis, the
other uses addition. I also was thinking this made the tilted square into five
equal but noncongruent parts. I was wondering if that was significant. Would
it be worthwhile to point this out to the class? You must know what it's like.
You're in class, thinking of the students and what's happening, and suddenly
a new idea emerges. Now you have to decide if it is worth commenting on.

Anyway, while all that was going on in my head, Bill said with exaspera-
tion, ''Oh, now I see what I did.'' None of us knew what he was talking
about. He looked up, surprised that he had spoken out loud. ''I didn't draw
the diagram right. Instead of going over four squares, I went over five. So my
picture looks like this.'' (See Figure 2.3.)

''Wouldn't the area be the same anyway?'' asked a girl sitting next to
Bill. She looked puzzled.

What a great question! I was wondering the same thing myself. I didn't
want Bill to tell the class his solution until we all had a chance to think about
it. Before Bill could answer, I turned to the class. ''What do you think? If the

FIGURE 2.2. Julie's Method for Finding the Area of the ''Tilted'' Square

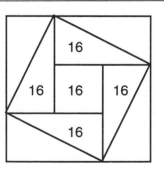

FIGURE 2.3. Bill's Variation of the Problem

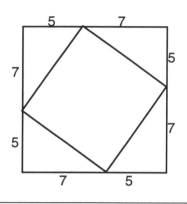

point is moved from partitioning the side of length 12 into sections of 4 and 8 and instead breaks that side into sections of 5 and 7, would the area of the tilted square stay the same? If not, does it get larger or smaller?"

I gave everyone a few minutes to form an opinion—and not just the students! I was giving myself time to think as well. I wasn't sure which way this would go, but I knew we were going to consider the possibilities. At this point I hadn't solved the problem for myself, but I liked the dynamic pictures this approach was creating in my head. Too often problems are just a single instance; here we had the opportunity to look at the mathematics of change.

Each individual had been deciding whether the area would stay the same, get larger, or get smaller. I wanted each student to determine what he or she believed before we investigated this further. When the class voted, it was an even split—about one-third for each possibility. I was thinking about a way for the class to resolve this when Briana said, "I wonder if we could do them all?" I asked her what she meant. "Well," she said, "I'm thinking of the point as being at 4 but Bill had it at 5. What is the area of the tilted square if that point is at 1 or 2 or something like that?" Briana seemed to get at the heart of the matter, and her comment helped me decide how to structure the rest of the class.

"Which cases do you want to try?" I asked, and the students began to call out while I wrote on the board: 1 and 11, 2 and 10, 3 and 9, 4 and 8, 5 and 7, 6 and 6, 7 and 5, 8 and 4 . . .

"Wait a minute. We don't have to try all those. They'll be the same as the others." This was from Sandra.

So we ended up with the first six situations. (They do like whole numbers, don't they?) I assigned a case to each group and reminded them that they had seen two ways to do these problems. I suggested each group do the prob-

FIGURE 2.4. Table of Values and Graph of Square-within-a-Square Problem

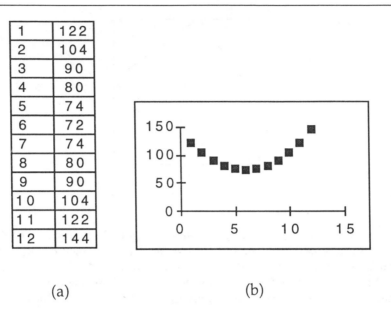

1	122
2	104
3	90
4	80
5	74
6	72
7	74
8	80
9	90
10	104
11	122
12	144

(a)   (b)

lem both ways and compare the results. I figured this way those who had tried one method would become familiar with the other.

As they were working, I walked around the room and checked the various groups. In fact I was using the time to figure out the problem myself. By now I was realizing this question would move us into an informal approach to maximums and minimums. It was clearly worth the time we were spending.

I recorded the values they reported in a table (Figure 2.4(a)) and suggested that we graph the area based on the placement of the point. (They had done little graphing this year and without my prompting I don't think they would have analyzed the problem this way.) There was a series of comments as they looked at the table of values. All I did was to record their work on the board. The students were carrying on the discussion on their own.

"What would happen if we kept going? Like with 7, 8 . . . "

"The values would just repeat."

"Put them in the table anyway."

"Can we have a value for 12?"

They were quiet for a minute. Then Juan said, "Yes, at that point the inside square fills up the whole square, so you could say they both have area of 144."

I was wondering if anyone would consider the meaning of zero for the placement of the point, but no one brought it up.

When they finished their graphs (Figure 2.4(b)), I asked the class if we could connect the points. I heard groans. "Do we have to do fractions?" (Actually I was pleased at that. To me it indicated they realized the implication of connecting the points was finding values for the point at 4.6, 2⅓, etc.) Then Gina said, "The area is smallest when the point is at 6 and the area is 72."

I asked, "How do you know the graph doesn't go below 72, maybe a little past 6, and then goes back up to 74 at 7? How do you *know* it is lowest at 6?"

I was expecting an argument based on symmetry, but that's not what I got.

Laura came up with diagrams from her group. They had tried Bill's case with the point at 5. "Compare the one we all did for homework with what Bill did," she said. "The four little triangles take up more space in Bill's. The little square in the middle is smaller when the point is at 5 than at 4." (See Figure 2.5.)

Briana piped up: "I don't see why that means that the lowest happens when the point is at 6."

Bill, who was now feeling good about his "mistake," said, "I see it. The little square is getting smaller and smaller until at 6 it is gone. The whole space is filled up with the four triangles." (See Figure 2.6.)

At this point, I introduced the word "parabola" and drew the continuous graph. I had thought about asking the class to compute some intermediate points like 1.5, 5.4, or 3½ for homework but I decided to let the physical beauty of the argument suffice.

Alice, you have to realize I had no idea this problem would lead us into

FIGURE 2.5. Comparison Between the 4–8 and 5–7 Cases

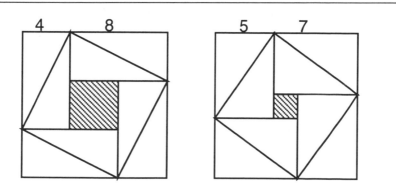

FIGURE 2.6. The 6–6 Case Yields the Minimum Area of the Inner Square

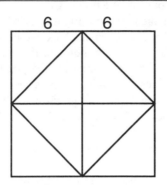

work they usually do in Algebra II. I just wanted them to practice area formulas! I know that next year I will design something like this, making sure that someone like Bill makes a "mistake."

Sorry for going on so long. I just had to share this with someone and I knew you would appreciate it. After all, it started with your problem.

Bye for now,

Meg

*   *   *

January 27

Dear Meg,

Wow, what a class! Did I say that my problems weren't brilliant? I take that back. Actually I just copied it out of a book. It took Bill's mistake to show us both what could be done with it. It was fun to read about your class even though my own experiences today have been very confusing.

Your class sounded so neat, so simple. Everyone contributed and stayed focused. Right now I'm feeling like my classroom is a confused mess. I've decided that I need to talk about it and you're elected. So pour yourself a cup of tea, sit in a comfortable chair, tell your family you are busy, and let me explain. I'm hoping that as I describe my situation it will make more sense to me as well.

As I mentioned before, my students come to geometry without a background in square roots. Each year as I plan this unit I remember an incident from the past . . .

. . . I was teaching over lunch time. My class met for half an hour, then we ate, then we had another half hour of class. I was leading a review of the Pythagorean theorem during the first part of class and planning a test for the last part. I was feeling pretty good about the review. I had started with an example of a right triangle with legs of 3 and 4 so that the answer for the hypotenuse was a whole number. Then I gradually increased the difficulty level, eventually posing problems with a missing leg and also irrational lengths. I had the sense the class was with me. They were calling out answers as I wrote on the board and they seemed quite attentive. (After all, they had a test in the next half hour!) I was feeling pretty satisfied with myself until Karl spoke up: "I see everything you're doing, but I still have just one question. Over there, where you wrote $\sqrt{10}$, why didn't you just write 5?" Then the bell rang and they all left for lunch—even Karl. He must have been hungrier for his lunch than for the answer. As for me, I just sat there, dumbfounded. Karl's question made me wonder what other students were thinking. I mean, how could they follow along with my presentation and then ask such a question?

. . . This memory stays with me. The incident made me determined that square roots will have meaning for my students. This year I decided to use a variety of "tilted square" problems to provide my class with examples of squares with irrational side lengths. I made up a worksheet with a bunch of problems like these (Figure 2.7).

I wanted my students to have squares with area 10, 40, 90, etc. I thought that once they had worked with the areas, I'd ask about the length of the side and that would introduce the need for the square root. My goal was for them to have a physical definition of square root: $\sqrt{a}$ = the length of the side of a

FIGURE 2.7. Worksheet Intended to Lead into Discussion of Irrational Numbers

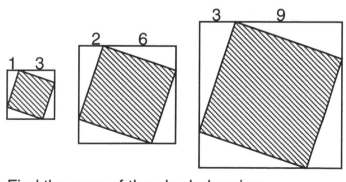

Find the area of the shaded region.

square with area a. I assigned the worksheet as homework—as far as they knew, it was some practice on area.

The same way you do, at the start of class I had them pair off and compare homework answers with each other. As the pairs were working I wandered the room, checking to see if they would be ready for my next step. They were finding the areas of the whole squares and subtracting the areas of the triangles. (No one drew in horizontal and vertical lines like Julie did in your class. I think it's because my class hasn't used Geoboards the way your class has.)

The bragging tone of one girl, Jeanne, caught my ear: "I can find the area of the tilted square without having to work with the triangles. I just look at the numbers."

"What do you mean?" asked her partner, Sean.

"Just test me," said Jeanne. "Make up one that isn't on the sheet."

"Okay. What if the numbers were 3 and 5?"

"Then it would be 64 take away double 15: 34."

Jeanne said this with great authority and pride. Her partner corroborated the answer by subtracting the areas.

"How did you do it?" Sean asked Jeanne.

"First I add the numbers and square that; then I multiply the numbers and double that. When you subtract you get the answer. It always works. It's a shortcut."

Suddenly images from algebra were running through my mind. Jeanne's shortcut reminded me of the formula for squaring binomials, but I wasn't sure what that had do with the problem. Nevertheless, I decided to let Jeanne show off a little. She had created a formula of her own and I thought I could use her example to make connections between algebra and geometry. I turned to Jeanne.

"I'd like you to show the class what you noticed. I'll call on you during the whole group discussion. Is that okay? "

Jeanne indicated that she would share her method with the class. When I left them, Sean was trying to practice the "trick."

As I write this now I find myself wishing that I had asked her how she came up with this pattern, but I was preoccupied with other thoughts at the time. I was thinking that I would have Jeanne do a few problems on the board, explain what her method was, and then have the class try her method in general, with a and b as the values, to see what was going on. This would be the way to connect the geometrical work they did and the algebraic symbols for it. After all, Jeanne's method was just an algebraic shorthand for the work: Find the area of the large square and subtract the area of the four triangles. I figured that solving the problem with a and b would give us a rule that was derived from their work. It would link what we were doing in geometry with the work they had done in algebra last year. Of course, that still wouldn't get us to square roots!

I started the whole class time by asking if anyone had a problem to discuss. There was no response. Taking that to mean each pair had agreed on their answers, I decided to go on.

I told the class that Jeanne had a way to do the area problems without drawing the diagrams. She came to the board and challenged the class to make up examples. Without writing anything on the board, she just reported the answers. The class was quiet, watching her, checking her answers, and trying to figure out her method.

After three examples, I was going to ask her to explain her approach, when Henry spoke up: "I see what you're doing. I can do it, too."

So I invited Henry to the front and the class made up another problem for both of them. So many people were involved, I decided to keep this going. I suggested that Jeanne and Henry do one more problem, this time writing out their computations so we could all watch them.

Someone suggested 2 and 6 as the numbers. Jeanne wrote: "$8 \times 8 = 64$, $2 \times 6 = 12$. Double the 12 and get 24. $64 - 24 = 40$." Henry wrote: "2 squared is 4, 6 squared is 36. $4 + 36 = 40$."

Was I surprised! I now saw that this problem must involve the Pythagorean theorem, which we hadn't even studied yet! But I was also confused. There was so much going on that I didn't have a clear idea of how to proceed. How Jeanne's and Henry's work were related wasn't obvious to me. Should I introduce the Pythagorean theorem now? What about the lesson on square roots I had planned?

The class was confused as well. Some of the students had no idea what was going on. Others were playing around with the numbers. Jeanne and Henry stared at each other's work, shrugged their shoulders, and looked at me. I knew I had to focus the class on one aspect of the problem, and so I invited everyone to look at Jeanne's way for the moment. What they didn't know was that *I* didn't see how Jeanne's and Henry's work were connected. I kept thinking Pythagorean theorem, but I didn't have a solid idea, and since we hadn't studied it yet, it wasn't on *their* minds at all. I thought I could at least get the class to look at Jeanne's method and match it with the diagrams they had drawn.

I said, "Let's stay with this 2 and 6 problem. Draw out the squares and solve it for yourself."

I waited at the front of the room and watched as they worked at their desks.

"Now do the same thing using 'a' in place of '2' and 'b' in place of '6.'"

As I said this I suddenly saw that Jeanne's method—$(a + b)^2 - 2ab$—would result in Henry's way—$a^2 + b^2$. Jeanne's and Henry's methods were not at all different. Henry's was the result of simplifying Jeanne's.

Clearly this problem was related to the Pythagorean theorem. I started looking at the diagram differently, focusing on the triangles. That's when I noticed the side of the tilted square was the hypotenuse of a right triangle. Meg, it's amazing what a shift in perception can do. Up to this point I had thought of the triangles as extraneous—we cut them off from the large square to see what was left. Now I was conscious that the numbers weren't just unattached values but rather the lengths of the legs of right triangles.

Suddenly I'm thinking, Well at least *I'm* learning mathematics today! I'm seeing connections that I haven't seen previously.

Meanwhile, the class was still working on the problem I had posed. Some students were getting wrong answers because they didn't multiply $(a + b)^2$ correctly; others were getting $a^2 + b^2$ but, even though they were right, it didn't mean anything to them. I was confused about what to do next.

My time for deciding was running out. Students were finishing the task, and my head was full of conflicting ideas. I could introduce the Pythagorean theorem now, but I didn't like the fact that we hadn't discussed square roots at all. I could have students come to the board and show their work on the problem, but I wasn't sure how those who did it wrong would learn anything aside from the fact that they were wrong. I did have on hand the homework assignment I had envisioned for this class, a worksheet on comparing areas. I supposed I could go with that.

But in the meantime the class was getting restless. It was almost time for lunch. After a half-hour break (we still have those split lunch classes), they would be back. I figured I would use my lunch time to decide what I wanted to do next. I collected the work each pair had done with the 2, 6 example and the *a, b* example—after all I didn't want them to think I wasn't interested in their work—and told them we would work on this some more after lunch.

So, Meg, you're thinking, what did I decide? My decision was to avoid mentioning the Pythagorean theorem and to go back to my focus on square roots. Actually, I was wishing I hadn't brought up this *a, b* scheme. I had planned on keeping an arithmetic focus to our discussion until I got a sense that my students were thinking of square roots as numbers. So I resolved that would be the focus of the next half hour.

When they returned from lunch I told them to work on a new example, a square with side length 3 broken into sections of 1 and 2. I would use this example to help them develop a sense of the irrationality of $\sqrt{5}$.

From this example they quickly derived that the area of the inner square was 5. I suggested that they talk to their partners and find a way to get a value for the length of a side of the square and gave them a few minutes to work.

When I asked for answers this is what I got: more than 2, 2½, 2.24, 2.236068, and $\sqrt{5}$. I asked how we could decide which, if any, of these were correct.

Maria said, "Well, the first one (more than 2) is right but it isn't really an answer—'cause it's not a number, really."

Henry said, "The last one ($\sqrt{5}$) isn't exact, because they didn't really do it. They just said it."

This was pretty interesting to me. It seemed that Henry thought of the square-root operation in terms of computations. This led him to conclude the $\sqrt{5}$ (the mathematically correct answer) was imprecise because it wasn't in decimal form. I wonder now if other students might have been thinking the same way. Do you see this in your students? I filed this away for later work and tried to keep the conversation going.

"What about the others?"

"I don't think $2\frac{1}{2}$ is right. It doesn't come out to 5, if you multiply it."

I wanted Krista to explain more. I hadn't heard anyone else express this.

"Can you show us what you mean?"

Krista came to the board and wrote: "$2\frac{1}{2} \times 2\frac{1}{2} = \frac{5}{2} \times \frac{5}{2} = \frac{25}{4} = 6\frac{1}{4}$."

She started to sit down. I said, "I need to hear more. How does that tell you that $2\frac{1}{2}$ isn't the right answer?" (It really takes a lot to get them to explain themselves. Even when they are right, I find they don't always include enough in their explanations.)

"The square has area 5. If the sides were $2\frac{1}{2}$ the area would be bigger than that, $6\frac{1}{4}$."

"I know that 2.236068 is right because I did it on my calculator." This was said rather impatiently by James. My sense is that he thinks math is straightforward and I make too much of simple ideas.

"Let's try Krista's test on this one," I said. "If the side of the square is 2.236068, what is the area of the square?"

As James started to push the calculator keys, I wrote it out on the board:

$$\frac{\begin{array}{r} 2.236068 \\ \times\ 2.236068 \end{array}}{}$$

and started to carry out the computation as if I were doing it by hand.

Before James could report his result, Marla said, "Well, it won't be exactly 5 because there will be a number in the end place, not zero."

I decided not to comment on the fact that she didn't seem to consider zero a number, because she was making an argument that could lead the class to understand the irrationality of square roots.

"What do you think of that, James?" I asked.

"It's pretty close to 5; it came out to 5.0027374."

I stopped the partial work I was doing on the board, drew a line and wrote James's answer. I was happy this happened. I had been afraid the round-off feature of the calculator might have made the answer exactly 5. That was why I wrote the problem out on the board so that everyone could see what it would be like to do the multiplication by hand.

"Yes, it comes close," I admitted. "Can we get a number that will make it exactly 5?"

"Let's try something just a little smaller," someone suggested.

James said, "But what is wrong with my calculator? I pushed the square-root button."

"I see that 2.24 comes out closer; it's 5.0176," added yet another student.

These comments came in simultaneously. I was having trouble keeping the whole group going in a linear fashion. James was bugged that his calculator wasn't good enough. I was wondering if my students' understanding of decimals was strong enough that they knew which of the answers *was* closer to 5. On top of all that I kept thinking that I shouldn't have let that statement about zero go by without comment.

Do you have days like this?

Okay, I know. You want to know what I did. Well, I took the route that seemed easiest at the time. I turned it back to them. This was the homework: "Determine the length of the side of a square that has an area of 5. Write a statement that explains your answer."

What would you have done? By the time you get this letter and respond, this particular issue will have passed, but I will still appreciate any comments you might have. How do you deal with a class discussion when so many issues are brought up? How do you choose which issues to address and which to ignore? These are my burning questions tonight. Please answer in 25 words or less. Seriously though, any thoughts?

Yours in confusion,

Alice

*   *   *

February 4

Dear Alice,

Do I have days like that? Oh yes, and when I do, I feel good about them. To me it sounds like your students are engaged, are sorting out their ideas, and are working hard!

You are, too. In spite of my positive comments, I do know how confusing it feels to be at the front of the class leading such a discussion, even though "leading" might be the last word you would use. It isn't easy deciding which ideas to pursue and which to ignore, or at least set aside. Sometimes it feels overwhelming, especially when you feel the need to "fix" everything you hear.

Let me give you another perspective. I'm going to describe what I see going on in your class. Your students are giving voice to their mathematical ideas. Sometimes they are right, sometimes wrong, but they are talking about what they are thinking. Since each student has his or her own way of thinking, the variety of comments and approaches can contribute to a sense of confusion. Yet in this confusion, sometimes through it, they can sort out their thoughts.

I am thinking about your classroom experiences and how they compare with the scenario you related about Karl and the $\sqrt{10}$. That was an orderly classroom. Students were quiet, watching your work. You didn't have the sense that it was confusing. But look what happened. Even while they were quiet, and, you thought, attentive, students were forming their own ideas. Again, some of these were right and some were wrong, but *you* didn't get to hear them. It just wasn't part of class to discuss them. Whatever ideas they had were left unchallenged. It was a matter of chance that you learned that at least one student thought $\sqrt{10}$ was 5.

As you indicated, Karl's question was just the tip of the iceberg. It made you wonder, "What else are they thinking?" So the order, the lack of confusion, was an illusion. The disorder was there in their heads. It always is. Each of us is forming our own ideas all the time. The question is, how do we, as teachers, get to hear what our students are thinking so that we can work with their ideas?

Your current classroom provides opportunities for students to talk to each other, both in small groups and through whole class discussions. In this way they have a chance to test out their ideas and modify them. Sure, it's bewildering when so many issues come up. In that last discussion, issues about decimals, zero, approximations, and square roots were swirling around. But looking at it from my vantage point, that seems natural. All those topics are connected, are a necessary part of the new understanding of number that you are asking your students to form.

When all these ideas come up, it is not possible to nail down every nuance of each idea for each student, but through discussions, students will take whatever piece makes sense to them depending on their past experiences. As you read what they write in their homework assignments, you will have a chance to address some of the individual concerns. Some ideas may even go by unnoticed. These will have to wait for their next opportunity.

I like the way you are approaching the irrationality of square roots. It seems your students will go away with the idea that no decimal or fraction form will be adequate to serve as $\sqrt{5}$. At this point you could explain that mathematicians made up a name and a symbol for this number that is the length of a side of a square with area 5.

I do think you can use this work to support the introduction of the Pythagorean theorem. As I was reading your letter I was working through the math myself. (Thanks for that chance, by the way. It was fun.) I used a diagram to show myself where the quantities 1^2, 2^2, and 5 are in the picture. I think the

FIGURE 2.8. The Pythagorean Theorem Embedded in the Square-within-a-Square Problem

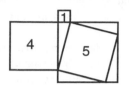

diagram (Figure 2.8) could provide a link between the traditional statement of the theorem and the diagrams with which your students are already familiar.

I wanted to respond quickly to your comments. The feelings you describe are so real to me. I hope my ideas help you sort out what is happening in your class. Let me know what you tried.

Supportingly,

Meg

*   *   *

February 12

Dear Meg,

Thanks for your kind words. It really helped to hear your analysis and to know you sometimes have the same feelings. It is so hard to know what a good class is any more. The old standards—students quiet, lots of problems being finished, right answers—are all inadequate. But it's not simply a matter of doing the opposite. Certainly not all classes with noisy students, few problems worked, and wrong answers are good! Somehow I have to figure out what my new set of standards will be. Your ideas are helping me through that process. As you indicated, verbalization of student thinking will be an important component. Thank you for showing me that was happening in the class I described.

Let me tell you what we did when we met again. Once I had defined square root, I decided to have them continue with this "tilted square" problem. I had something specific in mind. My class had done a lot of work with similarity so I wanted to capitalize on that experience. I saw I could use this problem to have my students explore the difference between doubling the perimeter and doubling the area. Additionally, they would be working with square roots and their simplification. I had them find the area and side length for a series of squares of varying sizes (see Figure 2.9) and asked the following questions:

1. Find the areas of the squares and triangles in the diagrams.
2. What patterns do you see?
3. What would diagram (d) look like?
4. Predict the areas of the figures in diagram (d).
5. How long is a side of the tilted square in each diagram?
6. What patterns do you see?
7. Predict the length of a side of the tilted square in diagram (d).

Students worked in groups of three. After a while, I suggested we compile the answers on the board, by saying, "Let's look at areas first." This was met by a bombardment of student questions and comments: "Do you want the areas of all of them?" "We only need to give two answers, 'cause all the triangles are the same." "But there are really two squares, a big and a small." "Put them all up."

I liked this interplay. The students themselves were deciding what information to record. However, I wasn't sure that we, as a class, had come to any agreement so I interrupted: "How many is all?"

Someone suggested we needed three values, one for the triangles and two for the squares. As I looked around the room visually checking in with each student, I sensed agreement. I drew a chart, labeled it, and asked for values (see Figure 2.10). Once the chart was filled, I asked, "What did you write for a pattern?"

"They go up by 4s."

FIGURE 2.9. Worksheet to Explore the Difference Between Doubling the Perimeter and Doubling the Area

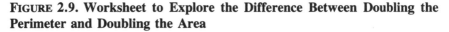

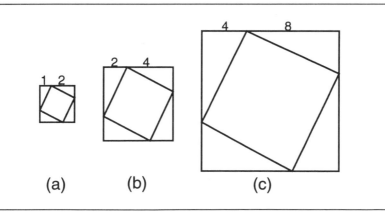

(a)   (b)   (c)

FIGURE 2.10. Table of Areas Taken from Diagrams in Figure 2.9

	Areas Triangles	Areas Squares	
Diagram (a)	1	5	9
Diagram (b)	4	20	36
Diagram (c)	16	80	144

"Each one is 4 times bigger."

As I wrote these on the board I asked, "Do these say the same thing?" To this, several students responded.

"Well, I see why someone would say that they go up by 4s, but I think that means like 1, 5, 9, 13."

"Yeah, that means they are 4 apart. These aren't 4 apart."

"They are sometimes, like 1 and 5."

"But that's the only time. And the 4 times bigger rule always works."

"No, it's really 1, 4, 16. We're looking down, not across."

I erased the first rule, feeling satisfied that the class accepted the second one. As I was doing that I overheard one student say to a neighbor, "The areas are easy. It's the perimeters I don't get."

This made me wonder how many other groups had worked with perimeter, not just side lengths. I was tempted to lead the class in this direction. I was excited that they had pursued this avenue and wanted to see what they had done. However, I decided to complete the area questions first since everyone had done those. So I asked, "What did you predict for figure (d)?"

Almost in unison, I heard "64, 320, 576." They all had the right answers, but somehow I was disappointed. It wasn't that I wanted them to have *wrong* answers, but I got no sense that the numbers meant anything to them. There was no sense of comparison, nothing about the way the shapes were growing. They were just answering the questions I asked. Now that I think about it, I realize that their answers were too pat, too easy. There was no confusion, no puzzlement!—there was nothing to work on.

I was thinking about your parabola class. In that activity the students were engaged, they were trying to answer a question for themselves. I was disappointed that nothing like that was going on here. As I asked them for their side-length figures, part of my mind was thinking about the perimeter comment and also how else to approach this problem.

Before I came up with something, I heard several comments that required my attention: "Some of it seems to be double, but I don't know what to do about the square roots." "Can we use the calculators and just have decimals?" "What would the perimeter be?"

I made a suggestion: "Before we try to answer those questions, let's get on the board what people have recorded for side lengths." (See Figure 2.11.)

When the second chart was on the board, Kevin said he had different answers for diagram (b). He explained: "When I did the area work I wanted to see how the square in (b) was 4 times larger than the one in (a). So I drew in lines dividing the square into 4 parts." He came to the board to show us (see Figure 2.12). Then he continued: "Each side of the little squares is $\sqrt{5}$, so the side length should be $\sqrt{5} + \sqrt{5}$. Can you call that $2\sqrt{5}$? Is it really twice as long?"

"Does that mean $\sqrt{20}$ is twice as long as $\sqrt{5}$?" Mei asked.

"What does the calculator say for $\sqrt{5}$ and $\sqrt{20}$?" This was from Sasha.

All these questions. All this confusion. I was feeling good. Now they were engaged. They were trying to figure out their ideas. I wasn't exactly sure what line to follow next, but I was remembering your comments, so I wasn't as worried as I was before. I knew I was conducting the class in a way that placed their ideas on the agenda. There were enough ideas to work with to keep us busy for a while, so I went back to the complex job of working with a class full of thinkers. I still find it hard, and sometimes I make decisions I regret. However, at the same time, I'm learning mathematics in a new way and so are my students.

I am really glad we are able to talk about teaching through these letters. Let's continue. It's almost time for February vacation. I am ready for a few

FIGURE 2.11. Table of Lengths Taken from Diagrams in Figure 2.9

Side Length	Inner Square	Whole Square
Diagram (a)	$\sqrt{5}$	3
Diagram (b)	$\sqrt{20}$	6
Diagram (c)	$\sqrt{80}$	12

days away from the daily work. I plan to do a bunch of stuff around the house and think casually about schoolwork.

What do you say we figure out what to do with circles next?

Warmly,

Alice

*   *   *

Notes from the Author:

While the letters you have just read are fictitious, the classroom stories are not. These letters are based on actual events that took place in a regional secondary school located in a college town in New England. The student body is 28% of color, including children of Asian-, Hispanic-, and African-American heritage. While there is a strong emphasis on college-bound students at the school, the classes described in the letters were grouped heterogeneously; that is, they contained students from the highest, middle, and lowest achievement levels offered by the school.

As I worked with this diversity of students, I was struck by how many times the so-called ''low'' student contributed significant ideas to the class. I became interested in pursuing the difference between mathematical thinking and mathematical knowledge. My belief is that while these can be deeply intertwined, one does not always imply the other.

At the same time that I was working on this piece, I was writing to a teacher friend in another context, sharing my classroom decisions. I chose this letter format for my classroom stories because I found this writing exercise stimulating. The need to explain carefully forced me to think hard about what

FIGURE 2.12. Demonstration that $2\sqrt{5} = \sqrt{20}$

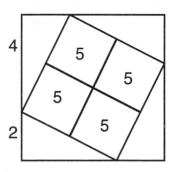

was going on in my classroom, and the opportunity to respond to my own letter made it possible for me to analyze my classroom at a distance. I recommend such correspondence to all teachers who view teaching itself as a problem-solving experience.

$$+ \quad - \quad \times \quad \div$$

ALGEBRA IS COOL: REFLECTIONS ON A CHANGING PEDAGOGY IN AN URBAN SETTING

Donna Babski Scanlon

I wasn't sure if those two guys were on task when I walked over to see if they needed some direction. I sat down with them and said, "How's it going?" as I took note of the fact that Alfredo was drawing something that had nothing to do with the problem I had given them. I groaned inwardly and tried to decide whether I should complain, when Narcisso said: "Ms. Scanlon, we're going to design a t-shirt for you. It's going to say 'Ms. Scanlon' on the front and 'ALGEBRA' in big letters on the back. And we're going to make a design to put on it. It costs 20 bucks but they'll make it for you at this place we know."

A seasoned teacher reading this may be thinking, "I hope she realizes that they're just trying to get her mind off the fact that they're not doing their work." But Alfredo and Narcisso are fellows who feel no need to charm teachers. They would feel comfortable saying, "This is boring. I'm not doing it." Teachers (like myself) of basic algebra classes are accustomed to hearing such comments.

My response to them was one of delight and I said, "Isn't algebra wonderful?" Narcisso responded, shaking his head, "It is, but it plays with your mind."

"I know what you mean," I laughed.

Bernie, a member of another basic algebra class, said to me, "I love this class. I don't want to change my schedule, but I'm not going to get credit for it. I took it in summer school and I passed. But I'm going to stay."

"I understand this. Can I explain it to the class?" This from Jose, who failed this course with me last year. His failure was caused by poor attendance, although he frequently had difficulty with the material. Algebra made no sense to him last year.

Jenn and Jackie shook hands and beamed smiles at one another after they figured out something with which the whole class was struggling.

These are the same students who, on September 6, responding to the question, "What is algebra?" wrote that algebra is confusing, impossible, mind-boggling, senseless, useless, a waste of time, and boring, boring, boring.

Why aren't my students rolling their eyeballs at me the way they used to, as I meticulously and enthusiastically explained each new algebraic idea? I was getting accustomed to my students being in pretty severe discomfort during class as they watched the clock and waited for the bell. And I was pretty used to having a majority of students in my basic class glassy-eyed, unmotivated, and hoping they could pass with a "D" so they wouldn't have to take this awful course again.

So, what's going on?

THE SETTING

I teach Algebra I at a high school in an urban community with a diverse population. This year I'm teaching six classes—four college preparatory (standard level) and two basic level—and have a total of 191 students. My large class size can be blamed on drastic funding cuts that have caused massive teacher layoffs system wide. The math department at my school has suffered a 40% reduction in staff.

The impossible situation is a survival test for myself and my students. Their fortitude and patience are amazing as they wait for me to take attendance and attend to management details. All the little things seem to take much longer with large classes. Just hearing questions or ideas expressed by classmates is a trying experience because students are not accustomed to raising voices to be heard across a large room with more than 30 bodies. Rustling papers, squeaky chairs, whispering are all in the background, distracting people from their own thoughts or someone else's. Seeing the board from those back corners of the room is difficult, but there is no alternative. The room is full.

So things are not as they should be. Yet somehow my students and I are getting pleasure out of working together to make sense out of mathematics. Certainly we hope that this situation will be resolved, but meanwhile we have so much to do, so much to figure out.

ALGEBRA I

Algebra has a reputation for being a mind-boggling series of steps and procedures and is often the beginning of the end of understanding mathematics concepts. I'm attempting to alter that expectation for my students. I have been searching for tasks that will allow algebra to become a natural and sensible extension of the mathematics my students have studied previously. Questioning them in a way that will cause them to struggle for clarity is a skill that I am working hard to improve. Sometimes that means I have to do some struggling for understanding, too. For me, the most exciting part of our process of change is that I am continually learning from my students—about mathematics, about myself, and about learning.

WHAT DO YOU MEAN BY "K"?

Using a variable to convey a mathematical idea is a rather foreign concept for many of my students. As I thought about how I could make algebra more meaningful, it occurred to me that we wouldn't get very far if students were not comfortable using letters in expressions in ways that seemed reasonable to them. They needed opportunities to see how a variable could be used to say something they would like to say, as in making a rule or generalization.

One of the problem sets they explored as they struggled to understand the concept of a variable was "Polygons All in a Row." Students were asked to notice the perimeters that were generated as the number of polygons increased. The first problem involves triangles, as shown in Figure 2.13. The class noticed that if you have 1 triangle, the perimeter is 3; 2 triangles, the perimeter is 4; and 3 triangles, the perimeter is 5.

The worksheet required that students organize their data in a table, and they were able to describe quite easily in words that if there were k triangles, the perimeter would be 2 more than k. Someone suggested that the rule for finding the perimeter of k triangles, in the language of algebra, would be $k + 2$. Students were comfortable with this because they could see in their table that the perimeter always turned out to be two more than the number of triangles. I was a bit uneasy about their understanding, but at this point I did not know why. After all, they had all completed the task correctly.

We went on to investigating squares in a row (see Figure 2.14). I called on various students to make observations, and they saw that if you have 1 square, the perimeter is 4; 2 squares, the perimeter is 6; 3 squares, the perimeter is 8.

At first, the students focused on one pattern they saw occurring—that the perimeter kept increasing by 2—and so they determined that if you have 4

FIGURE 2.13. Triangles All in a Row

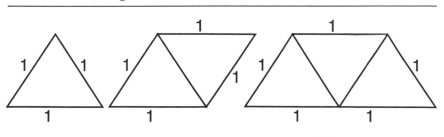

FIGURE 2.14. Squares All in a Row

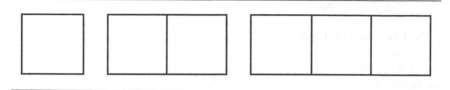

squares, the perimeter is 10; 5 squares, the perimeter is 12. But they found that information did not help them determine what the perimeter would be when they had 100 squares in a row. Finally, someone decided that you take the number of squares you have, double it, and add 2. Someone else offered that if there were k squares the perimeter would be $2k + 2$.

At this point, I realized why I had been uneasy earlier. Students were not seeing that they were adding the top length and the bottom length of the squares and that was why they were doubling the number of squares. They were not seeing that the two end-unit lengths were the reason for the "plus 2." In other words, I knew that $2k + 2$ was simply a formula that would get them the right answer, much as though they were playing a guess-my-rule numbers game.

I also realized that when we were discussing the previous problem, I had not asked them to look at their triangles to determine exactly why they added 2 on to the number of triangles they had. I believe that I may have taken that understanding for granted. For some reason, I, myself, was suddenly more aware not only of the connection between the components of the formula and the physical representation, but also of the importance of my students investigating the math in this way. *I* was beginning to look at math concepts and algorithms with a new purpose, and it felt good and it felt different. I wanted my students to experience understanding deeply and with clarity. It was no longer enough for me to hear them provide an answer, if that answer had no meaning for them.

I probed with questions, hoping someone would state these connections, but was confronted with blank stares and puzzled expressions. The period was over so I asked students to make sense out of $2k + 2$ for homework and to explore a progression of pentagons all in a row.

The next day, I did not manage to get someone to connect the formula to the picture, so I gave up for the moment and went on to pentagons. The students had a row of pentagons to interpret (see Figure 2.15).

This time, students were not given a table, and few used one to organize their data. I found as I checked homework that most were not able to decide the perimeter of 9 pentagons or 100 pentagons or k pentagons correctly, and yet many students had the same "wrong" answers, especially with reference to 9 pentagons. They thought the perimeter should be 33. I was puzzled by this. I was quite sure they wouldn't bother copying someone else's answer unless they could explain it, because that was an often-reinforced classroom expectation. Students knew that they would be asked for explanations. Also it was not a few students; it was many who had 33 for the answer. In addition, a significant number of students commented that they "didn't get it."

Since everyone was stuck at about the same place, I suggested we look at all of our data and try to make sense out of it. Students readily agreed that the perimeter for 1 pentagon is 5, 2 pentagons is 8, and 3 pentagons is 11, but students were reluctant to share an answer for 9 pentagons. Eventually, Nathan offered the above-mentioned 33.

"How did you decide that was correct?" I asked.

"Well, 3 pentagons have a perimeter of 11. So 9 pentagons should have a perimeter that is 3 times that," he answered quite cheerfully.

"Could anyone explain what Nathan is trying to tell us?" I asked.

Lisette offered, "He's saying that 9 is 3 times as big as 3 so the perimeter should be 3 times bigger and 3 times 11 is 33."

"How can we check to see if Nathan's idea works?" I asked.

"It doesn't work. I drew these [9 pentagons in a row] out and I found out the right answer is 29," said Katie.

"How else could we check Nathan's theory?" I asked, realizing that this must have been the theory of the others who got that same answer.

"It doesn't work because then it would have to be true for 8 and 2," said Madeline.

"What do you mean?" I asked.

"The perimeter of 8 [pentagons] is not 4 times the perimeter of 2 [pentagons]," she explained.

"Did anyone find another way to decide their answer was true?" I asked.

"Well, now that I see the chart, I see that the perimeters keep increasing by 3, and if we do all the ones in between 3 and 9, we'll get 29 for 9 pentagons," said Jose.

"I just added 18 onto 11 so I would not have to do all the ones in between 3 and 9," said Angel.

FIGURE 2.15. Pentagons All in a Row

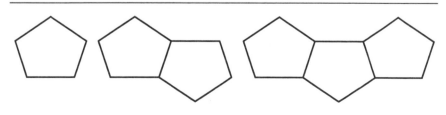

"Where did Angel get his 18?" I asked. No one could explain, so I asked Angel to explain where 18 came from.

"To get from 3 to 9 is 6. And the perimeters keep increasing by 3. So instead of adding three 6 times, I multiplied," he said. I knew some students got this but many didn't. I let it go. It was late in the day and late in the period.

"Now what about 100 pentagons?" I asked. Two students raised their hands. I asked Sarita for her opinion.

"It's 302, because the perimeter is always equal to 3 times the number of pentagons plus 2 more," she said as if this was quite obvious and this class was getting a little ridiculous. "So the formula is $3k + 2$," she added.

I let the class think about this for a little while. Then I noticed a conversation going on between two students and was just about to complain, when one of the students, Juan, said, "You add the bottoms, then you add the tops, and then you add the two sides."

As we were all caught up in finding the pattern from our numbers, Juan was cutting to the heart of the matter and dealing with the actual diagram. I know the look on my face registered some of the excitement I was feeling because Dori, a student I had last year, said "Uh oh, here she goes. Now she's gonna tell you how beautiful mathematics is. And she's gonna do this for 10 months."

I asked Juan to explain, and to expedite matters he came to the board and drew some pentagons (see Figure 2.16). He said, "Bottoms, 4. Tops, 8. Plus the two ends is 14."

I said, "What about if you had 10 pentagons?"

Juan said, "Bottoms, 10. Tops 20. Plus the 2 ends is 32."

The class responded with their attention. This looked like math they could handle.

"What about if you had k pentagons? What would the perimeter be?" I asked.

"Bottoms, k. Tops, $2 \times k$. Plus 2," said Juan.

I wrote "$k + 2k + 2$" on the board with "$3k + 2$" underneath. "Are they the same? Are they different? Explain your answer." These are the questions students explored for homework.

FIGURE 2.16. "Bottoms, 4. Tops, 8. Plus the Two Ends is 14"

I felt exhilarated after that discussion. Students had the chance to *see* (literally) for themselves why $k + 2k + 2 = 3k + 2$. Previously, I would have explained this equivalence by talking about "combining like terms" and "adding coefficients." I would have justified those procedures with the distributive axiom: $k + 2k = (1 + 2)k$. And students would have had plenty of practice combining other like terms. Although all this "formal mathematics" certainly needs to be addressed in my classroom, it will be more meaningful to my students now that they have had a chance to see how sensible it actually is. They can look at those pentagons and *see* how it makes sense.

This activity was done as a whole group discussion because students had had time exploring in small groups on other, similar problems, and I felt it was time for them to listen to and share understandings with the whole class.

Although at this point, students' understanding of the variable k was still shaky, there were important points about my own teaching of this concept that were brought to the forefront. What do I want my students to know about algebra? How should they engage in the mathematical ideas? How was I going to find more problems that allowed learners to "see" the algebra in action? How would I help them understand the importance of defining what their variable represented? We had gotten off to a good start, but I wasn't satisfied.

For lack of knowing how to answer my own questions, I resorted to providing them with more experiences that would require these understandings to emerge.

THE *Nth* STAIRCASE

Jose, Evilie, Jolene, and Arla were engrossed in their project. Evilie and Jolene were sort of nodding rhythmically as though to some beat that they could hear. I knew that meant they were satisfied with something and so I knelt near their desks to watch.

Their task was to make a poster that clearly showed everything they understood about the staircase problem (taken from Hirsch & Lappan, 1989; see Figure 2.17) and how they determined each of their solutions. The questions posed for consideration were

1. How many cubes are needed to build the next staircase?
2. How many cubes are needed to build the 10th staircase?
3. Explain how you worked out your answer to the previous question.
4. In what other ways could you look at the problem?
5. How many cubes are needed to build the *n*th staircase?

At this point, students had spent two days working on the problem. Everyone was able to answer the first two questions, but they were ignoring the third and fourth questions and were upset at having to think about the fifth

FIGURE 2.17. Figure for the Staircase Problem

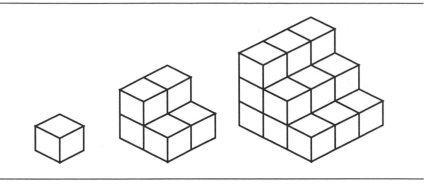

question—to deal with something as silly as an "nth staircase." That is why I asked them to make a poster to show how they worked out their answer to the question, "How many cubes are needed to build the 10th staircase?" My rationale was that if they had to clearly show all that they went through to get their answer so that someone else could understand it, then perhaps they themselves would see the problem more clearly. Perhaps they would discover the convenience of a generalization and would be able to determine what number of cubes they needed for "any" staircase. I was hoping this would be a good problem for them to realize that the variable is a useful tool for expressing a mathematical idea that they had discovered.

I chose the poster as the vehicle for them to express their ideas so that students in all my classes could benefit from seeing different approaches to the problem when the posters were displayed. But I also thought that it would be easier for students to take seriously the idea of showing their solution clearly if they knew someone other than me was going to have to understand their work.

As soon as I knelt down, Jose started, "Look teacher, n stands for the number of steps in the staircase, which is the same as the staircase number because the first staircase has one step, the second staircase has two steps, the third staircase has three steps, and so on." I opened my eyes wide and raised my eyebrows because I had been trying to get all 191 of my algebra students, college prep and basic, to define what their variable stood for. Many students were still floundering with this concept at all levels and were still intimidated by the idea of an nth term.

Jose paid no attention to my reaction and vigorously continued, pointing to his group's carefully drawn side view of the tenth staircase: "We want to say that you take the number of steps, n, and add it to the next smaller number and then the next smaller number after that and keep going like that all the way down to 1, and then you take that answer and multiply it by n because that's how wide it's going to be. It's going to be the same number of steps as it is wide so that's n." Jose was saying this as he pointed to their drawing (Figure 2.18).

Jose's group members, Evilie, Jolene, and Arla, were all looking at me as though of course they knew what was going on—it was obvious. There was something about their assurance that made me feel they would be insulted if I asked them if they were sure they understood. Evilie said, "We just don't know how to write that. Tell us how we can write that."

I asked them what would represent the "next smaller number after n" (Jose's own words). Jose answered "$n - 1$" right away. (Students have worked on this concept. A few weeks ago a likely answer would have been "m" or "o.") I wrote, "$n + (n - 1) + $," and asked what would come next.

A brief discussion among the four yielded "$n - 2$" so they made it easy for me. Evilie filled in the "$n - 2$" and someone said, "It's going to keep on like that until it reaches 1." I suggested they use three dots to express the "keep on" idea and showed them how to use brackets to say that the whole quantity was to be multiplied by n. Their finished expressions looked quite impressive: "The number of blocks needed to build the nth staircase is $[n + (n - 1) + (n - 2) + (n - 3) + \ldots + 1]n$."

Jose's group was justifiably proud of their project. The time they spent on making the lettering and colors just so, showed their pride. I told them that no one else in any of my classes looked at this problem the way they did, and so the uniqueness of their approach was another feather in their cap.

The scenario described above took place in one of my basic algebra classes. I've used many of the same problems and activities in both my college prep and basic algebra classes, with interesting and thought-provoking results. I feel sure that to "foster the view that algebra is a natural way of expressing

FIGURE 2.18. Students' Poster for the Staircase Problem

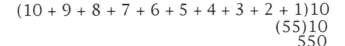

$$(10 + 9 + 8 + 7 + 6 + 5 + 4 + 3 + 2 + 1)10$$
$$(55)10$$
$$550$$

Sideview of the 10th staircase shows 55 blocks. Multiply by 10 because each square stands for 10 blocks.

what is sensible to arithmetic" (Kieran, 1991, p. 51) is worth pursuing in all of my classes.

Note: Another possible solution to this problem is n [n $(n + 1)/2$].

THE BAD NEWS

Learning to learn algebra for understanding is difficult. For some students more than others, it is stressful and threatening, especially early in the year when they have not had a chance to experience success. Below are some examples of students who are having difficulty coping.

> Jane's face was bright with the anger that she was trying to keep in check. "What kind of algebra class is this? He (last year's math teacher) told me I'd be using that book!" she complained, as she pointed to the shelf where the red Dolciani *Algebra: Structure and Method* books were collecting dust. "That's the stuff I know. That's what we're supposed to be learning. My parents never heard of this stuff we're doing. They can't even help me."
>
> Jane was fully expecting to start the year in Algebra I by simplifying complicated algebraic expressions, working with positive and negative numbers, and solving for variables in equations. She felt prepared for that. Instead, she was being asked to understand how variables can be used to find patterns and make generalizations from a variety of physical situations. In addition to that, she was constantly being asked to explain her ideas. Jane believes explaining is the teacher's job.

> "Why are we doing this? What am I going to need this for? This isn't even algebra. I can do algebra. How can I do it if you don't explain it to me?" This was Tim's standard complaint every time he came across something that required struggle. After he achieves understanding, he shrugs and says it's stupid and easy.
>
> Tim is a junior in a first-year basic algebra course. He has failed this class at some point for reasons other than academic and is there for the credits he needs in order to graduate. He was expecting to do homework for other courses while I taught and showed the rest of the class examples. He already knew how to do the work in the book and was planning to use the last 10 minutes of class to speed through whatever I assigned.

> Juanita was a "straight A+" student through eighth grade. She has never complained to me, but her older brother told me that she has cried from the frustration of being in my math class. It's stressful for her to be constantly guessing what I'm looking for and what I want her

to learn. If only I would tell her, she would do it. Her grades from me have been very good and I've always given her encouragement, so I was surprised to hear how unhappy she was.

I could go on like this for many pages, telling how, at this stage of their educational careers, so many students have difficulty adapting to different expectations from a teacher. I understand their reluctance, but I feel confident that they will eventually come to enjoy class. Some students take longer than others to recognize the power of their own thinking. In the past, I have seen some of my most resistant "critics" become avid supporters as well as independent thinkers. Although I strive for the type of effectiveness that stimulates my students to make sense of mathematics and take charge of their own learning, I also want them to think well of themselves and take pleasure in their explorations.

Meanwhile our struggle continues. The process of change is, at times, a strain for all of us. I believe, however, that we are growing even as we complain about its difficulty.

REFLECTIONS ON BASIC CLASSES

During my 17 years of teaching, I've noticed that students in "basic" and "remedial" homogeneous classes are actually quite heterogeneous with respect to their academic ability. Students are there for a myriad of reasons, which include absenteeism, learning disabilities, failure in college prep classes, unwillingness to do required work in college prep classes, personal problems, nonconformity, and a need for credits.

Basic classes often have very distinct personalities. Last year my third-period basic algebra class had 27 students in grades 9 through 12: five had special ed plans, three were soon to be parents, seven dropped college prep algebra after the first five weeks because they were failing, six were taking basic algebra for the second or third time, and six were average freshmen who were either advised or themselves decided that their math background was such that they ought to do a basic course before they tried college prep.

My success with that group was minimal at best. In retrospect, I feel that I might have been giving them mixed messages (something these students could not handle), as I was combining traditional lessons and assignments with small group problem-solving sessions and whole class discussions.

On the other hand, my sixth-period class had a majority of students who were average freshmen who had never been very good at math. They were anxious to understand algebra and open to new methods of teaching. Their reactions were positive and encouraged me to pursue my investigations into how I might begin teaching algebra for understanding.

I bring up these two classes because if I had not had the chance to see how very different class reactions can be, I perhaps would have agreed with those who say that basic classes cannot respond to improved instruction and that the problems inherent in those classes prevent both teacher and students from experiencing success.

The severity of the problems is sobering. This year, I have a group of three young women who often work together. The other day, when one of their male classmates showed astonishment upon learning that they all had babies at home, they laughed at his reaction.

I remember talking to Keith about the possibility of a conference with his parents. He was amused at my suggestion and politely told me that he lived with his girlfriend.

Evilie left home several weeks ago, but she still comes to school every day.

John frequently misses school because his girlfriend likes him to take her places during the school day.

Rachel needs to find a decent job. She also has a child and is often scanning the want ads during free moments in class.

Usually, I find these things out accidentally and I react in a neutral way. I feel the best way I can help is by stimulating their intellect and helping them come to the realization that there are options that become available with an education.

Unfortunately, I have not solved the dilemma of how to control the interruptive, often math-related outbursts during whole class discussions or how to get my students to be attentive to my instruction when I feel the need to speak to all of them at once. This sort of problem is peculiar to some groups more than others, but it jeopardizes the enjoyment my basic classes bring to me. My pleasure is often mixed with frustration and exhaustion as I try to work within the boundaries imposed by circumstances.

And so we try to make learning take precedence over everything else. I have seen such wonderful and frequent sparks of intelligence, curiosity, and intuition occur in my basic classes. In the past, it seemed that somehow I was never able to gather those sparks and use them to create an effective and promising learning environment. This year, although things are far from satisfactory, I am learning that improved instruction can make a difference in student achievement and level of involvement.

I am consistently rewarded by the creative thinking and quickness of these students when they are asked to do something other than listen to my thinking, take notes, and copy examples from the board. I have learned that planning meaningful activities, choosing engaging tasks, organizing small groups and pair problem-solving experiences, valuing thinking, and carefully assessing understanding promote an improved classroom atmosphere where learning is the objective for everyone.

REFERENCES

Hirsch, C. R., & Lappan, G. (1989, November). Transition to high school mathematics. *Mathematics Teacher*, pp. 614–618.

Kieran, C. (1991, March). Helping to make the transition to algebra. *Arithmetic Teacher*, pp. 49–51.

$$+ \quad - \quad \times \quad \div$$

MATHEMATICAL THOUGHT-IN-ACTION: RICH REWARDS AND CHALLENGING DILEMMAS

Joan Ferrini-Mundy

A mathematician, like a painter or poet, is a maker of patterns . . . and these . . . must be beautiful.

G. H. Hardy, *A Mathematician's Apology*

Seeing and revealing hidden patterns are what mathematicians do best. . . . Active mathematicians seek patterns wherever they arise.

Lynn A. Steen, *On the Shoulders of Giants*

For teachers who see mathematics as the study of patterns, the potential for exciting and rewarding classroom experiences with their students is enormous. However, once a teacher adopts this perspective, the practical challenges and dilemmas can be overwhelming. The stories offered by Virginia Bastable and Donna Scanlon convey both the rewards and the challenges. Furthermore, they provide insight into how these teachers have managed to continue to innovate and experiment in the face of those challenges, and they offer us glimpses of the persistence and confidence it takes to teach in the ways that they are teaching. These accounts should be viewed as stories of success.

Reading these accounts with a focus on the nature of mathematics, and what teachers do to bring such mathematics to their classrooms, has led me to four organizing themes for this commentary. These are: charting a mathematical course and making connections; building a mathematical culture; building from student understanding; and formality and evidence. Drawing on examples from the preceding stories, I will make some comments relevant to each theme, with attention to both the rewards and the challenges.

CHARTING A MATHEMATICAL COURSE AND
MAKING CONNECTIONS

The mathematician Henry Pollak speaks fondly of "cross country mathematics," by which he seems to mean moving about a mathematical territory, with its unexpected bumps, barriers, alternate routes, and unmarked paths. The classrooms we have seen here are places where the students are exploring a mathematical territory that is not fully charted. Having been provided this opportunity to explore, through the thoughtful and carefully crafted tasks and planning of their teachers, they are experiencing the satisfaction and rewards of discovering mathematical understandings. Moreover, they are growing mathematically in their pattern-finding sophistication and in their understanding of mathematical concepts.

Their teachers, having left the security of "doing the book," are now in the position of trying to elicit the mathematical discussion they feel is important, while at the same time responding to the students' questions and conjectures. This is very challenging for the teacher because it is difficult to plan, and the mathematics that emerges might differ greatly from what the teacher intended at the outset. It is clear from these candid accounts that both Bastable and Scanlon struggle with this issue. For instance, through "Meg's" letter, Bastable tells us about her thwarted scheme to introduce the Pythagorean theorem and her wish that she "hadn't brought up this a, b scheme."

Teaching in this style requires continual "reflection-in-action" (Schön, 1987), frequently without the time to assess the mathematical and pedagogical ramifications of possible choices. These accounts are filled with examples of such reflection-in-action junctures. A student's comments trigger an idea for the teacher, as we see in Bastable's story of Julie's solution to the square-inside-a-square problem. In her solution, she partitions a square into five non-congruent parts of equal area. The teacher must make an immediate judgment about whether this feature is interesting or potentially rich enough to pursue, must gauge how far afield they might go with this digression and whether there is "mathematical mileage" to be had.

To face such challenges takes courage and introduces the potential for constant self-questioning and second-guessing. Given that these judgment points occur so frequently, one wonders about their cumulative effect on a teacher's judgment, confidence, planning, and understanding. How can a teacher cope with the multitude of mathematical possibilities? Which opportunities should be pursued and which dropped? Both Bastable and Scanlon show us how they agonize, in split seconds, over those judgments, make their best decisions, move on, and reflect back later.

Many have argued that a deep understanding of mathematics well beyond the content one is teaching is the most critical factor in helping the teacher negotiate the mathematical terrain, but certainly the details of how that knowledge might help, if it does, are not well understood. Teachers who are working to move in these directions may need very new kinds of support, encouragement, and opportunities for sharing because of the self-questioning that this type of teaching may induce. A ripe area for research may lie in this domain of how teachers make judgments about which mathematical routes to pursue, what influences their decisions, and what the ramifications of their choices might be.

Related to the idea of letting the mathematical course develop out of the tasks presented to students, and out of their responses, is the notion of making mathematical connections. The *NCTM Standards* (1989) contend that "the mathematics curriculum should include investigation of the connections and interplay among various mathematical topics and their applications" (p. 146). It seems that the rationale might be both mathematically and pedagogically driven. Mathematical flexibility is sometimes optimized when looking at a problem in more than one context. Consider that the recent solution (or, at this writing, possible solution) of Fermat's last theorem, a simply stated result about numbers, rests on sophisticated arguments in the theory of elliptic curves. Devlin, Gouvea, and Granville (1993) call this "an amazing connection" (p. 3). Problems are solved, extended, and better understood by looking at them from quite different mathematical perspectives (Janvier, 1987).

Consider as an example Scanlon's efforts to help her students come to understand the notion of variable through "Polygons All in a Row." Throughout this account I am struck by how much the students seem to be learning about the concept of function, which is not the explicit goal of this activity. Scanlon's commentary indicates her awareness of the distinction between what Confrey and Smith (1992) would call the "covariance" and "correspondence" notions of functions. That is, while students are constructing the tables entry by entry, focusing on the pattern where the perimeter increases by 2, Scanlon realizes that ultimately they will need a way of answering the question about what happens when there are 100 squares in a row. This is a good example of the way that a single rich task can provide possible movement in several mathematical directions.

The lesson on the square-within-a-square, as described by Bastable, likewise has the potential for developing some beautiful mathematical connections. Connecting the points on the graph serves as a reminder that noninteger values have meaning; discussing how to be sure 72 is the minimum reassures me that the teacher is well aware of the need to help these students learn to justify their conjectures. The geometric argument for why placement of the point at 6 leads to minimum area of the inner square is brilliant in its visual clarity. The concept of function undergirds what is happening here, as we saw when the teacher brought in graphing. There are possible extensions of this problem that would enable the teacher to capitalize on this connection to function. One might look at the table and graph for the area of a single triangle, or the sum of the areas of the triangle, or the side of the inner square. There are many interesting functions lurking here: some linear, some quadratic, and perhaps others. What are they? Likewise with the polygons all in a row, the students could explore area, number of internal sides, issues about angle measurement, and probably other ideas in a quest for function.

People who love mathematics often find themselves naturally drawn to this kind of deep exploration, or "mining," of a single problem for its extensions, variations, and potential connections to other mathematical ideas. How much time and energy can we allow for a class in doing this, and how do we manage it? The challenges of finding a mathematical course and of building powerful mathematical connections are intriguing.

BUILDING A MATHEMATICAL CULTURE

We might argue that a defensible goal for mathematics education is to help children engage in mathematics the way that mathematicians do. Davis and Hersh (1981) summarize Lakatos's view of the development of mathematics.

> Instead of presenting symbols and rules of combination, he presents human beings, a teacher and his students. Instead of presenting a system built up from first principles, he presents a clash of views, arguments, and counterarguments. Instead of mathematics skeletalized and fossilized, he presents mathematics growing from a problem and a conjecture, with a theory taking shape before our eyes, in the heat of debate and disagreement, doubt giving way to certainty and then to renewed doubt. (pp. 346–347)

Many mathematicians do their work collaboratively, with false starts, with explorations along paths that may or may not lead anywhere, with the intention of refining and making more elegant their products, and with communication about their mathematics. The major vehicle through which the discipline grows is the testing of ideas and processes within the "community of discourse" (Lampert, 1990). Mathematicians share their hunches, test their arguments, and develop new ideas, whether at the outset or eventually in a public setting.

The classrooms presented in the accounts in this book demonstrate that a community of discourse can be created among young mathematics students. We see glimpses of students extending one another's ideas, arguing for their own positions, criticizing one another's conclusions, making conjectures, and applauding each other's triumphs. These teachers have constructed classroom settings where discussion about mathematics occurs and where the students listen to one another seriously. That this is possible, in particular in the challenging setting that Scanlon confronts, where students face enormous outside distractions and problems, is impressive.

Within mathematically promising classroom settings such as these, teacher and students may encounter challenging and difficult dilemmas. When mathematicians work together, before one solution is acknowledged for the group, a new problem often arises, and the group moves to it because it is intriguing. It's clear how this can happen with an individual, or even a group of two or three, but an entire class being transported en masse to a digression is difficult to facilitate and manage.

How do we acknowledge and encourage promising mathematical behaviors that students display? For example, in Bastable's story, does the question asked by the girl sitting next to Bill ("Wouldn't the area be the same anyway?") get the credit it deserves, in the teacher's mind and for the class, as being an important kind of question? It represents an untested conjecture and an interest in generalization, which is mathematically desirable. The teacher's instinct here seemed right: to pursue this very interesting idea by reformulating it more precisely for the class. Note that here we face the dilemma of who should reformulate—after all, it was a student's question. What might be gained by encouraging her to try to make a clear statement of the issue?

Another characteristic of working mathematicians is their complete emotional devotion to their discipline. In some ways, the strong sort of affective commitment to mathematical exploration one sees in mathematicians is replicated in Scanlon's classroom. Despite outside pressures, the students she describes are engaged in their activity, are proud of their accomplishments, and are learning some interesting things.

BUILDING FROM STUDENT UNDERSTANDING

Understanding what students are thinking is critical to the kind of teaching described here. The teacher's interpretation of student understanding can influence dramatically the shape and direction of the mathematics, as we saw in these examples. For instance, Bastable felt uneasy when Marla said, "There will be a number in the end place, not zero." The teacher was concerned that Marla didn't see zero as a number. I might generate a different theory. Perhaps she meant to say that the number in the end place would be nonzero, and this astute observation is key to her argument. The need to constantly monitor student thinking and to build mini-theories, on the fly, as individual students offer points of view, is further evidence of the demanding reflection-in-action this teaching requires.

How much energy should we invest in trying to think about different ways of seeing things? This would involve staying open in our own thinking, as well as in considering multiple explanations for what we think students are thinking. In the squares-all-in-a-row task, the teacher's way of thinking geometrically about $2k + 2$ is not the only way of thinking. Consider that $2k + 2 = 2(k + 1)$. This might be interpreted geometrically as twice the sum

FIGURE 2.19. Diagram to Show $2k + 2 = 2(k + 1)$

For the case of $k = 3$:

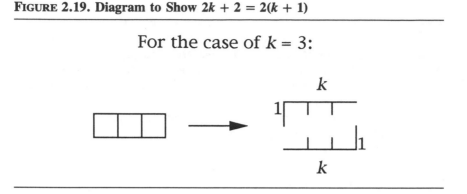

of the number of tops plus a side (see Figure 2.19). Being more adventure-some in our thinking, maybe $2k + 2 = 3 + 3 + 2(k - 2)$ is a nice geometric interpretation for someone. Okay, so it's not entirely obvious—this geometric interpretation (Figure 2.20) involves adding the three sides on either end, and then coming up with an expression for the length of the remaining sides, which is $2(k - 2)$. The potential for algebraic connections is very rich.

Developing situations that will cause students to "need" understanding of a mathematical idea is one of the most mathematically challenging parts of this kind of teaching. Despite the commitment Bastable and Scanlon seem to have to this notion, the stories don't go far enough in revealing how they have coped with this challenge. For example, I'd like to hear the teachers in Bastable's piece discuss *why* students need to have meaning for irrational numbers, at what level of meaning, and whether a geometric argument is the best way to go at it, or whether some other medium, like a calculator, might be better.

FIGURE 2.20. Diagram to Show $2k + 2 = 3 + 3 + 2(k - 2)$

For the case of $k = 4$:

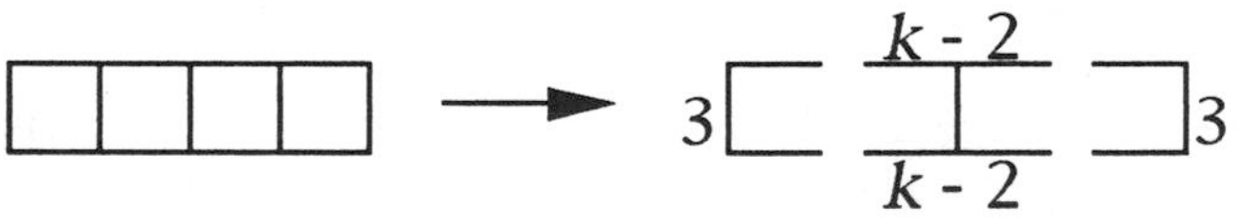

These potential conversations require the intertwining of mathematical issues and pedagogical ideas.

Perhaps the most mathematically challenging aspect of this sort of teaching is the interpretation of student understanding, and then the decision making that must follow in determining where to move next, what questions to ask, which mathematical thread to follow, and which to drop. Bastable's "Meg" commenting that "Jeanne's shortcut reminded me of the formula for squaring binomials, but I wasn't sure what that had to do with the problem," is a good example of how there are mathematical judgment calls to be made.

FORMALITY AND EVIDENCE

The problem about partitioning squares in Bastable's account is an example of a rich mathematical setting offering a great assortment of possibilities. I admit that I spent a moment convincing myself that the inner figure was indeed a square. My background in axiomatic Euclidean geometry always comes back to haunt me, and I wonder if high school students would be interested in or care about what appears obvious here. I also wonder about the teachers— did they think about these issues? What are the costs and benefits of letting this fundamental piece of the problem fall by the wayside? I think these questions could lead to good discussion.

Related to this issue is the dilemma of what constitutes an adequate argument. Is counting the squares on graph paper to be convinced you have a square okay? What's our measure of adequacy of an argument for tenth graders? What happens when students face geometric situations where all is not as it might appear in the picture? Something that convinces everyone? Something that would pass muster with the mathematician next door to me? Davis and Hersh (1981) provide some help.

> Proof serves many purposes simultaneously. In being exposed to the scrutiny and judgment of a new audience, the proof is subject to a constant process of criticism and revalidation. Errors, ambiguities, and misunderstandings are cleared up by constant exposure. . . . Proof, in its best instances, increases understanding by revealing the heart of the matter. (p. 151)

And, in mathematics, the nature of proof is evolutionary. Appel and Haken (1978), the solvers of the Four-Color Problem, acknowledge the challenges presented by the computer proof: "[Mathematicians] intuitively feel that if an argument contains parts that are not verifiable by hand calculation it is on rather insecure ground" (p. 178).

Getting stuck in details that are uninteresting to students can quickly derail a lesson, but helping students grow in their mathematical sophistication includes building their experience in making convincing arguments. How is this need woven into this type of teaching? The teachers here are *not* spending time proving the obvious and seem to have arrived at a suitable level of expectation for justification and evidence within the community of discourse in their classrooms. Over time, does this level of expectation increase? Should it? How is that accomplished?

Precision of language is another one of those "new math" habits so deeply ingrained in my own preparation to teach that I still struggle with what to do in the classroom and with what to make of what I see in other classrooms. Julie's solution to the square-within-a-square problem is loaded with opportunities for the compulsive mathematics editor. What does she mean when she says, "I wanted to see the rectangles—the ones that the triangles are half of"? Isn't a "tilted square" just a square? The inclusion of "tilted" is descriptive here, yet mathematically extraneous. Saying "the triangles are 16" really could mean they have area of 16 square units or they have perimeter of 16 units. Yet given the context, it's unlikely there could be a misunderstanding. So how does the teacher respond? This account is reporting a think-aloud protocol where the student virtually is solving the problem as she speaks. Polishing and careful language can come later, if necessary; this does not seem the time to be fussy, but is there ever a time? And, perhaps more significant, is there any way to gauge how effectively the student is communicating with her fellow problem solvers in this mathematical telegraphy? At what point, if ever, should we be concerned about enculturating students into the conventions and ground rules under which mathematicians communicate? Or is it enough to develop operating procedures that at least enable adequate communication among class members—telegraphic enough to be useful, not so telegraphic that meaning is missing?

Precision of language is closely related to issues of mathematical correctness. In Bastable's account, Briana asks what would happen if "we could do them all?" The teacher discovers through questioning that Briana means to try various integer values of a and b to get a sense of the pattern that might be present. Mathematically, her suggestion is good; it is in the spirit of the traditional "try extreme cases" strategy that problem-solving people have long encouraged. Nonetheless, there is a problem in that she hasn't really said what she meant—of course, we couldn't try "them all" in a concrete way, because we are talking about the set of real numbers between 0 and 12, and there are a lot of them. The integer mentality is definitely something of which teachers are aware. It gets students into trouble when they work with limits and derivatives; but Briana's suggestion was so mathematically "nice"—what do we do? The polygons-all-in-a-row exploration raised a mathematical question for me: How can we describe, precisely, the way that these polygons are arranged? Is the rule as simple as placing exactly one side adjacent? For instance, why

FIGURE 2.21. An Alternative Arrangement for "Triangles All in a Row"

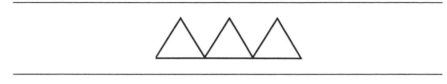

wouldn't the arrangement in Figure 2.21 work for the triangles? Did any students question this? Should they?

CONCLUSION

Mathematicians engage in problems in mathematics as intellectual activity; teachers engage in mathematical-pedagogical problem solving. Teachers, like professional mathematicians, can conduct discussions among themselves about pedagogical dilemmas and mathematical ideas. And the hidden patterns they try to expose are patterns of thought, of conjecture, and of engagement with mathematics, by their students. The challenge of this pattern seeking is enormous, and it would seem that the rewards of puzzling out what is really going on in a class are equally rich.

I keep thinking how fortunate these students are in experiencing mathematical communities as developed by Bastable and Scanlon. I wonder a lot about how it looks and feels to them. Do they see a teacher aimlessly wandering around following their suggestions? As high school students, are they so accustomed to the teacher as authority that they would subvert this sort of approach? Might they assume that the teacher isn't doing her job? How does she counter this?

Mathematically, the "content that we have to cover" has always been a sacred cow, and it prevails in discussions among teachers, mathematicians, and teacher educators. Teaching that values inquiry and student understanding, and is based in rich mathematical tasks is naturally orthogonal to the "cover-the-content" attitude. We are only beginning to realize that issues about which mathematical ideas, concepts, and procedures are part of the curriculum are deep and different in this kind of teaching. These accounts give us a glimpse into the decisions and choices mathematics teachers make on these issues in this context. A forum for discussing this is critical.

These are difficult and exciting dilemmas for teachers of mathematics in the 1990s. They make arguments over whether to teach the $Ax + By + C = 0$ form of the linear function, or whether it's okay to write AB meaning the line segment joining A and B, seem ridiculous. Pedagogically, there are other important challenges here that will surely be discussed in other chapters. These include issues of evaluation, of planning, of the stress caused by not quite knowing where you're going, of the challenges to teacher education to enable teachers to experience this kind of mathematics learning. But these accounts make it clear that such efforts are worthwhile.

REFERENCES

Appel, K., & Haken, W. (1978). The four-color problem. In L. A. Steen (Ed.), *Mathematics today* (pp. 153–190). New York: Springer-Verlag.

Confrey, J., & Smith, E. (1992). Revised accounts of the function concept using multi-representational software, contextual problems and student paths. In W. Geeslin & K. Graham (Eds.), *Proceedings of the sixteenth PME conference* (Vol. 1, pp. 153–160). Durham: University of New Hampshire.

Davis, P. J., & Hersh, R. (1981). *The mathematical experience*. Boston: Houghton Mifflin.

Devlin, K., Gouvea, F., & Granville, A. (1993, August). Fermat's last theorem, a theorem at last. In *Focus* (pp. 3–4). Washington: Mathematical Association of America.

Hardy, G. H. (1967). *A mathematician's apology*. Cambridge: Cambridge University Press.

Janvier, C. (1987). *Problems of representation in the teaching and learning of mathematics*. Hillsdale, NJ: Lawrence Erlbaum.

Lampert, M. (1990). When the problem is not the question and the solution is not the answer: Mathematical knowing and teaching. *American Educational Research Journal, 27*(1), 29–63.

National Council of Teachers of Mathematics. (1989). *Curriculum and evaluation standards for school mathematics*. Reston, VA: Author.

Schön, D. A. (1987). *Educating the reflective practitioner: Toward a new design for teaching and learning in the professions*. San Francisco: Jossey-Bass.

Steen, L. A. (1990). *On the shoulders of giants*. Washington, DC: National Research Council.

CHAPTER 3

"The Mathematics Classroom: A Community of Inquiry"

The theoretical tradition that has contributed most to shaping the reform agenda, notably through the work of Jean Piaget, has been criticized from within for neglecting the "social scaffolding" necessary to support individual cognitive development. In this view, learning is seen as "embedded in and enabled by socially constructed contexts." Invoking the social as "community," Martin Simon elaborates this point in his essay in Chapter 1: "Mathematical *communities* develop mathematical knowledge, rules for how mathematical knowledge is developed, and shared notions of what is important to the community" (editor's emphasis). Simon's invocation of "community" is echoed in the more rhetorically accessible injunction to shift away from classrooms as simply collections of individuals, toward classrooms as communities of mathematical inquiry.

At the beginning of each school year, teachers must establish the norms that will govern their classrooms over the next 10 months. In this chapter, Jill Lester and Mary Signet describe their efforts to interpret the ideal of "community of inquiry" in their second- and third-grade mathematics classes, respectively. Making the presence of other children a precondition of each child's learning requires much hard and thoughtful work, especially when, as Mary Signet and Donna Scanlon (in Chapter 2) testify, some students will stubbornly resist the introduction of new norms.

Lester teaches in a rural setting; Signet in a small city. Teacher educator and high school teacher Virginia Stimpson closely examines aspects of the process of "getting started" raised by Lester and Signet and then shares a "September strategy" of her own designed to "address resistance and confusion head on."

$$+ \quad - \quad \times \quad \div$$

ESTABLISHING A COMMUNITY
OF MATHEMATICS LEARNERS

Jill Bodner Lester

It's exciting. It's frightening. It's September and time for a new beginning. Every year I wonder what to expect from each of the unique individuals with whom I will share the next 10 months. Who are these children? How many of them are there? What are their strengths? There are only two certainties: We will have to work together to become a community of mathematics learners, and it will not happen overnight.

Before the children arrive, I spend weeks picturing what I would like math class to be and how I will approach math on the first day of school. I want to set a tone. I want the children to know that mathematics involves thinking and the development of problem-solving strategies. I want them to feel safe and to feel that they can risk asking a question or sharing an incomplete idea. I want them to listen to one another respectfully and to try to understand what their classmates are thinking and doing. I want them to learn to formulate their own mathematical questions and to take responsibility for their own learning.

It is also important to consider the mathematical content that must be covered in grade 2. Regrouping in addition and subtraction, measurement, time, fractions, and geometry are topics listed in the curriculum guide. It is through these topic areas that I hope to focus on big mathematical ideas: equality, part-whole relationships, patterns, relationships among geometric shapes, and relationships among the four basic operations.

Since I began to change the style of my teaching seven years ago, I have observed that the skills I'd like the children to acquire, develop slowly. Within the context of solving mathematics problems, the children gradually become more confident and more comfortable, and over time they learn that this classroom is a safe place to pose questions and to pursue answers. It is an environment in which curiosity, questioning, and exploration are respected and encouraged.

In order to engage children in thinking and discussion, I work to establish predictable classroom routines. Most days begin with a problem written on the board—which is read aloud twice, so that those who do not yet read well will have access to it. Then I ask the children to solve the problem mentally and to signal me when they have an answer. When everyone seems to be ready, I solicit answers and record each response on the board without comment. Our routine continues with a discussion of the answers that the children find troublesome or unreasonable. Then the children work in small groups to explore their ideas with concrete materials and to find alternative solutions that support the correctness of their answers. Finally, the children and I gather in a circle on the floor to discuss the small group explorations and discoveries. This routine is introduced over time and plays an integral part in the establishment of a community of mathematics learners.

I work in a rural town where there is only one second grade, so I teach groups ranging in size from 15 to 30. It is always a heterogeneous group, as we integrate all of our children (including those with Down syndrome) in regular classrooms.

PLANNING FOR THE FIRST DAY OF SCHOOL

This year, expecting to greet 25 nervous, but eager, seven-year-olds on the first day of school, I prepared a mathematics game using unifix cubes to find missing addends. With everyone (including me) seated on the floor, I would hold a train of 20 cubes behind my back, snap the train into two pieces, and bring one section of the train out for the children to see and count. It would be the children's responsibility to determine how many cubes remained behind me. I hoped the game would set the tone for our classroom investigations by raising questions about how different solution strategies result in the same answer.

I wanted the mathematics to be accessible, but I also wanted it to be a little beyond the children's easy reach. That is, for this game I wanted them to have to think about using what they already knew to solve more challenging problems. I chose 20 cubes because seven-year-olds are usually comfortable with number combinations up to 10, and they have 10 fingers with which to quickly check their calculations; 20 seemed to meet the criterion—challenging, but accessible.

DAY ONE: NEW EXPECTATIONS

On the first day of school, I greeted the new second graders (11 girls and 14 boys) on the playground. By midmorning the children and I had gotten to know one another a little better and were gathered on the rug for math. As I had planned, the large bucket of unifix cubes was nearby, and I had two stacks of 10 unifix cubes in my hands. I began by telling the children that I was holding 20 cubes. The room became uncomfortably quiet. No one moved or made a sound. They seemed to be trying to figure out what was expected of them; they had yet to realize that this was time for *their* ideas.

Slowly, Susan raised her eyes toward mine. I nodded. She nodded back. Then she eased her way through the middle of the circle and began to count the cubes as I held them in my hands. I wasn't surprised to see Susan touching each cube as she counted, "One, two, three, four, five . . . ," and I smiled as she continued to count all the way to 20 by 1s. She then inched her way back to her spot on the edge of the circle, nodded her head, and mumbled, "20."

Watching Susan count the cubes must have given Donald the courage to move toward me and remove the cubes from my hands. He sat down in front of me, placed one stack of cubes on the rug, and began silently to nod his head in methodical rhythm.

I asked Donald what he was thinking about, but he ignored my question and continued nodding. I was trying to formulate my next question when Donald carefully placed the second stack of cubes on the rug next to the first. He methodically compared the two stacks and said, "10 plus 10 more is 20," handed me the cubes, and returned to his spot on the rug.

Susan and Donald both had felt the need to count the cubes for themselves, as the cubes were a concrete representation of the number 20, and 20 is a quantity beyond the range of what these children can comfortably picture in their minds.

I looked around, but the children were not making eye contact with me, as if they were pretending that I wasn't there. I knew they were uncomfortable; this was unlike the math classes they had seen before. It wasn't the cubes—the children had used them in first grade to compute addition and subtraction facts. What was different here was the context in which the cubes were being used. No one was telling them exactly what to do. To lessen the discomfort, I asked if everyone was satisfied that I was holding 20 cubes in my hands.

Most of the children just sat. Nothing happened. It was so quiet that I could hear the clock ticking from across the room. After what seemed like an eternity, Keith leaned forward and said, "If you counted 5, and then another 5, and made all the stacks the same size, 5 + 5 is 10 and 10 + 10 is 20."

At this point, the children seemed to be satisfied that there were 20 cubes. There were nodding heads and the rustle of moving bodies as the children settled themselves into more comfortable positions, so I went on to play the game that I had planned. The children all appeared to be paying attention. Once again, they were quiet and focused on the cubes.

We played twice as a whole group without much conversation. I snapped the cubes in two pieces and held out one for everyone to see. Someone told how many cubes were still behind my back. Everyone agreed. I asked how they had arrived at the answer, but there was no response to my question. I hadn't really expected any, as the question was unfamiliar to them, and they would need time to get used to the kind of question I was asking.

At this time, I decided to divide the children into groups of three or four to give them the opportunity to play the game on their own without the pressure of performing in the large group. The children played the game for about 15 minutes, and then it was time for recess.

Later as I reflected on the day's mathematics, I realized that everyone had sat quietly and was apparently focused on what was happening, but there had been no substantive interaction among the children, no discussion of mathematical ideas. I was disappointed, although not surprised that the children had not become more actively engaged in the game that we had played together. This was exactly the reaction I had seen in previous years from other children who had had to work to figure out what the expectations of this second-grade class would be.

DAY TWO: WORKING IN SMALL GROUPS

On the second day of school we continued to explore the cube game in small groups. I joined Kelly, Nathan, and Isaac in a corner of the room. When I arrived, Kelly had one hand behind her back and was holding 7 cubes in front of her. Nathan was on his knees and leaning toward Kelly as he counted the cubes aloud one by one. Isaac was sitting apart from the group with his legs crossed. His attention appeared to be elsewhere.

I quickly assessed what I observed—Kelly and Nathan were actively engaged; Isaac was not—and decided to try to draw Isaac in.

Teacher: (I look directly at Isaac.) How many cubes do you think Kelly has behind her back?
Nathan: 13.
Teacher: What do you think, Isaac?
Isaac: (Isaac looks uncomfortable. He squirms and moves a little farther away, his response barely audible.) 13.
Teacher: What do you think Kelly?
Kelly: (Kelly responds without the slightest hesitation.) 13.

I knew that the children had solved their problem correctly, but I wanted them to begin to think beyond just answering—to focus on how they solved problems and why they chose their solution method. I looked from one child to the next, expecting my next question to be met with silence.

Teacher: How do you know that the answer is 13?

Nathan surprised me. He didn't seem to be the least bit put off by my question, and his explanation began to flow immediately.

Nathan: I knew it had to be 13. It had to be an odd number—3 or 5. There's no 2, 4, 6, 8, 10. 7 + 3 is 10. 10 − 7 is 3. We have a whole 10 left. That's 13.

From what Nathan was saying, I could tell that he knew something about odd and even numbers, that he knew about grouping 10s and 1s, and that he had used this knowledge to figure out his solution to the problem. However, I was still trying to understand the flow of his thinking, so I said, "I'm a little confused. I don't understand what you're telling us about odd numbers." Nathan's expression became a scowl. His left shoulder dropped, and he moved farther away from me. It was clear that he was annoyed with me and that my question made him feel uncomfortable. That was all right with me, as I wanted Nathan to think more deeply about his idea. I expected that he would eventually take on the challenge of my questions, if not today, then tomorrow, or next week, or next month.

Isaac now moved a little closer to the group. He had had time to think and appeared to be ready to risk sharing.

> *Isaac:* There are 7 here. I counted up to 13 and 7 more. That's 20.
>
> *Kelly:* (Kelly smiles and speaks quietly.) I started with the 20 cubes and I counted out the 7 behind my back. I counted backwards—20, 19, 18, 17, 16, 15, 14. The next number would have been 13. I knew there were 13 left behind my back.

Each of the three children had solved the problem differently. Kelly had counted backwards from 20 in order to figure out how many cubes remained behind her back. Isaac had counted up to determine his answer, 13, and Nathan had both added and subtracted as he manipulated the odd and even numbers in his solution. Now I wanted the children to think about how it was possible that three seemingly unrelated solution processes could produce the same answer.

> *Teacher:* It seems as if some of you solved the problem by adding and some of you solved the problem by subtracting, but you all got the same answer. How can that be?
>
> *Nathan:* We're smart. We like to do it different ways.
>
> *Teacher:* Why does it work?
>
> *Nathan:* (Nathan looks away and ignores me, directing his question only to the two children.) So, what's the answer?
>
> *Isaac:* Let's count them.

Kelly showed them the cubes that she had been holding behind her back. The children counted them and went on taking turns snapping the cubes apart behind their backs. I was feeling a little better as I left. In just a few moments, the three children had become involved in thinking about the cubes. It's true that they had not chosen to answer my questions. They were either too uncomfortable, or my questions had been inappropriate for them at the time. Still, my questions had served as a catalyst for the children to begin their work as a group. In their efforts to avoid answering me, they had begun to interact with one another. Nathan had directed his question to the other children, and Isaac had responded. Kelly had brought the cubes out from behind her back, and they had begun to listen to one another.

As I moved quietly away from Nathan, Isaac, and Kelly I saw that they were able to continue on with their explorations without the support of an adult. They were taking the first steps.

WEEK TWO: WHOLE GROUP DISCUSSION

By the beginning of the second week of school, the children appeared to be engaged in the problems I presented and were communicating with one another in the small groups, but I was still not comfortable with the large group interactions. Many different solutions were being offered, but the children seemed to be invested only in their own solutions. On the surface, it appeared that they were listening to one another. They sat quietly and looked directly at the child who was speaking. But there were no comments or questions. They were really waiting for that child to finish talking, so that they could explain "their way."

I decided to use another problem, one that had been successful in the past: Figure out the number of girls, the number of boys, and the total number of children attending our school. But this was not going to be a problem for which I provided all of the necessary information. I sent groups of children to the different classrooms in the school, each group with an index card that asked for two of the three bits of information (boys, girls, and total). Upon their return, the children recorded the information on a large chart that I had drawn up and put on display (see Figure 3.1). I asked the children to fill in all of the information they had gathered in blue marker; later, they would use a second color to record the information they acquired by solving the problems. I expected we would be working on this project for about two weeks.

After the information was recorded, the children were anxious to get started. I decided to have them begin by completing the information for grade 2, as it was our class and I knew that counting children directly was one strategy that was accessible. The children knew that there were 11 girls and that the total number of children was 25. Our problem was to determine the number of second-grade boys.

The class spent about 20 minutes working in small groups before we gathered in a circle on the rug to discuss our solutions.

> *Teacher:* Who would like to share a solution with the group?
> *Jerry:* (Jerry appears to be pretty sure of himself. His head is tipped to one side and his voice is strong.) We counted. We each walked

FIGURE 3.1. Data Collected for Week-Two Problem Solving

	GIRLS	BOYS	TOTAL
Kindergarten	11	9	
Grade 1		11	24
Grade 2	11		25
Grade 3	11	6	
Grade 4		15	22
Grade 5	8		20
Grade 6		7	15
TOTAL			

around the room and counted *all* of the boys. There were 14, counting Jack, since he's not here today.

Julie: (Julie, who has worked in Jerry's group, is usually more tenta-
tive in her actions, but she leans forward, pushes her hair back,
and speaks without raising her hand for recognition.) First we counted 14 boys. We looked around. We knew there were 14. We tried
to find out any other way. So we counted out 14 of the blocks. (Julie reaches forward and counts out 14 cubes, which she places in
the center of the circle.)

By counting the boys first and then by representing them with blocks, the
children had determined that the answer was 14. I was considering how I
might encourage further discussion when I heard Alec mutter, "Gotta count
to see if you have enough." Without lifting his eyes, he extended his hand to
count the blocks.

Alec had not been working with Jerry and Julie, so I was pleased to see
that he was trying to follow their thinking. I wondered if other children were

also trying to understand what Julie and Jerry had done, when Ellen interrupted.

> *Ellen:* Our group took all 25 and took away 11. We made all 25 and took away 11, because there are 11 girls.
>
> *Teacher:* Hold on to that idea for a minute, please, Ellen. Jerry and Julie aren't finished.

Ellen slowly moved back an inch or two. She nodded her head and sat back to await her turn to share a solution. Jerry grinned. He seemed to be pleased that his ideas were still being considered.

> *Jerry:* We started with 20 cubes.
>
> *Teacher:* I'm confused. Julie said you started with 14 cubes. (I am trying to figure out if Jerry and Julie are discussing the same solution method.)
>
> *Jerry:* (Jerry scowls, leans forward to touch the blocks, and then leans back.) We took, we took, I can't remember.

Jerry was stuck. He was unable to share any more about his solution, and Julie was unable to verbalize why she had chosen to begin with 14 cubes. I understood that the 14 cubes that Julie had chosen might represent the number of boys, but I was confused about Jerry's use of 20 cubes. Had he begun with 20 cubes or had he forgotten? I tried to get the other children involved in thinking about these ideas, but they did not seem very interested and the discussion went nowhere.

I repeated my statement of confusion and waited quietly for a response. While waiting, I looked directly at each of the 25 children in turn. There was no sound. There was no movement. I was met with 25 silent, immobile, and expressionless children.

I decided that it was no use pursuing this any longer and I turned to Ellen and asked her to tell us about her group's idea. Again, the children appeared to be listening intently, but after she finished there was no discussion and there were no questions. I was still faced with the problem of involving the children in the solutions of others, but based on my past experience, I knew that if I persisted in asking questions and in giving the children opportunities to engage with their classmates' ideas, this would eventually happen.

WEEK THREE: ANOTHER ATTEMPT AT WHOLE GROUP DISCUSSION

Over the next week, we continued to fill in the missing information in our chart. I was encouraged to see that groups were able to sustain interest in their work for longer periods of time and they were beginning to look for multiple solutions in order to check the accuracy of their answers. They were beginning to respond to other people's ideas and to relate them to their own solutions. I decided that this would be a good time to begin focusing on mental computations and estimations, as these skills would enable the children to assess their answers for reasonableness.

Using the information on the chart, I wrote the following problem on the board: *The kindergarten class in our school has 11 girls and 9 boys. How many children are in the class?*

I called on two children, each of whom read the problem aloud. Then I waited quietly for the children to signal me that they had an answer to the problem. As I waited, I looked around: Some of the children closed their eyes; some looked upward toward the ceiling, some moved their lips as if they were communicating with another being, and some were surreptitiously moving their fingers.

When the children appeared to be ready, I asked, "Is there anyone who has an answer that he or she would like to share with us?" Children offered the answers 18, 20, and 19, all of which I recorded on the board without response. I accepted correct and incorrect answers—in the weeks to follow, as this procedure became routine, I would begin to ask the children whether any of the answers volunteered bothered them.

> *Teacher:* How did you get those answers?
> *Zoe:* (Zoe smiles.) I like to work with 10s. I took 1 away from the 11. I added it to the 9. That made 10 + 10. That's 20. (Zoe's smile gets even bigger.)
> *Teacher:* That's interesting. Can anyone explain what Zoe did in his or her own words? (I want to be sure that the other children are following Zoe's thinking.)

As I waited for a response to my question, I looked around the room. The 25 children were looking right at me. This was different. Just two weeks ago they had been looking away and trying to avoid my questions. Slowly, a few hands rose. I called on Susan.

> *Susan:* (Susan always speaks softly. Her voice is very low, but the children are listening intently. The room is silent but for Susan's voice.) She started with an 11 and a 9. She took 1 from the 11. Now it's a 10. She added the extra 1 to the 9. That's a 10, too. Then she added the two 10s and got 20.
> *Teacher:* (I look directly at Zoe.) Is that what you were doing, Zoe?
> *Zoe:* Yes!
> *Teacher:* Does anyone have any questions? (I wait for a response.

There is none.) Who else has a solution to share? Several hands were raised, some waving furiously in my direction, others barely raised high enough to see. Isaac's was someplace in the middle, and I called on him.

Isaac: (Isaac sits upright in his chair. His voice is strong.) I added 11 and 9. I started with 11. Then I went 12, 13, 14, 15, 16, 17, 18, 19, 20.

Teacher: How did you know when to stop?

A puzzled look came over Isaac's face. He crinkled his eyebrows, squinted, and remained quiet.

Laurel: (Laurel leaps up out of her seat and shouts.) There are 9 numbers after 11!

There were nods and smiles everywhere. I was excited, too. Laurel had become so invested in figuring out what Isaac was thinking, she forgot that she is usually quiet and reserved. The other children—Sam included—who were nodding and smiling also must have been thinking about what Isaac was trying to do.

Sam: I did it that way, too!

Like Laurel, Sam had spoken out without having been recognized and looked around to see if there were any repercussions for speaking out of turn. There were none, so he smiled, wiggled in his seat a little, and returned his attention to the front of the room.

Keith: I have another way. I know that 9 is three 3s; 11 + 3 is 14; 14 + 3 is 17; 17 + 3 is 20.

Kelly: (Kelly is kneeling on one leg as she stands up beside her chair.) I pictured the cubes in my head. There were 11 of them, plus 9 more. First I counted them one way. Then I checked it by counting the other way.

Kelly walked forward and drew a picture of her solution on the board. There was a chorus of "Aah" and "Mmmm" after she finished. I thought about whether to look more closely at a particular solution, but I decided to let the children continue. They were discussing the math at hand in their own way, sharing their ideas and interacting with one another, and that was far better than their focusing on me!

After a while the interactions among the children slowed, and I decided to intervene in order to add a different dimension to their analysis—assessment of answers for reasonableness.

> *Teacher:* What if I were to say that there were 5 children in the kindergarten class? (My comments are greeted with laughter.)
> *Jeremy:* Five doesn't make sense!
> *Teacher:* Why not?

Jeremy shrugged, threw his hands up in the air, and grinned.

> *Alec:* (Alec clears his throat in order to get everyone's attention.) I think that what he means is that 11 is more than 5 + 5.
> *Jeremy:* (Jeremy is grinning from ear to ear. He nods.) Yeah!!!
> *Teacher:* What if I were to say there are 40 children in kindergarten?
> *Jeremy:* (Jeremy speaks out confidently.) 40 is way too much.
> *Jamie:* Even two 11s aren't 40.

I decided to stop there. The children had been actively engaged in mathematics for almost 40 minutes. They had been listening to and reacting to one another's ideas in a way that was respectful and kind. Alec had been listening to Jeremy in a way that was different from before. This time he was really trying to figure out what Jeremy was thinking when he responded, "I think that what he means is. . . . "

The children had been able to speak directly to one another in a way that until now had begun to occur only in their small groups; they had been able to listen to my conjectures about the number of children in the kindergarten class; and they had listened to my numbers and had evaluated them for reasonableness within the context of the problem.

ONE MONTH LATER: PUTTING IT TOGETHER

The children were sitting quietly awaiting the day's math problem, their desk chairs turned toward the front of the room so as to allow the best view of the board. I raised the screen and asked for two volunteers to read the problem aloud: *Grades 2 and 6 want to work together on some murals. If each of the 15 sixth graders and each of the 25 second graders need paintbrushes, how many shall I buy?*

I stood near the board where the problem was written, surveying the children as they mentally computed the answer to the problem. The only sounds that were audible came from the other classrooms in our wing of the school.

Hands began to go up. I looked directly at each child and nodded my head to acknowledge that I knew that he or she was ready to share an answer.

When asked, the children proposed 52 and 40 as solutions to the problem. As usual, I wrote the responses on the board without comment.

> *Teacher:* Are there any answers here that bother you?
> *William:* (William is small and he is sitting on his knees so as to be sure that he can see over the children who are in front of him.) 52 is too big.
> *Teacher:* Why?
> *William:* (His eyes crinkle and it is clear that he is considering a response to my question.) Hmmm.
> *Jamie:* (Jamie looks at William, who nods. It is as if she has asked his permission to speak.) There are only three 10s and two 5s. 52 is too big.

I watched to see if the child who had offered 52 for an answer was upset by this analysis, but she didn't appear to be distressed in any way. Instead, she was quietly counting on her fingers and appeared to be considering Jamie's explanation. Jeremy was busy looking around the room at the other children before focusing his attention on the board.

> *Jeremy:* I think so, too. There's one 10 in 15 and there are two in 25. That can't be 52.

William, Jeremy, and Jamie had all been considering the reasonableness of the answer. The other children were listening attentively and most were nodding their heads in affirmation. I decided that this was a good time to divide the class into groups of three so that they could validate their answers with manipulatives.

The children worked in their small groups for about 20 minutes before I asked them to gather on the rug in the rear of the classroom for a group discussion. As I worked my way to the back of the room, I overheard several animated discussions. Elise, a child who is only beginning to develop confidence in her ability to do math, stopped by to show me a sheet of paper. Her paper had the number 40 written three times in three different colors. She said, ''These are the answers we thought it was. We proved it three ways.''

Once everyone was settled into a circle on the floor, I asked who would like to share a solution. Almost every hand waved back at me. The children were stretching their bodies so that their hands would reach higher in the air. It was clear that they wanted to share their ideas with their classmates. Because it was unusual for her to raise her hand in the large group discussions, I decided to recognize Elise.

Elise: We have this! Me, Zoe, and Donald started to make ideas and wrote down our answers. They're all 40.

Teacher: How did you figure that out?

Elise: We counted up to 25. We counted 15. We counted the cubes up and it was 40. (Elise doesn't even look at me. Her face is beaming with pride as she moves to get unifix cubes. She makes a train of 20 cubes. Then she adds 5 more cubes to her train.) One, two, three.

As Elise began to count the cubes one by one, she was joined by a chorus of voices. Four, five, six . . . all the way up to 25. I looked around at the children. They were leaning forward watching intently as Elise pointed to each cube. Some of them were even moving their fingers in the air as if they were themselves pointing at each cube. It was clear that they were working and thinking right alongside her. It was also clear that they were paying absolutely no attention to me.

Elise continued to make another train with 15 cubes, and the children continued to work with her to check the accuracy of her counting. Then Elise joined her two trains and was about to begin to count the cubes in the long train.

I'm not sure Ben was speaking to anyone in particular, but as he leaned forward to join in the group counting, he said, "I think it's 40."

The children continued their chorus of counting. When they reached 40, they moved back and the circle of children enlarged to its original size. Elise looked like the Cheshire cat; her smile extended from one ear to the other.

There was no lull in the discussion, and no one looked to me for recognition.

Zoe: Well, another thing we did was, we made the 26 and the 15. Uh—I mean the 25 and the 15. Then we took the two 5s—one from the 15 and one from the 25. We added them together. That made 10. 20 is two 10s. There's a 10 from the 15. That made it 40.

Jack: (Jack is bouncing up and down in his place. His voice is almost too loud.) I like it!

Keith: (Keith is up on his knees and pulling on his earlobe.) I think it's right. I think it's right, because—

Kelly: (Kelly continues on as if she were the one who has been talking.) There's four 10s in 40.

Isaac: (Isaac doesn't pause either, as he continues working with Kelly's idea.) Four 10s make 40.

Jeremy: (Jeremy giggles.) That's a neat way to do it.

I was feeling very pleased. The children were working together. They were listening to each other's ideas and were finishing each other's sentences. No one seemed to mind. Everyone seemed to be involved in the process.

I looked around at the circle of children, wondering who might have another solution to share with the group. I needn't have bothered. No one was waiting for me!

> *Melody:* (Melody is another one of the quieter second graders. She takes a very deep breath and begins to speak.) We, Robert, Julie, and me, we took 10 cubes and another 10 and 5 more—
>
> *Robert:* (Robert speaks without any hesitation.) To make it 25.
>
> *Julie:* (Julie is just as invested in the sharing as her partners.) And 15 more—

Robert reached forward to demonstrate his group's solution with the base-10 blocks, 25 pairs of eyes following his every move. Robert placed two 10-sticks on the rug.

> *Melody:* (Melody counts out 5 unit cubes.) We need 5 of these.
>
> *Jeremy:* That's the 25 for grade 2.
>
> *Robert:* (Robert reaches for another 10-stick. Melody gets 5 more 1s.) We added another 10 and 5 more. It added up to make 40—10, 20, 30, 31, 32, 33 . . . [all the way to] 40.
>
> *Ben:* (Ben runs his tongue all the way around the edges of his mouth.) Well, my group used three 10s and one 5. Then we counted another 5. When we added them all together, we counted 40.
>
> *Keith:* (Keith's eyes look upward. He seems to be deep in thought.) We had—wait—we took the 25 and the 15 and we took away the 10 from the 15 and the 20 from the 25. That made 30. Then we measured the two 5s on one 10 thing: 30 + 10 is 40. (He pauses and holds up his hand as if directing traffic.) Then we knew it was the same as 10. We traded it in. It's still 10—10, 20, 30, 40. (He looks up and then from one child to the next.) What do you think?
>
> *Nathan:* (Nathan claps as he speaks.) Keith has 40. Yeah!!!
>
> *Isaac:* I think he's right 'cause four 10s always adds up to 40.
>
> *Kelly:* (Kelly knits her brows. She appears to be thinking very hard.) Four 10s adds up to 40. Three 10s that are all together and 10 little separate ones. You can take the 10 little ones and trade.
>
> *Jamie:* We did the same as Keith, but we made sure we were right by taking the 40 and seeing if we had 25 and 15 in it.

I was amazed at what had transpired during the processing of the problem. The children not only had shared a multitude of solutions and strategies,

but they had traded in 10 unit cubes for a 10-stick. They were in the preliminary stages of reinventing regrouping in addition and they were excited about
their discovery.

I was impressed by the mathematical content of the discussion, but I also
was pleased to see how the children were functioning as a group. The children
had listened to one another in order to figure out ideas and how they related
to their own solutions. And they had validated each other's solutions without
looking to me for direction or support.

CONCLUSION

During the first two months of the school year, the tenor of mathematics
learning had changed for these second graders. Mathematics was no longer a
solitary activity to be completed independently in order to get the correct answer.

The children were immersed in thinking about the multitude of possible
solution strategies that were accessible to them and they considered how the
strategies were related to one another. They were no longer frightened or
timid about tackling unfamiliar problems; they were energized by the challenge.

The children had learned to listen respectfully to the ideas of their classmates; they had learned to listen in order to figure out the problem-solving
strategies of others and how those strategies were supported or refuted by their
own ideas and solutions.

They also had learned that they were in an environment in which it was
safe to take risks. Answers were accepted without judgment, and it was all
right to make mistakes. In this environment, the children felt capable and confident that they could solve problems. They had the power to use what they
already understood to solve problems that were more challenging and less familiar, and they were able to formulate their own questions and to raise these
questions for the whole group to discuss and ponder.

The problems that I created gave the children a common focus for discussion, but the children took it from there. By taking responsibility for their own
learning and pursuing the answers to their own questions, the children were
able to turn even the most mundane problem into a meaningful and challenging
exploration.

During the rest of the year, the children will continue to explore the topics listed in the grade 2 mathematics curriculum—regrouping in addition and
subtraction, measurement, time, fractions, and geometry. As a community of
mathematics learners, they have the confidence to look beyond rote skills and
to search for meaningful patterns and relationships in mathematics.

$$+ \quad - \quad \times \quad \div$$

FOOD FOR THOUGHT – AND TALK

Mary Signet

Formulating plans for a new school year was especially exciting this term as I was to teach more mathematics classes than I usually was assigned. As a Chapter I teacher, I was going to collaborate with the classroom teacher, sharing classroom responsibilities for mathematics. However, early into the school year my well-laid plans to take over the class were dashed. We had scheduling conflicts and a solution was not readily available. Instead, I was to pull out a small group of children who were functioning well below grade level in mathematics. This solution would be more in keeping with my role as a Chapter I remedial mathematics teacher.

Chapter I provides federal money to school systems that demonstrate, using AFDC and Free Lunch figures, a high level of poverty. Once the poverty levels of the system are determined, children are enrolled in the program only on the basis of academic need. As in many other old industrial cities in the northeast section of the country, my school system relies heavily on funding from outside sources to provide many of its education services.

This writing is an attempt to share the struggles I faced in trying to develop a community of mathematics learners with children who, even before they reached third grade, had already gone down a path of failure. The children, who are all nine years of age and all taken from the same third-grade classroom, had been deemed eligible for instructional service provided by Chapter I because they performed well below grade level. It was my job to help them find a new path, one that could lead to success.

THE PROBLEM

At times, having a small group comes with its own set of problems, and this group of four children certainly did. There were many varied problems but the most outstanding at this time was one of communication. When we all came together for math class, they didn't talk to one another; nor did they talk to me. When I was able to get a few words out of them, they were of the monosyllabic variety. It's not that they didn't want to come with me—they ran to the door when they saw me standing there—but that was the end of any signs of animation. Every morning, at the appointed time, I would arrive at their classroom door and the same scene would unfold.

Sandra, a willowy, light-skinned African-American child is usually the first one to note my arrival. She slowly looks around and moves toward the door. She makes no comments and shows no expression as she leans against the door jamb waiting for the others to assemble.

Pedro sits quietly in his seat until my eyes come in contact with his and

I signal for him to come to the door. He is a very reserved, well-dressed little boy of Hispanic background whose big black eyes seem to be focused straight ahead. He, too, shows little sign of animation.

Vicky, a blond, blue-eyed Hispanic-American child, yells across the room, "Wait a minute!" and begins to clear off her desk. This usually leads to confusion in her area of the room. On initial observation, it is very apparent that Vicky exhibits many problems in gross motor skills. She finally arrives at the door, usually in an agitated state from a problem at her desk area.

Joel, the smallest of the group, has a warm, accommodating personality. As he is seated farthest from the door, he is usually the last in line. He is white and has a mop of shiny black curls that frame his tiny face. His jet black eyes twinkle as he inquires, "Are we going downstairs today?"

Picking up my little group was the easiest part of the time we spent together. "You look like a gaggle of geese," noted the librarian one day as we paraded to our area in a corner of the library. I was first in the parade and the children followed, usually in the order that they arrived at the door. There was no conversation as we walked along—even when I tried to engage them in one.

Each day I labored to get the children involved in some type of mathematical exploration and discussion, but what I got was eight eyes staring, as if into space, past me. I brought out tubs of manipulatives for them to play with, but that didn't work. One day while I was reading them a story, hoping to involve them in some kind of discussion about the book, one of them fell sound asleep.

"What can I do about this group? How do I focus on this problem?" I wrote in my journal. At that moment, thinking and reflecting were not putting the problem into perspective for me.

Some time during the second week of my work with them, I brought out the manipulatives again. Something happened—I'm not quite sure what—but I could see Sandra peering through her arms trying to get a glimpse at what I was doing. She usually sat with her arms wrapped around her head while it rested on the table. After I placed the tub of unifix cubes in the center of the table, the following incident took place:

Sandra (with little or no excitement in her voice): I know, those are to play with when your work is done.
Teacher: Have you ever used them at math time?
Sandra: Nope. (pause) Only when your work is done.
Teacher: Would you like to play with them?
Sandra: Nope. I don't like them.

My hopes to keep her talking ended with her final statement, and her head went back into her hands. Needless to say, I was very close to my frustration threshold, my concern for Sandra greatly increased.

Discussing my worries with her classroom teacher later in the day, I got some sense of what was going on there. Sandra was doing the same thing in her class—communicating very little verbally. In both of our classes, the other three children at least had started talking to one another, but not Sandra. The others were not talking about mathematics, but at least they were talking to one another.

Nightly, while writing in my journal, I would question what was happening with this group: What is going on here and how can I solve this problem? Since not all of the children had gone to the same lower elementary school, but had been transferred to this school from different schools, perhaps once they got to know one another this talking thing would change. While this might be partially true, two weeks felt like a long time to have children acting like this. I continued reading and rereading my journal as if it would draw me a map of how to solve this problem. Thinking back on my 25 years as a first-grade teacher, I reviewed all the little tricks I have used to get children involved, but they didn't seem to fit as a solution to my problem. I was preoccupied with how I might get my four third graders to talk and couldn't seem to find an answer.

PROGRESS

One Sunday in October, my husband and I stopped at a roadside farm stand and saw a large variety of seasonal vegetables and fruits. What caught my eye was a basket in the far corner with a sign that read, "Watermelon, 4/$1.00." They were the size of softballs and resembled squash rather than melons. A bargain, I bought eight of them.

The next morning on my way out to school, the watermelon sitting on the kitchen table caught my eye once more. "I wonder if the children would like some of this melon," I thought aloud to myself. Maybe, just maybe, they would.

Later that morning I collected the children in the usual fashion and we walked downstairs to the library. The children spied the watermelon sitting in the middle of the table.

"What's that?" Joel asked in an inquisitive tone of voice. I thought to myself, They *can* act like regular kids. Pedro said, "That's something you put in the oven and cook." Vicky added, "It ain't ripe, but I don't know what it is." Sandra said nothing, but she was wide-eyed, looking at the watermelon.

It turned out to be a delightful 25 minutes as we struggled to figure out what this green sphere was. The consensus was that we should cut it to see if that would help identify it. Cutting into the melon brought forth a gush of juice from inside, and the children were standing to get a better look at this thing in the center of the table. When I cut into the watermelon, exposing the light red flesh dotted with tiny white seeds, their little eyes lit up and smiles broke across their faces. "Is it a watermelon?" Joel asked, first hesitating and then looking around for consensus. "Wow, it is a watermelon," added Pedro. "Can we eat it?" Sandra was still staring at the fruit in the middle of the table and finally stated emphatically, "It don't look like the watermelon in the store. Can we eat it now?" Vicky, who was very quiet up to this point, blurted out, "I've gotta have a piece of that watermelon!" I then cut the melon into chunks and we all sat down to enjoy the fruit. I was so happy, I couldn't believe my eyes. Here we were, talking and eating—together.

The children returned to class that day relating stories about the watermelon that looked like a softball. What I didn't realize at the time was that this was to be the beginning of their mathematics lessons with me.

My journal entry for that day read, "We're talking!" I had reached my first goal, to get the children engaged in some type of conversation. Looking back on the experience, I don't know which of us was more excited. Now I had to think of another project that would keep the children interested and talking and maybe even have some mathematical value. Evidently food worked today, so I decided to follow up with another lesson concerned with food.

MORE FOOD, MORE THOUGHTS

The next day I brought in two small packages of Cheez-its. "Oh, boy!" exclaimed Pedro. "We're going to eat every day!" He had a broad grin and his face glowed as he looked at the crackers on the table. I just smiled at him; I was pleased to see some of yesterday's enthusiasm returning that morning. "Yes," I replied. "We are going to eat, but first there are a few things that we need to figure out about the crackers."

Handing one bag to the two girls and the other to the boys, I continued, "First I would like you to look carefully at the bag. Think about how many crackers are in that bag." After a brief discussion about the word "estimating" and what it means, the children began to look ever so carefully at the bags, rubbing their hands over the outside wrapper. To my surprise, they began chatting to one another and soon came up with reasonable estimates—35 and 30. I actually hadn't been looking for anything reasonable; I just wanted to keep the children engaged in conversation. But they were doing better than that, and so I printed the numbers next to their names on the large sheet of paper I had taped to a nearby board. They were excited when I next cut open each bag and said, "Think about how you plan to split up the crackers in the bag."

I watched as the children sat in pairs trying to figure out what to do. Joel took over in his group and announced, "I'll take one; then you take one." This they proceeded to do. When they finished, Pedro suggested, "Let's count. I'll do mine and you do yours." Soon they had two neat piles of crackers in front of them, but they still had to come up with a total before they could eat them. They were working and talking together about the crackers, so I moved on to the table where the girls were sitting.

Vicky: I got 15 and she got 11.
Teacher: Who has more?
Vicky: I do.
Teacher: How many do you have altogether?
Vicky: I dunno. I'll count them.
Teacher: Sandra should help, too.
Sandra (picking her head up from her hands, begins in a grumbling
    tone): One, two, three, four, five, six . . . (Her voice gets quieter
    with each succeeding number until she gets to 21.) There's 21.
    (Then she immediately puts her head in her hands.)

I really wanted to arrange the crackers so that they could count them more easily but restrained myself. It was clear that they needed to come up with their own counting plan. I guess one would say that their strategy was not very visual—just piles in the middle of the table. Neither of the girls seemed to be able to make any sense out of trying to count the crackers. Both were counting by touch and coming up with different answers each time. Sandra was still hiding behind her folded arms, but she was well aware of the fact that she had the smaller pile. When I suggested that they try to make their piles even and then try counting, I saw a spark of life in Sandra as she peered through her arms at the two piles in front of her. Finally, a small smile broke across her face and she lifted her head. She would participate in making equal piles of crackers. Oh, I do wish Sandra were a bit more verbal.

Realizing that time was running short, I returned to the boys, who were beaming now that their crackers had been arranged and counted. Joel explained to me that they had an extra cracker, but they had put it in the trash. They were ready to eat and did so very quickly. The girls were still counting, but they had come up with a plan to show how many crackers they had. They had evened off the piles of crackers, Vicky reporting that she had given Sandra two of her crackers. "Now we both have 13."

Wanting to bring some closure to the day's lesson, I began to write the numbers the children had given me on a chart. Vicky volunteered to come to the chart and place the greater-than sign between two numbers to show which one was bigger. "We did this in our class: '>' always goes to the littlest number. Ain't that right, Joel?"

I wasn't quite sure how much the children understood about the sign, but they initiated the discussion and that was a step in the right direction. I finally felt that there was hope for my little group and that we would be able to accomplish some things in mathematics. There were many options opened to me now. A few weeks before, the only thing on my mind was to get the children communicating. That we had accomplished.

STILL MORE FOOD AND THOUGHTS

We have eaten our way through a box of pretzels and have started on the second box. The children bring snacks, which they dutifully count before they eat them. When we go to the cafeteria to buy milk every Friday, the children convert pennies to different coins and keep track of this in their journals. They discuss with one another different ways they can pay for their milk, since I told them they cannot use the same configuration more than once.

Counting the food every morning has become second nature to the children. I didn't plan that the morning snack would become a ritual, but it has. The children bring in snacks and will attempt to share the smallest bag of goodies. The time I spend with these children has become a pleasant interlude in my day. They are learning to be kind to one another and polite when one of them is speaking.

The past few days find us back to pretzels as we explore addition with carrying and odd and even numbers. They count the pretzels to determine how many each of them has and combine the amounts to come up with one grand total. Some days we try to predict if the total will be an odd or an even number. Other days we try to decide how many more pretzels one group has than the other. We work against the clock (one of the drawbacks of a pull-out program), as we have so much to do in so little time. Some days I assign homework so that we can begin our discussion immediately.

Sandra and Pedro were the only members of the group present one day recently. As they were getting ready to leave, I gave each of them a small box of raisins. "What are these for?" Sandra asked. "What do you think?" I replied. "Snack?" she asked with a twinkle in her eyes. "They're to count and all those other things," Pedro shot back. "You mean homework?" giggled Sandra. I explained that they could eat them at recess once they had counted them. With that statement they were off to their classroom.

Later that day, while I was on bus duty, I noticed Sandra standing across the street yelling something to me. At first I couldn't hear what it was, but I finally made out "103" as she scampered through the empty lot on her way home. I had no idea what she was talking about.

That evening, as I sat writing in my journal, I realized what she was saying. She was telling me that there were 103 raisins in the box. I smiled to myself thinking about Sandra and our earlier classes when she was unwilling to raise her head from the desk. How good it was that she was talking now, even if it was only a little.

$$+ \quad - \quad \times \quad \div$$

GETTING STARTED

Virginia Stimpson

Most students enter our mathematics classrooms in September having been socialized as passive recipients of knowledge. They expect the teacher to model the solution procedure to be followed in the day's assignment—usually a set of closely related exercises—and they know that they are supposed to keep quiet during teacher presentations and individual seatwork (Ball, 1988; Schoenfeld, 1985). No wonder, then, that students are puzzled by the demands of teachers like those whose stories are included in this book.

In these teachers' classrooms, students are expected to pose and address mathematical questions, explain their thinking, and actively attend to the reasoning of their classmates. They are to take the initiative in finding various methods for solving problems and in analyzing the connections among them. Their teachers do not show them the way, but by presenting problems or asking questions, point them in a direction.

To minimize the confusion and frustration caused by these clashing expectations, teachers must prepare themselves and their students for such drastic changes in instructional practice. Essential to the creation of classrooms in which students actively explore mathematical ideas, are the development of a clear vision, selection of appropriate mathematical tasks, and the establishment of new routines of student behavior. In this essay, I use Jill Bodner Lester's account to illustrate these elements of the process, and then discuss some of the difficulties Mary Signet encountered as she worked with her group of troubled third graders. Finally, out of my experience as a high school teacher committed to engaging her students in mathematical inquiry, I offer one of my own September strategies.

In the beginning of her account, Lester describes her vision of her classroom as a community of mathematics learners.

> I want the children to know that mathematics involves thinking and the development of problem-solving strategies. I want them to feel safe and to feel that they can risk asking a question or sharing an incomplete idea. I want them to listen to one another respectfully and to try to understand what their classmates are thinking and doing. I want them to learn to formulate their own mathematical questions and to take responsibility for their own learning.

However, Lester's class will not learn how to become the community she envisions by listening to her explain what they should do. Rather, this learning will take place through their work on mathematical tasks and in interaction with their teacher and among themselves.

For the first day of school, Lester selected a mathematics game using unifix cubes to find missing addends. This task would meet several necessary criteria: It was likely to be accessible to all of her students but "a little beyond the children's easy reach"; it would provide an opportunity to raise questions about how different solution strategies result in the same answer; it would lend itself to cooperative activity; and it would introduce some of the mathematical content of the second-grade curriculum.

With goals in mind and task selected, Lester was ready to meet her students and begin working to establish new classroom behaviors—this would be the real challenge of September, for the children would be arriving without experience of the kind of classroom she intended to build. And, sure enough, in contrast to her vision of a group of children curious about mathematical issues and engaged in lively debate, on those first days Lester's class sat in silence: "I asked how they had arrived at the answer, but there was no response to my question."

Readers may have been frustrated at the students' initial lack of responsiveness and Lester's unwillingness to fill the silence with her own talk. But within a short time, students did begin to speak up; and within a few weeks, they were interacting easily with one another. What had she done to effect this dramatic change in classroom culture?

Some of Lester's critical teaching behaviors are easily identified. For one, in contrast to the traditional classroom in which the teacher responds immediately, providing "positive feedback" for correct answers and dismissing wrong ones (Rowe, 1974), Lester remained nonjudgmental as various solutions were offered. Instead, she encouraged elaboration and found ways to foster conversation among her students. By praising persistence and creativity rather than correct answers, she taught her students a new set of values for mathematics class.

Furthermore, Lester's nonjudgmental attitude communicated her belief that her students were capable of making sense of mathematics. As she listened to them, she was not waiting for a single, correct answer or steering the conversation toward one or two standard methods of solution. Rather, she worked to understand what they were thinking. Although it took weeks, her students learned to follow her example, listening to their classmates and taking their ideas seriously. Through their conversations, they discovered that they themselves, and not just the teacher, could assess the validity of various solutions and strategies. And they found that they could pose their own questions and make new mathematical connections.

The children's mathematical investigations were supported by the predictable classroom routines Lester established over the first few weeks of school.

Students knew that each day they would be given a problem and be asked to consider it, first without the aid of pencil and paper or manipulatives; then they would be invited to discuss their preliminary thoughts about the problem and consider one another's approaches, before they broke into small groups to explore it with whatever tools were available; later, they would gather again to discuss their discoveries. With the predictability of these routines, students could concentrate on mathematical ideas and were better able to participate in the risk-taking activities of sharing and evaluating one another's solutions.

Rather than assign workbook pages filled with repetitious exercises, Lester selected two big problems that the class worked on for several weeks. The problems were noteworthy, not so much for their drama or excitement, but for the mathematical issues that were embedded in them. She knew that ideas worth pursuing in depth would arise from exploring them.

Some of Lester's actions are quite subtle and their effect on classroom culture less obvious. Her willingness to tolerate silences is one. For it was in the space made available by those very silences, that students discovered their own mathematical voices.

On the first day of school, the class timidly tested this space. Susan was the first to venture to speak and then "inched her way back to her spot on the edge of the circle, nodded her head, and mumbled, '20.'" Following Susan's example, Donald moved into the middle of the circle. But when he was finished, there was more silence, which "seemed like an eternity," before the next child spoke up.

Lester tells us that the silence was uncomfortable for her students, and her descriptions indicate that it was uncomfortable for her as well. But it was her tolerance of the discomfort—her own as well as theirs—that allowed that space to stay open. By the third week of school, the children still needed to check its boundaries—"Sam . . . looked around to see if there were any repercussions for speaking out of turn"—but were excitedly filling the space with their mathematical ideas.

Lester's treatment of silence provides one example of an understanding of the significance of emotion for learning that contrasts with that of the traditional classroom. For her, discomfort is not necessarily an evil to be extinguished as quickly and efficiently as possible; nor is it necessarily an indication of failure on her part or the students'. Instead, discomfort can actually be a positive aspect of the very process of learning.

Another example is found in Lester's response to Nathan. On the second day of school, after he had explained how he knew that, if Kelly had 7 of 20 cubes in front of her, she had 13 behind her back, Lester told Nathan that she was confused, and needed further explanation. "Nathan's expression became a scowl. . . . It was clear that he was annoyed with me and that my question made him feel uncomfortable." Yet Lester felt satisfied with the interaction.

She had communicated her expectation that he think more deeply about his idea and, although he did not take on the challenge at that moment, she believed that eventually he would.

Implicit in the episode is her belief in her connection to these seven-year-olds. She knew that within minutes Nathan would be past his annoyance. And she knew that soon Nathan and his classmates would come to recognize that she valued their ideas, and the trust between herself and the class would grow strong.

Two months into the school year, the reality of Lester's classroom matched her vision. During the initial eight-week period—through the silence, annoyance, and discomfort—she felt confident: "Based on my past experience, I knew that if I persisted in asking questions and in giving children opportunities to engage with their classmates' ideas, this would eventually happen."

Similar goals, strategies, and teaching behaviors are at issue in Signet's piece. Yet, where Lester never doubted that her fairly typical class of 25 children would become the community she envisioned, Signet felt no such assurance about her troubled group of four. And her story starkly demonstrates how, in working to enact the new pedagogy, teachers are so much more dependent on their students. In the traditional classroom, once teachers have performed their demonstrations and handed out worksheets—while keeping the class quiet—they are said to have taught. However, when teaching for understanding, "if students do not do the work, have good ideas, and engage in lively discussions, the class will fall flat and the teacher will have failed publicly" (Cohen & Barnes, 1993, p. 246). This is the nightmare Signet faced.

While it took only a few days for Lester's students to begin to discuss the mathematical questions she posed, Signet's students remained silent for weeks. And in contrast to the silence that grows out of confusion over classroom norms, the silence in Signet's class seemed an active refusal of connections. Were these young children depressed, suspicious? We don't know—and neither did Signet as she pondered and fretted, day after day, trying to figure out just how her students might be drawn out.

In the face of the children's uncommunicativeness, it is striking that Signet did not retreat to a more traditional teaching approach that did not depend on students having and voicing mathematical ideas. After all, she was a 25-year veteran and must have had available to her packages of drill sheets that could have filled the 40-minute math period with something that looked like work. Apparently, once she had begun teaching mathematics for ideas, she had come to believe that filling in drill sheets had little to do with real learning. Thus, if she had any hope that her group of nine-year-olds would progress mathematically, they would have to begin talking.

Signet's persistence paid off. We don't know whether, after weeks of silence, the children had begun to trust their teacher and each other, or if they had become unbearably bored, or if that little watermelon was simply too intriguing to be ignored. In any case, they began talking—even if it wasn't about mathematics.

Once the silence was broken, Signet could begin teaching. She started by having her students share bags of Cheez-its, a task that could be accomplished by a variety of approaches, lent itself to cooperative activity, and was connected to the mathematical concepts and skills mandated by the third-grade curriculum. Withdrawn Sandra still needed to be coaxed into participating, but once she realized that taking part in that activity meant that she would get her fair share, she too became interested.

In order to make sure student thinking remained central in her teaching, Signet still needed to check old teacher behaviors. She commented, "I really wanted to arrange the crackers so that they could count them more easily but restrained myself." She made the task easier for Vicky and Sandra, but she did not take over the solution of the original problem. Like Lester, Signet knew that eliminating frustration would not help her students learn. Suggesting how to arrange the crackers might have provided immediate relief, but it would not have communicated her confidence in their ability to reach a solution. Her restraint provided room for her students to think and to grow.

And the rewards for her high expectations for her students came surprisingly quickly. Already on that day when Signet brought in Cheez-its, Vicky volunteered to write on the chart at the front of the class and added to the discussion by including a greater-than sign between her numbers. The students had learned that the discussion was theirs and so could take it beyond their teacher's initial focus. These children were thinking about numbers and symbols, aided by a context that they cared about.

Reading these teachers' reflections reminds me of my own experience as a high school mathematics teacher in suburban Seattle (Minstrell & Stimpson, in press). Each September, I, too, have the task of working with new students to change their expectations and behaviors. I have not faced a situation quite like Signet's, but my tenth-, eleventh-, and twelfth-grade students are, in some ways, strikingly similar to Lester's second graders: They too are initially confused by my questions and unsure about how to respond.

One difference between high school and second grade, however, is that my students have had many more years experience with traditional teaching practice. Like Donna Scanlon's students (described in Chapter 2), mine enter class with well-defined expectations and agendas that conflict with my own.

To address resistance and confusion head on, I have developed a document that I give to my students and their parents, as well as to administrators and new colleagues who enter my school system. That document describes my goals for engagement, empowerment, and problem solving and discusses the rationale of each. It includes a description of students' abilities to gather and organize data, to look for patterns, to generate and test solutions, and to evaluate ideas presented by others. I suggest that these abilities rarely are tapped by paper-and-pencil exercises, and I work to allay fears about nontraditional activities by emphasizing that familiar mathematical topics will continue to be addressed. Parents and students are assured that although there may be an awkward period as new behaviors are learned, students generally find satisfaction in having their ideas respectfully considered by their teacher and their classmates. And now that I have been teaching this way for over a decade, former students are around not only to pass on stories about their initial concerns, but also to attest to their ultimate success and gratification.

REFERENCES

Ball, D. L. (1988). *Knowledge and reasoning in mathematical pedagogy: Examining what prospective teachers bring to teacher education*. Unpublished doctoral dissertation, Michigan State University.

Cohen, D. K., & Barnes, C. A. (1993). Conclusion: A new pedagogy for policy? In D. K. Cohen, M. W. McLaughlin, & J. E. Talbert (Eds.), *Teaching for understanding: Challenges for policy and practice* (pp. 240–276). San Francisco: Jossey-Bass.

Minstrell, J., & Stimpson, V. (in press). Creating an environment for reconstructing understanding and reasoning. In L. Schauble & R. Glaser (Eds.), *The contributions of instructional innovation to understanding learning*. Hillsdale, NJ: Lawrence Erlbaum.

Rowe, M. (1974). Wait-time and rewards as instructional variables: Their influence on language, logic, and fate control. *Journal of Research in Science Teaching, 11*(4), 291–308.

Schoenfeld, A. H. (1985). Metacognitive and epistemological issues in mathematical understanding. In E. A. Silver (Ed.), *Teaching and learning mathematical problem solving: Multiple research perspectives*. Hillsdale, NJ: Lawrence Erlbaum.

CHAPTER 4

"Teaching Mathematics to *All* Students"

There is widespread agreement that mathematics has functioned as a social fil-
ter, discouraging and even excluding large numbers of students from a range
of promising career paths. Many, both inside and outside the movement for
mathematics education reform, argue that for economic as well as ethical reasons, mathematics should now be recognized "as a new civil right."

One interpretation of the challenge to "reach diverse learners" or "teach
mathematics to *all* students" has been the call for the elimination of "ability
grouping" or "tracking." But contributors to this chapter place any simple
equation between "heterogeneous grouping" and "successful learning for *all*"
into question.

Two of the following three narratives focus on the sort of student that
"all" or "diverse" is generally taken to imply: learning-disabled third and
fourth graders in Alissa Sheinbach's class, Spanish-speaking urban high
schoolers in Allen Gagnon's. More provocative, though, is Margaret Riddle's
assessment of the opportunities "mixed-ability grouping" offers to the "math
stars" among her college-town fifth graders. Teacher educator Raffaella Borasi interrogates accepted interpretations of "homogeneity" and "diversity"
and, drawing from her own work in middle schools, suggests "student diversity can be turned into an asset for mathematics instruction."

$$+ \quad - \quad \times \quad \div$$

JUGGLING MATH AND MAINSTREAMING

Alissa Sheinbach

Teaching reminds me of one of those jugglers who spin plates atop
broomsticks. The first couple of plates are easy, but just about the time the
juggler starts spinning plate number five, the first one has started to wobble,
so he has to go back and give it another twirl. Soon there are 20 plates spin-

ning and the juggler is furiously running back and forth trying to keep them all in motion, his heart racing and sweat pouring off his brow. It's a wonder teachers are not all skinny.

In my math class I often feel like most of those plates are spinning beautifully, but I am constantly lunging for those two or three that are about to fall and shatter. I teach a combined third- and fourth-grade class in a small, rural school. There are 15 children in my class, almost all white and middle class. The school is well-known for its fine special education program. Classes are grouped heterogeneously, and students with special needs are mainstreamed.

There is no resource room. Instead, the special education (SPED) teachers work closely with classroom teachers to adapt the regular curriculum for children with special needs. The great majority of the time, these children stay in their own classrooms working alongside their classmates, sometimes using adapted materials and/or supported by SPED staff. A great effort is made not to label children. SPED teachers and classroom teachers discuss students constantly, both formally and informally.

I believe that much of the success of this program is due to the dedication and talents of a very small SPED staff and to a principal for whom SPED is a very high priority. Money is a significant problem for the school, however. Even though the mainstreaming model is more cost-effective than the pull-out model, the school still cannot afford to hire as many SPED teachers as it needs.

For the past three years I have been working to create a math program based on problem solving and student-centered discovery, as opposed to a more traditional one emphasizing algorithms and lecture/demonstration. The structure is heavy on partner or small group work integrated with whole class discussion. The teacher plays the role of facilitator more than that of disseminator of information.

I feel confident that most of my students are understanding mathematics, but I cannot escape the nagging fear that Anna is wobbling dangerously; that I cannot get to Sean soon enough to give him another spin; that Justin is starting to topple.

Anna, Sean, and Justin all struggle a good deal with math. By traditional standards they would be failing. In many schools they would be in special classes or in a resource room, but the trend in education is toward heterogeneous grouping—mainstreaming students who have trouble learning or have different learning styles.

I watch Anna, Sean, and Justin. In reading and writing I feel confident that the whole language model of immersion works for them. They are surrounded by language of all different levels and styles. They enter the learning environment wherever they happen to be—through a poem, a story they listen to, a piece they write. If what we are working on is easy for them, it works well as reinforcement; if it is very difficult for them, and they miss much of it, they usually can still find some part of it that they can get meaning from to make it worthwhile.

But then there's math. My confidence in this heterogeneous model is a bit shaken. Is math too sequential for this model? If they do not understand place value yet, can I just throw regrouping at them and hope that they will pick up something? What if the problem is too hard? Will they let their partner do all the work? Will they be turned off to math? Will they learn what they need to know? Is this just the wrong model for them? If it's the right model, what do I need to do to help them succeed?

ANNA

Anna says she doesn't like math. She told me one day while holding onto my elbow. In fact, she spends a good deal of the day within arm's length of me. I often notice that after we talk she will walk away and then look secretly over her shoulder to see if I'm still looking at her. It always makes me think that she does not trust me; that she will catch me in a lie or that I will have forgotten her by the time she gets to her desk.

I worry about calling on Anna in math. She rarely volunteers to speak in discussions and often appears distracted. I am frustrated because *she* is one of the students who most need the reinforcement and clarification of these discussions. Anna is easily confused in math. Her sense of number is very weak, as is her memory. She has trouble seeing patterns, numerically and spatially. She does not easily intuit relationships between operations.

One day Anna was working on a set of multiplication word problems with a partner. I noticed from the other end of the room that her partner, Katie, had the paper in front of *her* and was doing all the writing. Anna sat across from her, looking at the problems upside-down.

I approached Anna. Instinctively her arm curled around the paper to block my view, and she turned away.

> *Teacher (T):* How are you doing with these problems? (No eye contact from Anna.) Anna, could you talk me through this one?
> *Katie:* It's 4×7 because . . .
> *T:* Katie, let Anna talk about this problem, okay?

Anna had looked relieved to have escaped my question but I was not going to let that happen. Now she was annoyed.

> *T:* Let's read it together. It says, *David bought 4 sets of rubber stamps. The stamps came in plastic cartons, 7 stamps to a carton. How many rubber stamps did he get?*

Anna has substantial difficulties with reading and writing, so I will often try to read the problem to her or restate it. I suspect that sometimes her failure to understand math problems stems more from a language misunderstanding than a math misunderstanding. She does read, but it is laborious, and she often gets bogged down in all of the steps for writing. (She is, however, an amazing and inventive storyteller with a deep, theatrical voice.)

Fine motor skills like handwriting and drawing are also very difficult for her. She is a large child and, although very athletic and a great swimmer, she is often clumsy with her hands. She sometimes walks with a bit of a slump, her curly blond hair falling into her face.

Anna does not see herself as having girlfriends. In fact, when she's not alone, she spends most of her time with boys. She is something of a tomboy, more comfortable with the boys' physical play. Yet some of the girls are very supportive of her and consider themselves friends. Katie is an example.

T: Anna, how would you attack that problem?

Anna hesitated a few seconds, and then she looked up to see if I was still there. I was. She gave me a quick but piercing stare.

T: Anna, do you notice anything about equal groups?
Anna: The rubber stamps.
T: What do you mean?
Anna: They come 7 in a carton.

Anna fingered the unifix cubes on the desk. She bit her lip and looked up at the clock and then began arranging the cubes into rows. I asked her to explain the model to me (see Figure 4.1(a)).

Anna: These are the groups (pointing to the 7 rows).
T: What does each cube represent in your model?
Anna: A rubber stamp.
T: Where are the cartons?
Anna (counting the rows out loud): One, two, three, four, five, six,
      seven cartons . . . oh, no . . . there should be 4 cartons. (Anna re-
      arranges the cubes. See Figure 4.1(b).)
T: What do you have to find out in this problem?
Anna: How many stamps. (counting the cubes one by one) 26.
T: What did you do to find the answer?
Anna: I counted them all up.
T: Do you feel very confident or do you want to count one more time
      to be sure? (I want her to find her own mistake in counting.)

FIGURE 4.1. Anna's Two Representations of the Rubber-Stamp Problem

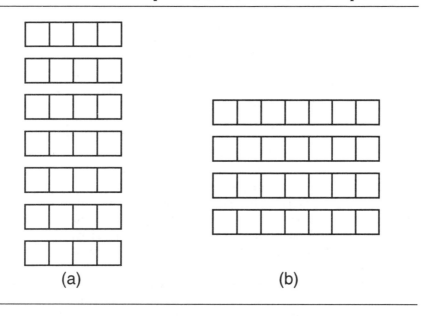

(a)   (b)

Anna recounted the cubes, this time moving each one away with her finger after counting it. She got the correct total of 28.

T: It sounds like you understand multiplication, Anna.

She eyed me carefully, as if to see if my compliment was truthful or false. I did believe Anna understood. At first, she had confused the number of groups with the number of items in a group, but then she caught her own mistake. She had made a counting mistake, but that was not unusual for her. Still, she represented the problem by modeling equal groups, and that was one of the main concepts that I was trying to convey. She did solve the problem by counting by 1s, but counting by groups of 7 was beyond her capabilities and she did not know the multiplication tables by heart yet.

Later in the year, to review the concepts of multiplication and division, I gave the following homework assignment: *Write and solve eight story problems: two addition, two subtraction, two multiplication, and two division. Use numbers that are challenging but not too hard for you to solve.*

The next night, I looked over Anna's homework. For her two multiplication problems Anna wrote: ''(1) Kelly has 1 fish and Kate has 5 fish. They put them together and got 5. 1 × 5 = 5. (2) Tom is 8. Wendy is 9. 9 × 8 = 72.''

I sat at my kitchen table trying to figure out how Anna was thinking when she wrote these problems. During the multiplication unit Anna was slow to catch on to the concepts, and she needed to work with the numbers as concretely as possible, modeling even very simple problems and laboriously counting out totals. The children had written many multiplication and division problems as a class and in pairs during the unit. Anna and Katie had written successful problems together. I wondered whether Katie had written them without much help from Anna.

The task of writing problems is certainly more complex than solving problems. It requires one to know the different parts of a multiplication problem and the correct order that they come in. It demands that one have a solid understanding of how the four operations are different. A number of children had some difficulty remembering how to write these problems, but Anna's examples seemed to reveal more significant confusion. The first problem was clearly addition, and the second was not really a problem at all. When I asked Anna about it on Monday, she was not able to explain her thinking, and she was able to create a successful problem only when I gave her a good deal of structure and prodding.

Looking back, I need to ask myself again, what did Anna understand about multiplication? Something of the concept of equal groups was there but not solidly. It is doubtful that Anna could have successfully applied what she knew about multiplication to help her solve problems in the real world.

Anna would have benefited from more practice with simple multiplication and division. She needed to solve and write many more problems before she actually mastered these operations. However, the rest of the class was ready to go on to more complex problem solving, utilizing multiplication and division concepts. I thought of letting Anna work on simple problems, but she is very defensive about doing work that differs from that of the rest of the class. In other subjects, she often does have different assignments or different materials, and she resents it.

I also wanted the whole class to work on the same problem, so that it could be the focus of our discussion and we could refer to it later. I decided to have Anna and Katie work together on the problem selected for the class: *How many seconds in a week?* They sat, with both calculators and counters in front of them. But Katie worked on the problem with no input at all from Anna. When I asked Anna about the problem, she did not know where to start or how to use multiplication or addition to solve it.

Without a good deal of help, this problem was clearly too difficult for Anna. Her partner, Katie, is also a weak student in math, but she was working on a higher level than Anna and, after a good deal of work exploring the new concept, Katie was ready to attack more sophisticated problems. She might not have been able to get the correct answer, but she was ready for this kind of exploration. On the other hand, I think that Anna was not getting anything out of this lesson. Katie was actually adept at including her partner and working cooperatively, but Anna's weak skills and resistance seemed to thwart Katie's attempts.

I have tried pairing Anna with another student who is at about her level of understanding in math. It sometimes works but then I usually have to give them a simpler problem, and I want to avoid making them the "slow pair." I also want Anna to work with students who are more advanced than she, so that she can learn from their strategies.

I seem to think about Anna constantly. I worry about her, push her, tease her, and try not to show that she's one of my favorites. And I wonder, what works for Anna?

SEAN

Sean was working on an exercise with pattern blocks, wooden blocks that come in different colors and geometric shapes. The assignment was to copy designs on the worksheet, upside-down. It was part of our work on rotations for the geometry unit.

Sean's face was very serious, and his knuckles were white where he gripped the blocks. I sat down by his desk and saw that the design he was drawing did not match the one on the paper in front of him and that he was clearly having a lot of trouble seeing the rotation in his mind. I asked him if there was a short cut he could use that would make it easier to draw the design. I was hoping that he would build the design with blocks first, exactly as it was shown, and then physically turn the block construction around and copy it down on the paper.

When Sean tried that, I realized that he had trouble copying the design even without a rotation. He was now many pages behind his classmates and visibly anxious and impatient about this. I picked up some of the blocks and started working the puzzle with him, leaving him to fill in the outside of the design. We both felt defeated because I really had done the exercise for him, but at the time I was stumped for a way to help him.

Sean is a gregarious child. He lives for soccer, but he has a lot of trouble with his aim. It is certainly a source of great frustration for him, and it doesn't seem to be for lack of practice. Earlier in the year I had observed him when the class had a few modern dance lessons, and I was very aware of how much trouble he had following steps and knowing where his body was in space.

Sean's written work shows signs of trouble as well. He often has trouble tracking across the paper, leaving big, blank spaces or squeezing the words into a corner. It is difficult for him to follow patterns and directionality while writing letters.

On the other hand, Sean reads quite well and has a good imagination for stories. He is quick to grasp concepts in science and social studies. Sean has been tested for learning problems, and it is clear that there are some deficits in spatial skills and short-term memory. It was obvious during the pattern block assignment, and I noticed it again during a lesson on measurement.

The assignment was to cover a small box with contact paper. The rules were: (1) All of the outside faces must be covered exactly without overlapping; (2) The faces of the box may not touch the contact paper or be lined up with the contact paper until after the pieces are cut out; (3) Use as little contact paper as possible.

My objectives with this assignment were to have students practice using standard measuring tools and units of measure and to undertake the spatial task of matching shapes and dimensions. Rule number two was designed to ensure that the students would actually measure the dimensions of the different faces and not simply trace them onto the contact paper.

Sean and his partner, Justin, had been working on the problem for about 10 minutes before I came over to their table. I noticed that the pieces of contact paper that they had already cut out did not seem to fit the faces of the box. Both boys seemed perplexed, and Sean was already showing some frustration. He picked up a pair of scissors and started trimming the sides of one piece to make it fit, but he still was not getting satisfactory results.

T: Can you show me how you're doing this?
Justin: We measured the box and it's 13.
T: Do you mean 13 inches or 13 centimeters?

Justin looked confused. He pointed to the centimeter side of the ruler and measured it against the face of the box once more.

T: Those are centimeters. So that side is 13 centimeters. Is that all the information you need from the box before you can cut out the contact paper?
Sean: Yea, now we measure the [contact] paper like this.

Sean put the ruler down and measured from the edge to the middle of the contact paper (see Figure 4.2(a)). He proceeded to cut out a rectangle without measuring the adjacent side.

T: How do you know that will fit?
Sean: Because I measured it.

The contact paper was about one inch too narrow when he fitted it onto the box. Sean looked amazed.

T: Why do you think it didn't match exactly? (He shrugs.) Let's look at the piece that you cut out again. Which sides were 13 centimeters like you measured?

FIGURE 4.2. Sean's First Two Attempts at the Measurement Task

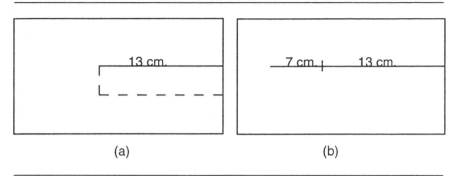

(a)   (b)

Sean pointed to the two sides and measured them again.

> *Sean:* The other two sides didn't match. (Then he measures them. He
>   is regaining some of his enthusiasm.)
> *T:* Why don't you try to cut out another piece of contact paper to
>   match your 13 centimeter by 7 centimeter dimensions?

This time Sean measured 13 centimeters from the middle of the contact
paper and then measured 7 centimeters in a straight line above that (see Figure
4.2(b)). He was not sure where to cut now.

I demonstrated how to measure and cut out a 13 cm × 7 cm rectangle
from the corner of the contact paper. I was disappointed with myself for taking
control again and giving away the method. Still, Sean was clearly frustrated at
this point, having experienced obvious failure each time that his paper did not
match up to the box face. He did not know how to remedy the situation himself, and his thinking and sense of space seemed so different from mine that I
really did not know what to ask him that would help him make the corrections.
Justin, his partner, also has a difficult time with spatial tasks, and he had already given up in confusion.

The advantage to pairing Justin and Sean in this activity was that each
was actively trying to solve the problem without taking over from the other.
The boys also did not feel intimidated by one another, as they would have with
a partner who could whip through the problem quickly and easily. Unfortunately, neither boy could come up with an effective strategy for solving the
problem, and they seemed to confuse each other.

Sean and Justin will probably never be *good* at spatial tasks but it is beneficial for them to have a lot of practice with different types of materials and
problems. I wish that I could have given them the same activity a few times
so that after they had learned the method, with some one-on-one help, they

could repeat it on their own. I felt compelled to go on to something new, however, because repeating the activity would not have been a good use of time for the rest of the class. If Sean and Justin had one-on-one time with me or another teacher at a different time during the day, this would have been a very good reinforcement activity. Perhaps a better strategy would have been to pre-teach this activity to them before the class tried it. Then they would have been able to keep up with the class and feel successful as they worked alongside their classmates.

Many people have a weak spatial sense, and I would not necessarily be concerned about the difficulties Sean had with these geometry and measurement activities, except that he seems to have a good deal of confusion in other areas of math as well. However, Sean is clearly a bright child. It is obvious in language-oriented subjects that he is a good thinker, often understanding complex ideas, but he is stymied by problems involving sound-symbol processing and short-term memory tasks.

It is also clear that Sean is bright in nonspatially oriented math. He notices sophisticated relationships in operations that elude many of the other children. He is very quick with addition and subtraction in his head, and often impresses other children with this ability. He seems to have a good understanding of such concepts as place value and regrouping when we are representing them concretely, but confusion sets in when we work with numbers on paper.

Sean believes he is a very good math student. Especially because of his problems in other subjects, it is important to confirm his strengths in math. However, I can't ignore his weak spots because they are significant and affect how he is able to learn new concepts. Sean is strong-willed and can be very defensive about any weaknesses. His style is to hide them whenever possible. In fact, sometimes I've seen him actually sink lower and lower under his desk until only his neck and head are showing.

It would be a mistake to put Sean into a resource room for math or even to have him in a separate group with a special education teacher in the classroom. More than anything, he needs to show off his talents to the whole class during math and to work on sophisticated problems.

The puzzle, then, is how to fill in the gaps in his skills and understanding without making him doubt himself as a mathematician. Sean's processing is sometimes so unusual that I have trouble myself understanding how he is thinking. In addition, he often will reject help from me and from his peers. I really cannot expect even the most sensitive and skilled nine-year-old partner to be able to work effectively with Sean in math.

JUSTIN

Justin, a beautiful child with big, blue eyes, is shy and secretive. He has a slight physical disability that makes his gait awkward, and he seems to be very self-conscious about this. Language has always been a struggle for him, but he is making great strides in reading and writing.

Still, it must be pointed out that Justin's weaknesses in language are significant. He is reading and spelling at least two years below grade level, and he has a very difficult time putting words on a page. Justin gets one-on-one or small group help from the special education teacher in reading, writing, spelling, social studies, and science, although most of this work is integrated into the regular class program.

The children like Justin; he is very loyal to his friends. In general, school is difficult for him. He does not seek his teachers out for help when he has trouble with something, but neither is he resistant to help. He is almost always willing and good-natured when I sit down to give him some reinforcement or when his classmates offer help. Instead of telling me where his confusion is, however, he usually will try to guess his way out. For example:

> *T:* Are there any more possibilities, Justin?
> *Justin:* No.
> *T:* How do you know?
> *Justin:* I mean yes. (pauses) No, it's no.

Justin seems to have a weak sense of number. He has a lot of trouble intuiting relationships and patterns in the number system, and he rarely finds or uses shortcuts to solve problems. When we were working with base-10 blocks, Justin continued to count the number of 1s on each 10s rod for weeks, instead of just assuming that all of the rods had ten 1s.

The following exchange took place when Justin and his partner, Heather, were working on a palindrome problem. (A palindrome is a number that is the same backwards and forwards, such as 252 or 9449.) The problem was to find all three-digit palindromes the sum of whose digits is 10.

> *T:* So you got 505 and 181. Are there others? Could there be one starting with a 6?
> *Heather:* Yea, that's what I was trying to figure out.
> *T:* (after some wait time) It would have to be 6-blank-6.
> *Justin:* 686?
> *T:* But all three numbers together have to equal 10.
> *Justin:* 626?
> *T:* 6 plus 6 is 12; plus 2 is . . .
> *Justin:* 14.
> *T:* Could it be that?
> *Justin:* No.
> *T:* It doesn't equal 10.
> *Justin:* It couldn't be 606. That equals 12.

T: Could it be anything else that starts with a 6?

Justin: Yes. . . . No.

T: Why not? . . . (after wait time) Could it start with something bigger like a 7?

Justin (thinking for a moment): It couldn't because that's already 14.

T: If it's 4-blank-4, what would the middle number be?

Justin: 424.

T: Yeah. Now you have numbers that start with a 4 and 5 and you said it couldn't be bigger than 5. How about one starting with a 3?

Justin: 333?

T: What does that equal?

Heather: 9.

Justin: Oh, 343.

T: Could there be another one starting with a three?

Justin: Yes. (thinks) . . . 323? No. (continues to think) How about zero? Umm, 0 10 0?

Heather: That's not a three-digit number.

Of course, the fact that Justin has a weak memory for number facts makes it even harder for him, but I'm sure that his difficulty conceptualizing number makes memorizing facts much more difficult. It's as if he is asked to memorize arbitrary bits of information, one at a time. But there is more going on here. First, Justin was not working with any kind of system. After getting 505 and 181, he did not know where to go next. He did not think to try numbers with 2, 3, and 4 in the ones and hundreds places. Second, after finding that a number starting with 6 would be too big, he did not quickly intuit that to start with any number bigger than 6 also would be too big. Third, he also did not automatically intuit that there could be only one possibility for 3__3, where the digits add to 10. (We were working only with positive numbers.)

Still, this was a good problem for Justin because he not only had to manipulate numbers and think about relationships between them, but he also was challenged to find a system to solve the problem. He did, however, need support to be successful and make it worth the time. In this case, Justin's partner, Heather, was also slow to see the patterns and use effective strategies for the palindrome problem. A stronger partner would have been a better model for Justin in solving the problem. But he needed more than that, because Justin tends to "shut down" and not really attend when he sees someone solve a problem that is difficult for him. He needed someone to ask him questions and pull him along in the problem. That is not something that we can expect other third and fourth graders to do. Justin would profit from an adult tutor in the classroom.

Because of Justin's language difficulties, the special education teacher decided to give him some individual time three days a week. Since the special education staff was spread so thin, the teacher worked with Justin for language during the only time that fit her schedule: 15 minutes at the end of the math period on Monday, Wednesday, and Friday.

When she came into the room she would ask Justin to explain to her what he was working on. Her goal was to help him strengthen his ability to communicate clearly with spoken language. Since she also could help him structure his math work, these sessions had the added benefit of supporting his understanding of the math concepts.

This teacher worked with Justin throughout our unit on place value and regrouping. She gave him extra support in representing regrouping problems (e.g., 89 + 43) with the base-10 blocks. By the end of this part of the unit, Justin was very proficient at solving these problems with the blocks and had a good understanding of the base-10 system. When we moved onto abstract problem solving with paper and pencil, he had more trouble and was easily confused, but he had no trouble going back to the concrete level when he needed to.

My objectives for him during this unit were to be able to solve regrouping problems using manipulatives and to understand the concepts of place value that these manipulatives represented. In fact, Justin met these objectives quite well. Even a short amount of one-on-one attention from a teacher seemed to make a difference for him. More one-on-one help would yield even greater success. Fifteen minutes at the end of math class three times a week is certainly not ideal for meeting Justin's needs in math. And what about the other children in my class who also needed this kind of support? There was no special education staff available to help them.

CONCLUSION

Readers may recognize the Annas, Seans, and Justins in their own classrooms. Perhaps they are labeled "special education" students, "learning disabled," or "slow." Perhaps, as in my school, they are not labeled at all, but special plans or modifications are made for their individual needs. Maybe they are just ignored and left to sink or swim by themselves. Where do they belong?

I believe that they belong in the regular classroom for math, alongside their peers. There are a number of reasons for this. First, these children are complex learners. Sean is a good example of this. He has some significant weaknesses, but they are balanced with some very strong skills and abilities. A heterogeneous classroom is the best environment for these children, because it provides sophisticated challenges and opportunities to shine in front of their classmates.

Second, the other children also get a more rounded picture of their "differently abled" classmates instead of seeing them simply as slow learners. It may be Sean, Justin, or Anna who comes up with the creative, novel solution or insight during a math discussion.

Third, there is the issue of self-esteem. If these children were in pull-out programs they would likely lose confidence in themselves and their abilities. In a separate program they would see themselves as different and slow.

Fourth, Anna, Sean, and Justin need good models for clear and competent thinking in math. If they are isolated, they do not get to learn from their peers.

Fifth, these three children desperately need to be integrated into the social and intellectual community of the class. The more time they spend living and working with their classmates, the more connected they are to this community.

But being mainstreamed is not enough. The learning must be appropriate for them if they are to thrive in the regular classroom. If it is constantly too difficult they will not only lose confidence in themselves, but also learn to hate the subject.

One answer to this dilemma is to individualize the classroom work so that each child can work at his or her own level. Thus, many of the social benefits of mainstreaming are maintained, and the children are learning what they should. However, this solution does not seem to work well for the kind of math program I use. Instead of individualizing instruction, I emphasize whole group and pair work.

I do not want to give up the benefits of this type of grouping and instruction for a number of reasons. A community of learners is created that values clear communication and cooperation skills. In addition, learners turn to each other for support instead of being dependent on the teacher. By working with a partner, learners more safely and confidently attack difficult problems too intimidating to try solo. Also, children in the group learn to appreciate each other's strengths and weaknesses.

In addition to wanting to maintain the benefits, I also have to admit that creating an individualized curriculum is a daunting task. As a ready-made curriculum does not really exist for this type of problem-solving-based math, it is very intimidating for me to think of creating different problems, activities, and evaluation for all of the different academic levels in my class.

If not by individualized programs, how do I make mainstreaming work? One answer is to individualize the objectives rather than the programs or activities. For example, in the regrouping unit I expected Anna and Justin to master the concept of regrouping with concrete representation, but not necessarily to master the algorithm.

Another key to making it work is for the regular classroom teacher to use methods and structures that are effective with "difficult to teach" students. Examples of these are: (1) repetition, review, and rephrasing; (2) combining visual, auditory, and kinesthetic modalities to appeal to different learning styles; (3) using concrete representations of math concepts; (4) making conceptual connections explicit; (5) using games and mnemonics to help memory tasks; and (6) pre-teaching important concepts.

Teachers need to be trained in these techniques. I have found training I have had in some of these methods for language arts easily transferable to math. There is much we can learn about these methods from special education teachers, but we must adapt them to make them work for the whole classroom.

There is another piece missing, however. At some point the Annas and Seans and Justins need more one-on-one time with a teacher. Pre-teaching the concepts and skills to these children is an effective tool. Tutoring or reinforcing the concepts one-on-one after introducing them in class is also important.

I have seen this kind of pre-teaching and tutoring work wonders. Years ago, I had a student in my class with a full-time, one-on-one aide. The aide spent a lot of time pre-teaching math concepts to the student and then going back later to practice and reinforce the same concepts. This child, who was at least four years behind her age group in math abilities, caught up at least a year, in large part because of this one-on-one help.

Of course, teachers do a lot of one-on-one teaching regularly, but we do not have as much time to do it as is necessary, especially if there are a few very needy students in one class. Teachers need to be supported by extra staff in order to give these students the time they need. In many schools, this boils down to an issue of money. Mainstreaming may be less expensive than pull-out programs but it is still expensive. If regular classroom teachers are not supported with staff, it will not work. We need to do what is necessary to make a math instruction based on problem solving and student-centered discovery accessible to the Annas and Seans and Justins. They deserve it as much as everyone else.

$$+ \quad - \quad \times \quad \div$$

THE PICTURE UNFOLDS

Allen Gagnon

As I work with student ideas rather than text materials, I keep learning to test my assumptions about what my students know. This story points out the need to learn about students in the beginning of the school year. Who are they? What are their backgrounds? What would they like to accomplish in the coming school year?

This year, I wanted to start my College Algebra II class with new material. I felt by starting the year with a review of Algebra I (my traditional beginning), I send a bad message. I tell the students that they can go to sleep for a while. Nothing new or worth their attention is going to happen for some time. I didn't want to send that message to my students, so I decided to start with an investigation that would provide them with an opportunity to build on the geometry they studied last year. I also realized that many of the algebraic concepts I wanted my students to study this year could be brought into this investigation at various times. What could I start with that would help me accomplish this? I usually teach trigonometry during the second semester of the course, but this year I decided to do it first. How should I start? What would they remember that would be useful? How could I build on that knowledge? These are but a few of the questions that came to mind as I prepared for the year to begin.

I structured the worksheet shown in Figure 4.3(a) to get the exploration started. I placed students in groups, hoping that working together would help them recall as much as possible from their study of geometry. I wanted to see if they could remember the Rule of Pythagoras and some of the special right-triangle relationships. I was delighted when they did. My next worksheet (Figure 4.3(b)) took off from what had been discussed in order to see if they could use these ideas.

I wanted to include problems for which students would need to make decisions. In problems 3 and 4, they needed to realize that protractors and rulers were necessary to measure each side and angle. They also needed to decide whether to use inches or centimeters. I was interested to see what they would do with these two problems and I was pleased as I worked my way around the room. They realized the need for the tools. This was great! I sensed they understood the difference between a diagram that is drawn to scale and one that is not. But on the first two problems they did not use protractors or rulers to assign the missing values. I judged that they seemed to understand the background information necessary to open our investigation of trigonometry.

It was Thursday, and I considered giving them some kind of a test, after a large group wrap-up. I decided to have the wrap-up the following day and made up a test that could be used as a take-home over the weekend or as an exam in class on Monday. I would base my decision on the results of Friday's class.

I did not realize the surprise that lay in wait for me—the kind of surprise that reminds us teachers that we have a lot to learn about understanding our students. It points out the need to listen carefully as they talk to us. It also provides us with insights into ourselves.

On Thursday, at the close of the school day, I hold office hours. The main purpose for this time is to let students come for individual help or to make up missed tests or work. That Thursday, during office hours three of my Hispanic students came for some help. They wanted to go over some of the problems. They felt they were having a lot of trouble with this work.

FIGURE 4.3. Gagnon's Two Worksheets

Write all you can remember about the following right triangle. You are free to use the geometry texts on the table in the front of the room for a reference. Other materials (rulers, compasses, and protractors) are also available if you wish to make use of them.

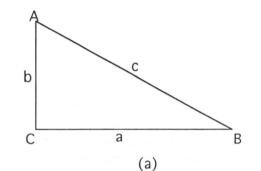

(a)

Find the missing sides and angles in the given diagrams.

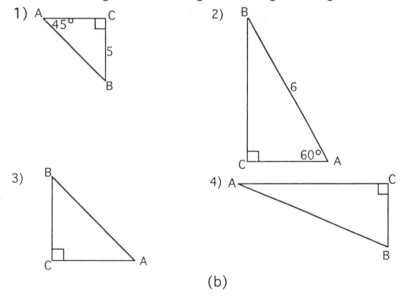

(b)

When these students entered the room I felt a certain sense of apprehension. I have not had a lot of experience working in class with students who have very limited English-speaking ability. Many of my encounters with Spanish-speaking students have occurred in the halls of the school. Occasionally, these encounters have not been positive and have resulted in disciplinary action. The Hispanics whom I had in class before were always able to converse in English. I didn't know if these students would be like them. Would they be well behaved? Would they be cooperative? Would they be able to communicate their ideas and concerns? I realize now how foolish these thoughts are, but they were my thoughts at that time. No two students are really alike. Every student comes to class with his or her own set of experiences and feelings. Why did I feel this way?

At the beginning of the school year, the guidance counselor had informed me that several of the Hispanic students who had been assigned to my class were in the mainstream for the first time. I realized much later that this information had some effect on my thoughts and concerns at the time. These three students (Maria, Yvette, and Jesus) were taking their first math course outside of the bilingual program. (This program is called "bilingual" but the instruction is all in Spanish.) My class was their first experience at learning math in a setting that must have been both difficult and frightening for them. This caused some of my anxiety. Their ability to communicate in English was very limited. I was scared that I would not be able to make myself understood. And I was frightened that they would not be able to tell me what was troubling them.

I was also conscious of the cultural differences between us and of the way my city has been struggling with these differences for a long time. There are many Anglos in the city who feel the Hispanics have made little attempt to learn English. The Hispanics have a deep sense of culture and want to retain their native language. These opposing attitudes sometimes cause a certain amount of friction and struggle. Were my students and I going to have a problem because of language? I just didn't know what to expect. I also didn't know how I really felt about this issue of culture.

Where should we work? Should Maria, Yvette, and Jesus try to stand around my desk or should we get together as a group? This was the first issue I needed to decide. I felt that they would be more comfortable if we could be a small group away from my "teacher's desk." I wanted them to feel that I was going to work with them. I wanted to foster the group work concept even in this setting.

We sat at a grouping of desks (this year I have four desks arranged in such a way that pairs of desks face one another) and began with a problem that was typical of those we were working on. First I gave them a leg and hypotenuse of a right triangle and asked them to find the trigonometric functions for both of the acute angles in the right triangle.

I sensed that these students were very anxious. Trying to calm them and at the same time open the lines of communication, I attempted to be deliberate and not too pushy as we began to work on the problem. I asked Maria to try to solve it. I encouraged the others to become involved in the discussion and to let us know points of confusion. I asked Maria how she would begin, and she replied that she would start by drawing a diagram (I had stressed being able to draw the triangle in different positions) and inserting the given information into the diagram.

As she started to attach numbers to the various sides it became clear that she and the others were not sure of the terminology that is usually associated with right triangles. They were confused about the distinction between the longest leg and the hypotenuse, the longest side in a right triangle. I gently questioned them to see what background they had and I was surprised to learn that they had spent the first half of their geometry course last year without a teacher. In fact, the class had gone on for almost half the school year without any instruction in mathematics at all! This information was very upsetting to hear. How could this be allowed to happen? What will be the ramifications of this for these students? This was a serious obstacle. I was glad, however, that they were opening up to me and giving me this information.

All three of these students let me know that this was their first time in the mainstream and that they were very anxious. I already knew this but their sense of anxiety was something I really needed to pay attention to. I also remembered my own earlier anxiety and I realized that I had to try to build their confidence in their ability to succeed. They seemed sincere about wanting to do well, but they also displayed a lack of confidence that they could succeed. They had never worked with some of the concepts I thought we were just reviewing. With such a handicap, I was awed that they were able to follow the discussions as well as they did.

We talked about the labels for the sides of the right triangle and how the Rule of Pythagoras is used. As we did this, they conversed in Spanish among themselves. I encouraged this and had them help me with my limited understanding of Spanish. (I had two years of Spanish in college but am very rusty.) They would tell me the English word and its Spanish equivalent. This process helped me to know what they were thinking. I asked them if it would help to have someone in their group who could speak both Spanish and English. They answered with a definite YES. This was especially true for Jesus. As we talked, I could sense that they were becoming more comfortable. Without realizing it, I also was relaxing. This was encouraging, and I tried to keep up this comfortable atmosphere as we talked and explored the problems.

I don't remember exactly how we got onto the topic of why I had become a math teacher. But I do remember telling them that I enjoy doing math and like being a teacher. Maria couldn't remember ever hearing anyone say that they enjoyed doing math. I pointed out to her that enjoying doing math and understanding math are two different things. I told them that there were many things in mathematics that I did not understand and needed to work on. I also shared with them the knowledge that trying to teach has helped me learn a lot of mathematics. Maria commented again that she doubted if she would ever be good at math. I told her that she could be, that she needed to be patient and just do her best. I realized that having some successful experiences doing math would have a tremendous impact on her feelings about mathematics. I vowed to do something about that.

As we talked and worked on the problems, the students were beginning to understand how to use the Pythagorean theorem to find either leg or the hypotenuse. However, as they apparently had very little experience simplifying radicals, they needed help with this. By questioning them, I was able to verify that they did understand the idea of prime factors and saw how to factor the radicand with primes. We talked about how this could be used to help simplify the radicals. When they got excited at one point in our conversation, it was apparent that a light bulb had lit up for them. We tried several examples of this sort, and they were able to simplify the radicals without too much difficulty.

Next we turned to the definitions of sine, cosine, and tangent. I reminded them that, before simplifying, they could use the definitions to form the ratios. I am trying to get my students away from the idea that they need to memorize a bunch of formulas and definitions. What I want them to be able to do is to choose the right formula in a given situation. This new strategy is certainly different from what I did in the early days of my teaching—I vividly remember how I used to tell my students the importance of memorizing these formulas. Now, to accomplish my new goal, I encourage them to use index cards to write the definitions and formulas. They are free to refer to these index cards at any time. The index-card approach accomplishes several things: It acts as a form of organization for the material; it encourages students to consider what they have available as they solve a particular problem; and it also takes some of the pressure off them. I want the emphasis to be not on remembering the formula, but rather on knowing which formula to choose and how to use it.

My group of students used the information on their cards to find the ratios they needed. It was nice to see them handling this part of the problem so well. The thought crossed my mind that, if I had not promoted use of the index cards, it would have been impossible for them to remember everything they needed. I believe that eventually they will not need to look at the index cards, but will feel supported by the knowledge that they can, if they need to.

At this point we ran out of time. I really felt sorry to see the session end. Yvette asked if I would make up some new problems for her to practice on. I gave them one and told them we would do more the following day.

As I thought about the session later that night, I realized that I had learned a lot about these students and their needs in just a short time. The experience of working with these Hispanic students made me realize that my earlier fears were senseless. In many ways, these kids are just like others and yet they are each unique. Their limited ability to communicate in English was going to be a problem only if I allowed it to be one. I needed to make sure they understood my directions, and this meant being aware of the possibility that I was not communicating clearly. This was a problem for which we all needed to share the responsibility.

I also realized that they were going to need more time to think about the mathematics we had discussed. If they could benefit from more work on these concepts, then I was sure that others in the class would also. The next day I had the large group discussion focus on some of the problem areas that had come up in the after-school session. We talked extensively about simplifying radicals and did several examples. We also explored rationalizing the denominators. I concluded class that day with several new problems. My original intention had been to wrap up this topic and then test the class. My office-hour session showed me that, before I gave that first test, the class needed time to explore and experience further.

My reflections on that session created other questions for me. Should I stand by my policy of grouping students randomly or should I make sure that these students always have someone in their group who speaks Spanish and English? What about the testing situation?

I learned a lot about my students that day. Maria is a senior and is very concerned about getting into college. As we talked, I sensed her nervousness, although her command of English is good. She was the most talkative of the three students that day. Yvette is very quiet and shy. She speaks English but, at times, has some trouble finding the right words. She is a junior and is conscious of her grades and considers the possibility of going on to college. Jesus is the quietest of the group and has the hardest time communicating in English. He is also a junior and is very aware of the importance of grades for his future plans. Jesus is a very serious student and has proven himself to be a good thinker. Once he understands a concept he seems very proficient at using the information. His computational skills seem to be the best of the three. Also, I saw that the three students made new connections and were able to advance a few steps on their journey toward understanding math. We had started to know one another better. But this was just the beginning, and I needed to listen carefully in the days that followed.

The story I just related focuses on what I learned that day and how it affected my planning. In the past, help sessions were for the students. Now I use them to inform my decisions. In the early years of my teaching a very different story would have been told. I would have asked the students what specific problems were giving them trouble. I would have gone over these same problems again in the same way or tried using some other explanation. I believe that sooner or later they would have said they understood, even if they didn't. They would have done this to save themselves embarrassment. We might have tried a new problem if they had not had enough of my help. I would have felt that I helped them solve their problems only to find they failed the test. I would have gone ahead with the test as planned, since they needed to stay "on schedule." I would have wondered why the extra help in office hours was not successful, but would not have dwelled on it. I would never have heard the background information that helped me to assess what to do next.

This new story shows the struggle that I am involved in. It is easy to slip back into old habits. It is possible to be blind to what is happening right in front of me. When my teaching was based on lecture, I didn't feel that I was shortchanging students. I really tried to "tell it" in a way that made it easy for them to understand. I just didn't see that they were not understanding. Or, I just never gave it a lot of thought. It is harder to teach now than it was in the early days of my career. I need to deal with a lot more. It is more effort and work in some ways. But I believe that I get more enjoyment out of my labors.

+   −   ✕   ÷

BEYOND STARDOM: CHALLENGING COMPETENT MATH STUDENTS IN A MIXED-ABILITY CLASSROOM

Margaret Riddle

One of the ways I get to know my new fifth-grade students each September is by asking them to fill out a math inventory. This two-page sheet instructs them to circle adjectives that describe how they feel about math, to find and explain the errors in a subtraction problem, and to write a story that matches a given long-division problem. As I review these inventories, I usually notice three or four students whose responses indicate that they enjoy and feel competent at math. Often they also appear to already understand some of the concepts that will be explored in fifth grade.

Like many other teachers, I think about my students a great deal, and it is often these competent math students who give me the most sleepless nights. At the age of 9 or 10, these girls and boys perceive themselves to be top students in math. However, although they appear to learn math quickly and easily, I also have observed that they frequently do not go beyond getting "the right answer." Since I myself was such a student, when they complain that math class is "boring" or "too easy," their dissatisfaction haunts me.

Most recently, my own professional studies have focused on improving my methodology in science, math, and language arts teaching. I have studied whole language, writing process, and constructivist theory as it applies to math and science. My work has led me to believe that there is much more to elementary mathematics than most elementary teachers and students ever thought, and that the riches that are available are particularly exciting for competent math students. Furthermore, my classroom experiences in the past few years have convinced me that these students can best be inspired and reached within a heterogeneous classroom. Interestingly, it is often the pursuit of alternative strategies and the persistence of their "less able" peers that open up for them the fascinating possibilities that actually exist in studying mathematics—even in elementary school.

What are the characteristics of these young math stars? First of all, they are able to figure quickly and accurately in their heads and on paper. Their self-esteem has been enhanced by knowing they are often first with the answer. They are not used to listening to and considering the alternative strategies of their peers since they have come to think their quick answer is THE one. They think they understand concepts when they are able to work algorithms.

I believe that it is often their very success as elementary math students that works against these students beginning to develop into truly competent young mathematicians. They have a vested interest in maintaining their position at the top of the class, and they certainly don't perceive that they have a problem as math students. The feeling of disequilibrium that comes from wondering and exploring alternative solutions is one with which they have had little experience. It takes practice and courage to understand that confusion can be an opportunity to learn, and they have had little opportunity for practice. Through no fault of their own, these students are ill-equipped to reap the benefits available in classrooms that ask them to consider alternative solutions in pursuit of deeper conceptual understanding.

Enrichment programs that have separated such students from their classmates so that they might do advanced work make them even less interested and aware of the richness of thinking that is available right in their own classrooms. They are able learners, after all, and they have learned well the implicit lessons taught in traditional classrooms: If you are first with the answer, you are smarter than your classmates, who probably have few ideas and theories that will interest you. Your job is to memorize facts and procedures, pursue the right answer, and work quickly and accurately. Pull-out enrichment programs convey the clear message that math class is too easy and too boring for "math stars."

Although I am convinced these students are best challenged within a regular, heterogeneously grouped classroom, in the fall I often doubt my own convictions. By the time of parent conferences in late October, I am frequently tempted to buckle under pressure from these students, their parents, and administrators. Might it not better meet their needs to offer them an enrichment program, perhaps mentored by a mathematics major from Mount Holyoke College? During parent conferences I hear myself saying, hesitantly, "Your child is an excellent math student. I want to make sure to challenge her this year."

When parents respond, "She participated in an enrichment program in her other school in third and fourth grades, and she really loved it," I begin to doubt my own philosophy and start to worry.

However, several years of facing this situation have given me plenty of evidence that these students can be well served in a heterogeneous classroom, but that it takes time for them to become open to the possibilities that are available in that setting. When I have given the process time to work and have carefully encouraged these children, I have seen them become more hooked on this type of learning than I ever thought possible in October.

"Why should I work with a partner when I can get the answer on my own?"

In last year's class Nate was a "math star." A quiet, responsible boy with a quick, straightforward mind, Nate entered class in September in active pursuit of right answers. He was competent at problem solving and accurate in computation. Nate was almost never stumped in math and seemed to have unending self-confidence. He had a wonderful way of setting his own agenda in activities—working as hard and completing things as well as he wanted to for himself. He enjoyed working outside of school on math problems that affected his own life. He averaged his weekly profits from his paper route, for instance, and created a graph to project them into the future. He was also generally kind and respectful of his classmates.

However, in the beginning of the year, Nate was completely uninterested in working with classmates to solve math problems. When he was assigned to work with a fellow student, Nate typically would choose to go ahead on his own, checking neither his thinking nor his answers with his partner. He often finished his work early, and the look on his face was one of resigned boredom.

After watching him for several sessions, I decided to give Nate a gentle nudge. I purposely partnered him with a student who was neither quick at figures, nor good with facts, nor capable at computation, but who had some skills Nate lacked. Like Nate, Brian was kind, respectful, and extremely well liked by his classmates; but, unlike Nate, he felt he was a poor math student who usually didn't understand much. He was a strongly visual learner who was also artistic, athletic, and extremely persistent. Brian's strength was in being able to visualize a problem and to use pictures and manipulatives to work his way through it. He would solve problems by making the math fit his pictures and his common sense understanding. Having been supported the previous year by a teacher who had encouraged these skills, Brian had some real strengths, and they were different from Nate's.

In previous years, I never would have had the courage to partner such students together. To my mind, Nate's competence would have demanded an equally able partner. I would not have asked that he "help" a less-skilled classmate, and I never would have believed that he could actually learn from a student who wasn't as quick as he was. However, in Nate's case, I noticed that, although he was quick, he didn't ponder, question, look for patterns, try different methods, or collaborate with his colleagues. In other words, he operated more like an accountant than a mathematician. I believed he was capable of more, and his bored look bothered me.

My own experience in problem-solving groups in courses offered by SummerMath for Teachers at Mount Holyoke College had taught me that working with others whose abilities were different from mine was both challenging and fascinating. As I had struggled to understand the diagrams and reasoning of my teacher-peers, I found myself excited by mathematics in a new way. I wanted Nate to have a similar experience.

On their first day as partners, I noticed that Nate and Brian had literally turned their backs to each other and were working independently on the problem shown in Figure 4.4. Students had been provided with manipulatives—buttons and unifix cubes—and plain paper for drawing pictures. Brian was floundering a bit, but he was trying to make sense of the problem using the manipulatives. He had used 14 scraps of paper, torn from the large sheet, to represent the 14 baskets. He had started by placing 2 buttons on each scrap to represent the bananas, then added a third button for the apples. Nate, meanwhile, was sailing ahead, relying strictly on his computational skills, oblivious to Brian's discomfort and unaware of his alternative methods. Although I was somewhat threatened by Nate's confidence and ability, I took a risk and talked to them about working together. "I see you aren't really working together," I said. They looked uncomfortable and made excuses. I went on:

> You know, I put you together for a reason, and this is it. Nate, you are really good with numbers and figuring, and Brian, you are really good with drawing pictures and figuring out what math means by using the objects. I think if you two put your heads together you will both learn a lot from each other, and you will find this problem much more interesting than you thought it was. You know, it's really the thinking and looking for patterns that makes math interesting, not so much just getting the answer.

Nate and Brian were used to hearing me say things like this about working together in science and writing workshop, as well as in math. Posted above our bulletin board was a favorite classroom quote: "We're smarter together as

FIGURE 4.4. Fruit Basket Problem

HOLIDAY FRUIT BASKET PROBLEM

I decided to make up fruit baskets for my relatives for the holidays. I want to make 14 baskets for all the different families. In each basket I want to put these things:

2 bananas
3 apples
4 oranges
8 dates
6 figs
25 nuts
10 peppermint candies

Use the objects to figure out how many of each thing I must buy in order to have enough for my fruit baskets. Be sure your partner understands how you solved the problem. Be ready to show the class your solution. Write your answers in the space below.

I should buy:

_____ bananas

_____ apples

_____ oranges

_____ dates

_____ figs

_____ nuts

_____ peppermint candies

a group than we are by ourselves.'' They also knew that I enjoyed working with other teachers in my evening math class because I often talked about it. They frequently heard me respond to a student's idea about a book we were reading with a comment like, "Now isn't that interesting? I never have thought of that before." In other words, they were used to seeing me do what I was asking them to do.

Being the agreeable kids they were, they listened and tried hard to actually work together in a meaningful way. Brian explained to Nate about his paper scraps and buttons. Nate listened, and as I walked away I heard him suggest, "We could just double the answer we got for oranges to find the number for dates because 8 is the double of 4." He checked to make sure Brian understood. Later they explained to the class that they had simplified the process to make one button stand for 25 nuts. They had then grouped their baskets into 4s and counted by 100s to find the number of nuts that were needed.

This particular problem is a wonderful opportunity to investigate the concept of multiplication. When manipulatives are used to approach it, patterns, combinations, and relationships emerge visually to make it quite fascinating. Simply computing the answers does not reveal the mathematical structures in the same way. Since Nate was receptive to Brian's ideas, he began to see these things in a way he found exciting. There is little doubt that Nate's computational expertise helped Brian on that day and on those that followed. However, I also noticed that Nate took a real interest in the patterns that became evident as Brian worked with the manipulatives. He seemed fascinated to find different ways to solve the problems.

Gradually, Nate became more and more open to working with other students, and he also maintained his interest in finding alternative ways to do problems. Sometimes he would even work on problems long after the class had moved on, looking for different solutions and patterns. He stopped being "finished" when he got an answer. During class discussions, Nate listened intently to his colleagues' ideas and eagerly shared his own, making sure that others understood his method. He would often add enthusiastically, "Of course, you could also do it this way . . . or you could do it this way." The bright look on his face and his intense concentration led me to believe that his mind was always working and that the natural curiosity he had about mathematics was becoming fully engaged at school during math class.

While we were studying division in March, the class focused considerable time on interpreting remainders in different types of problems. One day Nate became interested in predicting whether a large number would be divisible by a given number without a remainder. These sorts of questions come up regularly in a math class like ours, and the enrichment possibilities are built right into the mathematics at hand. Beyond the teacher perceiving the students' interest and the possibilities inherent in the topic, no extra books or materials are required. The whole class tossed around the idea of divisibility and possible rules for it for about 15 minutes that day. We quickly realized it was quite easy to predict divisibility by 1, 5, and 10.

On the way to lunch I mentioned to Nate, "It might be fun to see if you can predict divisibility with other numbers." He took hold of the idea and pursued the problem, working on it for over a week on his own. He even invited one of his friends, another former "right-answer" math student, to stay in during recess to search with him for rules of divisibility. Their work included pages and pages of math problems, work on the board, and experimentation with a calculator. They held some theories quite passionately for a while, until they realized their misconceptions and revised them. They made lists, explored patterns, and talked about their theories at lunch, recess, and on the bus. They did come up with some rules, which they outlined on charts and shared with the class. However, they never did finish the problem. The process of solving it had been all-consuming for a while, but it wasn't just a search for an answer—it was joyful experimentation with the true essence of mathematics. Their persistence and fascination, as evidenced in their work on this problem, was the outcome I had hoped for when I had partnered Nate with Brian in November.

I suspect that if Nate had simply been advanced in math or had participated in a pull-out enrichment program, he might not have learned to use his mind as flexibly as he did when he struggled to understand what Brian was thinking with his manipulatives. The richness of mathematics might have remained buried treasure as far as he was concerned.

"Why do we have to use these blocks when we already understand how to multiply?"

It is important for teachers to understand their students well—especially what and how they think. But in classrooms in which students are encouraged to actively construct their own understandings of mathematical concepts, this is crucial for success. One of the tools I use to probe students' thinking is the Learning Log, a journal in which they are regularly asked to express their ideas about what we are studying.

As the year goes by and students come to trust that their thoughts will be respected and listened to, they become more candid about their feelings. Their frankness helps me to plan an appropriate program for them, even when they say things I don't really want to hear. One day in January, after a problem-solving session in which base-10 blocks were used to work on multiplication, Meghan wrote me: "Why do we have to keep using these blocks when we already understand how to multiply?" That day I responded to her question by telling her that blocks can help you to understand at a deeper level something you thought you understood before. However, her sincere question stayed in the back of my mind. I wondered if I was requiring her to work concretely on concepts she already understood abstractly. I worried that she was bored and not learning as much as she could. I paid close attention to Meghan's work and her questions as I searched for ways to challenge her.

Although she was very quiet in class, since the beginning of the year I noticed that Meghan was a very able math student who was definitely at home with figures and problem solving. As the oldest in a large family, she had excellent social skills and, in a cooperative-learning situation, could get along with any child in the classroom. She had many friends, was respected by her classmates, and had been selected as a class leader by them. Meghan was extremely self-motivated and took each academic task that was assigned and did her best. A logical, organized thinker, she had unusual skill at revising all her written work—crafting it until she was satisfied that it really communicated her thoughts. Although she very rarely shared her own ideas with me during conferences on reading or writing, she listened carefully and applied every suggestion in a meaningful way. Because of what I knew about Meghan, her remark particularly worried me. Here was a "model student" who was usually challenged and inspired at school, but who was hinting she was bored in math class.

A few weeks later, I chose Meghan to be a member of a small group that I removed from class for a few days for a multiplication challenge. I asked these students to work with a partner to try to figure out $.6 \times .7 = ?$ and to use graph paper or blocks to explain their thinking. Decimals had been introduced just a few months earlier, but both Meghan and her partner had seemed to understand them. They had worked confidently with addition and subtraction of decimals as well as with some simple problem solving. However, during their exploration of this problem they were both completely baffled. They could neither apply the problem to a real-life situation nor even begin to approach it using the graph paper or base-10 blocks. They were joined by two other girls, but after about 20 minutes, none of them could get anywhere. They were not able to find any tools for building a concept for multiplying decimals.

The next day I supplied a context for them in the hope that it would make the problem real. First, I directed the whole class to mark off a 10 by 10 square on a piece of graph paper, while I drew the same picture on the board. Under the picture I wrote, "giant cake." "Suppose you are a caterer who does wedding receptions," I proposed to the class. "You make huge cakes that will serve 100 people. Could this be a picture of such a cake?" They nodded yes. Next I held up a base-10 flat and asked, "Could this represent a cake like that, too?" They agreed it could. I asked, "Show me a signal indicating how many cakes this picture or this flat represents." Most students raised one finger. "After a particular reception," I went on, "let's say you have .7 of this cake left. The rest was eaten, and now you have .7 left. What would that look like on our picture?"

Peter, a quiet student who has a strong conceptual understanding of math

FIGURE 4.5. Representations of (a) .7 and (b) .6 of .7

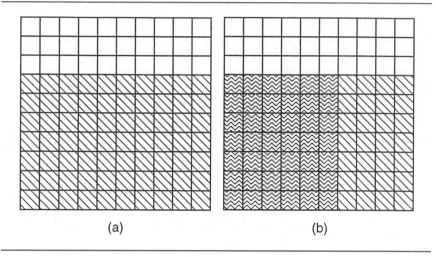

(a)   (b)

based on his ability to visualize problems, quickly suggested that we should color 7 of the 10 blocks in each column to look like Figure 4.5(a). Peter explained that if .7 of each column was left, then .7 of the whole cake would be left, too. I colored my picture on the board according to Peter's directions and asked each of the other students to complete her or his own. "Now," I said, "since your employees had worked particularly hard that day, let's say you told them that, after their shift was ended, they could take home .6 of what was left of the cake. What would that look like on our picture?" After some discussion and some more help from Peter, the class agreed to color over .6 of each of the rows of 10 pieces, completing a picture like that in Figure 4.5(b), which showed that .42 of the cake was to be taken home.

For many students this story opened up a way to understand the multiplication of decimals. For several days, the class practiced using graph paper to solve simple problems, writing stories of their own to explain the solutions. Eventually, we wrote some rules together to explain how to multiply decimals. I realized that very few of them would have a solid understanding at the end of this brief period of study, but they were beginning to construct some meaning for the operation.

At the end of our study of multiplication, I asked students to complete a test that probed their conceptual understanding of both multiplication and decimals. When I took a close look at Meghan's test to see how she was doing, the story she had written to explain 4 × 24 demonstrated a solid understanding of the multiplication concept: *Every year I give out 24 Valentines. How many*

Valentines will I have given out after 4 years? So did the picture she drew (Figure 4.6(a)) to show that 13 × 4 = 52.

However, in the section of the test about multiplication of decimals, I could see that Meghan was still shaky about some concepts. When asked to draw a picture and find a solution for .6 × .2, Meghan had correctly listed the solution as .12 and accurately drawn the picture shown in Figure 4.6(b). However, she had written this story: *Jacqueline bought a gigantic wedding cake for her sister. Most of the guests didn't like the flavor, so only .2 was eaten. The bride's family kept the rest. How much did the guests eat?*

At the very end of the test, students were asked to tell what new things they had learned about multiplication during the year. Meghan's response was unlike that of any of the other students: "At first it's easier to understand, when you don't know what's going on."

Her statement reminded me of one made by Dan, a student in the previous year's class. In many respects, Dan's way of thinking and his strengths were similar to Meghan's. Going to lunch one day, early in our study of division, he had remarked, "When we began to study division, I thought I understood it, but now I'm not so sure." We had shared our feelings about how unsettling it can be when you realize that you don't really understand something that you had thought you did. That feeling of disequilibrium is one with which most competent students have little experience. They are often uncomfortable with it and react with expressions of boredom, which can mask their lack of deep understanding.

FIGURE 4.6. Meghan's Representations of (a) 13 × 4 = 52 and (b) .6 × .2 = .12

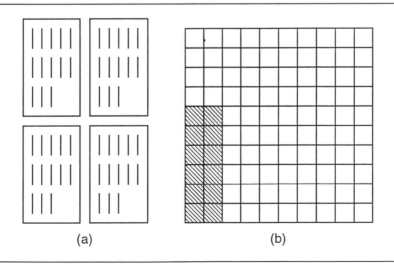

(a)   (b)

About three weeks later I saw clear evidence that Meghan was getting excited about math class. She was starting to use diagrams, stories, and blocks to work her way through a problem. We were exploring the concept of factorials through the problem described in *Anno's Mysterious Multiplying Jar* (Anno & Anno, 1983).

> On the sea was 1 island. On the island there were 2 countries. Within each country there were 3 mountains. On each mountain there were 4 walled kingdoms. Within each walled kingdom there were 5 villages. In each village there were 6 houses.

We had stopped at this point to try to figure out how many houses there were. Although Meghan generally worked beautifully with any partner, this time she asked her partner, Jessica, if she could get started on her own until she had a picture she could explain. When I came by she was busily working on her picture. Later she explained her picture (Figure 4.7) to Jessica and me.

> The whole paper is the island. I divided it in half—that's the two countries. Then I took one half and divided it in three—that's the three

FIGURE 4.7. Meghan's Drawing for Anno's Problem

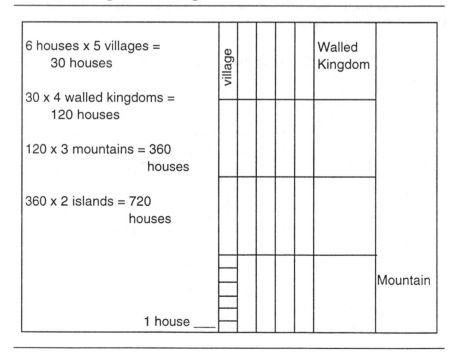

mountains. Then I divided each mountain into four to make the walled kingdoms. Now I'm not going to draw all the rest, but I will just figure them back in at the end.

She proceeded to explain her picture to Jessica and me, along with the computations at its side, in a way that was so clear and organized that we both easily understood what she was thinking. In fact, Jessica had processed the problem in a quite similar way, and they took pleasure in sharing their solutions and noting the parallels. Many of the students in the room had difficulty even getting going on the problem, although in general they enjoyed the activity.

For homework that night, I asked the students to think of an Anno's problem of their own, as easy or as difficult as they wished. "I want you to write a story, draw a picture, and find the answer for your own problems," I said. They seemed eager to try it. I sensed their enthusiasm again the next day as they shared their problems with their partners. Jessica raised her hand to volunteer Meghan's problem as an especially interesting one, and it certainly was. Meghan's story was complete with distractors, and she had worked it through in the same absolutely clear way, using a picture that she explained so beautifully she made it seem simple. Here is Meghan's story.

There was a building. Inside the building there were 3 rooms. In each room there were 7 desks. Next to each desk was 1 wastebasket. In each wastebasket were 4 walkmans. In each walkman was 1 tape. On each tape were 6 songs. How many songs were there in the building?

Meghan's explanation revealed how strong she was at logical thinking. When she came to the desks and wastebaskets, she said, "Now these are the desks, but I can just pretend they are also the wastebaskets, since there is one beside each desk." I asked Meghan if her picture had helped her think about the problem, and she replied, emphatically, "Oh, yes!"

I added, "Remember there was a time not so long ago when you were wondering why we needed to draw pictures and use blocks in math?" As I mentioned, Meghan isn't one to volunteer her thinking, but her enthusiasm for the problem she had written, her confidence in her thinking as she explained her picture, and her smile gave me the answer I'd been seeking since she raised that question in her Log several months before. Sometimes, students like Meghan don't really know how much there is to understand until they find themselves in a classroom that gives them the time and space to probe their thinking and conveys the expectation that they will do so.

"I love the challenge that comes with math!"

The opportunity to work closely with students like Meghan and Nate over the past several years has strengthened my belief that a math class like mine can offer the most capable students much more than would the traditional ability-grouped class. These students used to think that getting right answers quickly was the goal in math. But as they explore concepts through real-life problems, using pictures and manipulatives to search for alternative solutions, they are mining previously buried treasure.

The daily dialogue I have with them as they work together on problems gives me insight into their thinking, their questions, their wonderings and theories, and their excitement for learning. The private conversations they have with themselves and me in their Learning Logs helps me know how to encourage, challenge, and support them. Their comments reinforce how important the classroom atmosphere of collaboration and exploration is to real conceptual learning. Students show they are open to alternative solutions and they are looking for sense. They build on each other's ideas. They aren't afraid of confusion—sometimes they are intrigued by it. They express playfulness, frustration, satisfaction, and joy. They write:

> I think the answer has to make sense. What helped me understand was the picture Sarah drew. I was very confused before I saw her picture.

> Peter's idea makes sense, but it's hard to understand. Scott's idea is easy, but it doesn't make sense.

> Here's the problem: is it 23 kids or 23 minutes?

> > Yours truly,
>
> > Confused

> Do I understand? Well, sort of. It's kind of like looking out a window for your mom, but it's foggy and rainy. You see a woman's shape, and you think it's your mom, but then again, maybe it isn't.

Reflections from among the most capable students include ones like these.

> I kept getting confused about if it was 23 kids or 23 minutes. I find this so interesting. . . . I love it. When I looked at the picture and really understood, my mind was repeating "oh and ah" a million times.

> I realize now that although I will continue to listen to my students and try to challenge and support them in ways that fit their learning styles and interests, my sleepless nights are probably over. It is clear to me that each student, including the most able, can thrive in this setting. I know that to be true when

I read entries like this one, from a student whose mother had, early in the year, described her as needing a challenge in school.

> At first I was a little wishy-washy, but then I jumped right into the problem! I think this was one of the most interesting problems I have ever worked on at school! Math really makes you look deeper into a problem that you thought didn't even involve math. I love the challenge that comes with math! It's my favorite subject.

REFERENCE

Anno, Masaichiro, & Anno, Mitsumasa. (1983). *Anno's mysterious multiplying jar.* New York: Philomel Books.

$$+ \quad - \quad \times \quad \div$$

THE REALITIES, CHALLENGES, AND PROMISE OF TEACHING MATHEMATICS TO ALL STUDENTS

Raffaella Borasi

A mix of ethical, economic, and political reasons has brought the issue of equity in school mathematics—that is, empowering ALL students to learn mathematics—to the forefront of many recent educational debates and policies. The issue of equity is explicitly raised and addressed in two of the most influential reports recommending directions for change in school mathematics—the *NCTM Standards* (National Council of Teachers of Mathematics, 1989, 1991) and *Everybody Counts* (National Research Council, 1989). The latter, in particular, points out the discrepancy between the expected composition of future U.S. work force(s) and the failure and/or avoidance experienced by many minorities and women in school mathematics today. Consequently, it argues for the need to rethink mathematics instruction to make it more attractive and accessible to students of both genders and of diverse ethnic backgrounds. The need for mathematics teachers to confront a more diverse student population has been heightened by several recent initiatives, at both state and local levels, to mainstream larger numbers of students previously served in self-contained special education classrooms. These initiatives have been motivated both by the financial need to contain the growing expense of special education programs within reduced school budgets and by the mandate of the Regular Education Initiative that as many students as possible be placed in regular classrooms so that they can be given the same exposure to curriculum content as their peers.

While most mathematics educators would agree with the rationales behind the current call for heterogeneous classes and for increased attention to serving the needs of a diverse student population, many have raised concerns about the considerable implications for mathematics instruction that this move would involve. Is it really possible to teach mathematics effectively in such "inclusive" classrooms? Would students with special needs—because of learning disabilities, emotional problems, inability to speak adequately the language of instruction, or simply "lower math ability"—be well served in such an environment, or instead end up feeling lost and frustrated? Would the "good" students be "slowed down" and kept from reaching their full potential in such classrooms? How should mathematics instruction be reconceived in order to meet the demands of a diverse student population?

Indeed, these concerns were explicitly voiced by Sheinbach, Gagnon, and Riddle, whose stories about inclusion are presented in this chapter. While the successes reported in those stories should encourage us to believe that it is both possible and beneficial to teach students in heterogeneous mathematics classes, it seems worth addressing explicitly the concerns that this proposed reform raises. In this essay I discuss just a few of these concerns.

Are heterogeneous math classes a choice or a necessity?

The first thing that struck me while reading the previous three narratives was the fact that each of the experiences reported dealt with students who were "different" in quite different ways. Indeed, thinking of these experiences, as well as others of my own, I could identify at least the following areas with respect to which mathematics students could present considerable differences: ability levels, background knowledge, learning styles, strengths and weaknesses (such as learning disabilities), cultural/ethnic background, and primary language.

It is crucial to keep this "diversity within diversity" in mind when approaching the issue of "reaching diverse learners in school mathematics." Once we realize all the possible sources of difference among students, we may begin to question whether the effort to achieve a "truly homogeneous" mathematics class is indeed realistic. Even when "special education students" are carefully labeled and kept aside from the mainstream classroom, and the other students are further "tracked" on the basis of their perceived ability or their performance on predetermined tests, a lot of diversities (some of them equally affecting learning and performance in the mathematics classroom) will still remain and will need to be dealt with. For this "practical" reason alone (if not for ethical and economic ones), I believe administrators and teachers today have no choice but to redefine the problem presented by student diversity in mathematics classes in terms of "how we can we capitalize on it" rather than "how we can eliminate it."

Why and how can students' differences become an asset in the mathematics classroom?

Somewhat contrary to common expectations, the narratives by Riddle and Sheinbach provide some powerful anecdotal evidence in support of the claim that it is indeed possible to capitalize on student diversity in a number of complementary ways, to the benefit of ALL students. Sheinbach's examples, focusing on students who could be easily identified as learning disabled, show that even the "slowest" students can not only "survive" in the mainstream classroom but even benefit from exposure to a richer variety of learning opportunities, while at the same time avoiding the stigma often associated with a special education label. At the other extreme, Riddle's story shows how the best students can also benefit in many ways from interacting with their less able peers: by recognizing the possibility and value of alternative approaches to the same problem, by learning to respect alternative learning styles, and by becoming aware of—and learning to address—their own weaknesses. My own observations in several classrooms participating in a research project entitled "Supporting Middle School Learning Disabled Students in the Mainstream Mathematics Classroom" (Borasi, 1994; Borasi, Anthony, & Smith, 1994; Borasi & Smith, 1994; Fonzi & Rose, 1994; Woodward, Borasi, & Packman, 1991) have confirmed that the experiences reported by Riddle and Sheinbach are by no means unique.

Consider, for example, the following event, which occurred in an eighth-grade "blended" classroom of 30 students (18 "regular" and 12 "special education") co-taught by Vincent Bobin (a mathematics teacher) and Mark Lint (a special education teacher) in a suburban middle school. At the beginning of a unit on area, the students were presented with the task of figuring out the number of squares in the picture shown in Figure 4.8. While a good number of students simply counted the squares, others came up with creative shortcuts like breaking the figure into rectangles and triangles and applying known area formulas, or using "compensation" strategies such as recognizing that the two right triangles on the top could be "moved" to form a rectangle. To the teachers' surprise, an equal number of "labeled" and "nonlabeled" students relied on counting, while some of the learning-disabled students in the class came up with the most creative strategies!

In sum, my experiences, as well as those reported by Riddle and Sheinbach, suggest that student diversity can be turned into an asset for mathematics instruction in the following ways:

- "Brighter" students can serve as "models" for their peers.
- Students with learning disabilities and/or weaker math backgrounds may occasionally devise creative, nonstandard solutions *precisely because they do not know or remember the standard taught procedure*. This, in turn, may

FIGURE 4.8. Living Room to Be Carpeted

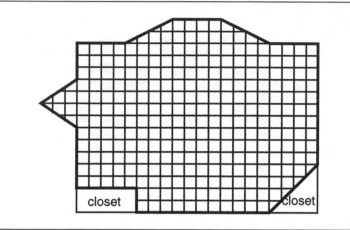

allow everybody else in class to recognize novel approaches to solving the problem—an experience that can be extremely beneficial not only for the authors of such solutions, whose self-esteem is likely to be increased, but also for the "brighter" students, who can thus be made to experience some valuable "cognitive disequilibrium."

- By being exposed to and explicitly discussing different learning styles and approaches, all students can become better aware of their own. Consequently, both teacher and students can take better advantage of their strengths and address their weaknesses. (Note, for example, how the students in Gagnon's class were able to articulate their needs and propose constructive ideas about how to address them.)
- As a result of all the above-mentioned experiences, one can hope that all students would learn to better appreciate and respect each other, as well as to recognize the value of diversity.

However, it is important to realize that these advantages may not materialize if the instructional goals, mathematical tasks, and overall teaching style remain the same as in traditional mathematics classes.

What kind of mathematics instruction is needed to meet the challenge of serving a diverse student population?

Key elements of the success stories of inclusion reported in this chapter can be found in the very nature of the mathematics curriculum these teachers tried to implement and the learning environments they created with their students. Their hands-on, student-centered, open-ended activities are quite different from the traditional routine: teacher explanation followed by student practice, with periodic evaluation on sets of exercises that admit only a single right answer and, often, one efficient way to achieve it.

Indeed, one could reasonably argue that the "ideal" of the homogeneous classroom is a logical consequence of the theoretical assumptions of the "transmission paradigm" (Borasi, in press; Neilsen, 1989) informing traditional mathematics instruction. If mathematics is perceived as a highly hierarchical collection of procedural knowledge and skills, and instruction is essentially identified with the transmission of small chunks of such knowledge in an orderly sequence, it is no wonder that an audience of students with the same background knowledge, as well as ability and speed for assimilating information, would seem ideal. However, not only is this ideal unrealistic (as argued earlier), but also the very foundations of the "transmission model" have been challenged on philosophical as well as empirical grounds. (See, for example, Borasi, 1992, in press; Neilsen, 1989; NCTM, 1989, 1991; NRC, 1989, as well as earlier chapters of this book.)

In contrast, an approach to mathematics instruction based on a constructivist view of learning provides an alternative that can facilitate the goal of accommodating and capitalizing upon student diversity. The following characteristics of such an approach are critical:

- An emphasis on process over product—for example, valuing alternative ways of solving the same problem—may help students value the contributions of a wide variety of classmates.
- The use of open-ended and complex mathematical tasks, which can be defined in alternative ways and do not have just one right answer and a unique way to reach it, can allow students with different strengths to find their "niche" and achieve success within their specific limitations.
- The use of more student-centered activities as the main vehicle for learning mathematics also could enable different students to go at their own pace and/or understand alternative assignments that are appropriate to their mathematical knowledge, ability, and interests.
- The introduction of groupwork and cooperative learning can further enable students to benefit from one another. Groups might be formed by complementing the strengths of group members—for example, putting together students with complementary learning styles (as in the case of Nate and Brian in Riddle's story), or different degrees of proficiency in the language of instruction (as in Gagnon's experience)—or by matching the students' ability levels (as in the case of Anna and Katie, or Sean and Justin, in Sheinbach's narrative), depending on the nature of the task assigned.
- A decreased emphasis on computation or, more generally, on specific skills

and content knowledge, may enable some students with weak computational skills and number sense to show their mathematical abilities for the first time (as illustrated by Brian in Riddle's story).

A move toward a more "constructivist-based" or "inquiry-based" teaching approach should be perceived as a prerequisite for teaching mathematics effectively in heterogeneous classrooms. However, such an approach may not be *sufficient* to guarantee successful learning on the part of all students in an inclusive classroom.

What are realistic expectations and appropriate instructional modifications for "inclusive" mainstream classrooms?

In our zeal to break a tradition of segregation, and in our enthusiasm to expose all students to the benefits of working in heterogeneous classes, we should be careful not to forget how real and handicapping some of the conditions actually are that initially caused a student to be considered in need of special instruction. Not being proficient in the language of instruction can indeed constitute a great obstacle, not only to understanding teachers' lectures and explanations, but also to participating fully in large group discussions, small group work, and even more individualized help sessions organized by the teacher. Physical handicaps such as deafness or blindness can considerably limit the learning modalities a student can rely on and the kinds of learning activities he or she can fruitfully participate in. Students with learning disabilities can experience similar limitations, although their disabilities may be somewhat less evident and, thus, often more difficult for teachers, parents, and other students to identify and take seriously. Consider, for example, how a severe writing disability can affect a wide range of learning activities: keeping a Learning Log, doing a technical report, taking notes, or even just responding to essay questions on a test. In some cases, the learning disability can be even less visible yet more severely handicapping, as in the case of students affected by memory and processing problems (such as Anna in Sheinbach's narrative). (For more information about the most common kinds of learning disabilities that may affect students, see Levine, 1990.) Cultural and gender differences, and their potential consequences for succeeding in traditional mainstream classrooms, may be even more subtle and difficult for teachers to detect and take into account. Furthermore, students who are mainstreamed later in their academic careers often are also handicapped by the fact that they may have been exposed in the past to a different curriculum from that of their classmates (as in the case of Gagnon's students, who had come to his course from a "bilingual" program where some areas of the mathematics curriculum had not been addressed).

How can students with the kind of handicaps listed above be expected to succeed when suddenly mainstreamed? Obviously, they cannot, unless considerable *modifications* are made for them both in terms of instruction and expectations. For example:

- *Teachers should be aware that certain kinds of tasks are too demanding, or even impossible, for students with certain physical and/or learning disabilities, and instructional modifications are required.* For example, teachers who use journal writing in their classes should consider the possibility of offering students with severe writing disabilities alternative or modified assignments, such as having such students report their thinking orally and/or suggesting that a parent, tutor, or resource room teacher scribe for them.
- *Whenever mainstreamed students come with considerable gaps in background knowledge* (because of exposure to a different curriculum and/or as a result of their disabilities), *a different and individualized set of goals would need to be put in place.* It would be unrealistic to set the same learning goals and use the same evaluation measures for such students as for their peers. Consider, for example, the case of an eighth-grade student who has not yet understood the basic concept of fraction and the rules for operating with fractions. It would be silly, as well as damaging to the teacher's and the student's self-esteem, to expect this student to be able to solve equations with fractional coefficients as well as his peers could—even at the end of a unit on equations. In this case, the teacher might choose to assign the student practice and evaluation exercises that avoid the use of fractions, or allow him to use a calculator that manipulates fractions, in order to facilitate the student's understanding of equations (the focus of the unit) as well as to better assess what he has learned in the unit.
- *"Compensating for" rather than "remediating" a student's disability should be the goal of classroom instruction.* The impossibility of remediating a student's disability is quite obvious and accepted in the case of a physical disability like blindness or deafness. Yet there are many teachers, parents, and administrators who would insist on asking a student to "improve" her writing when her difficulties in that area are due to some learning disability and are thus unlikely to disappear, or even improve considerably, no matter how much she practices. Rather, both teacher and student should learn to "live with" the disability and try instead to minimize its effects on the student's performance. They—teacher and student—should identify, build upon, and consistently use her strengths and learn to make efficient use of supports appropriate to her needs (such as calculators, manipulatives, mnemonic devices and strategies, etc.).

Implementing the recommendations listed above is not easy. Even teachers who agree in principle with the above points may feel inadequate to putting them into practice because of their limited understanding of their students' strengths and weaknesses and/or their unfamiliarity with appropriate instructional techniques. In addition, district policies, such as student evaluation criteria and procedures, may conflict with the goals of inclusion. Indeed, the points listed above call both for specific training for teachers assigned to teach mathematics in heterogeneous classrooms and for the support and close collaboration of mathematics teachers, special educators, administrators, parents, and students.

It would be quite unrealistic to ignore the need for extreme flexibility and considerable support that inclusive classrooms demand in order for all students to experience some success. Teachers and administrators who truly care for *all* their students and want to offer them the best possible learning environment should recognize up front that "inclusive classrooms cannot do it all"—although, when appropriately used and orchestrated, they may be the best alternative available.

Note: The reflections and insights reported in this essay have been informed by the results of work supported by the National Science Foundation under Grant No. TPE–9153812. Any opinions, findings, conclusions, or recommendations are those of the author and do not necessarily reflect the views of the National Science Foundation.

REFERENCES

Borasi, R. (1992). *Learning mathematics through inquiry.* Portsmouth, NH: Heinemann.

Borasi, R. (Ed.). (1994). *Developing area formulas—An opportunity for inquiry within the traditional math curriculum: Detailed reports of three classroom implementations.* Preliminary report to the National Science Foundation for the project, "Supporting Middle School Learning Disabled Students in the Mainstream Mathematics Classroom" (TPE–9153812).

Borasi, R. (in press). *Reconceiving mathematics instruction: A focus on errors.* New York: Ablex.

Borasi, R., Anthony, D., & Smith, C. E. (1994). *Developing area formulas—An opportunity for inquiry within the traditional math curriculum: In-depth story of a classroom experience.* Preliminary report to the National Science Foundation for the project, "Supporting Middle School Learning Disabled Students in the Mainstream Mathematics Classroom" (TPE–9153812).

Borasi, R., & Smith, C. F. (Eds.). (1994). *Remodeling—Experiencing mathematics in a real-life context: Detailed reports of three classroom implementations.* Preliminary report to the National Science Foundation for the project, "Supporting Middle School Learning Disabled Students in the Mainstream Mathematics Classroom" (TPE–9153812).

Fonzi, J., & Rose, B. J. (Eds.). (1994). *Investigating tessellations to learn geometry: Detailed reports of three classroom implementations.* Preliminary report to the National Science Foundation for the project, "Supporting Middle School Learning Disabled Students in the Mainstream Mathematics Classroom" (TPE–9153812).

Levine, M. (1990). *Keeping ahead in school*. Cambridge, MA: Educators Publishing Services.

National Council of Teachers of Mathematics. (1989). *Curriculum and evaluation standards for school mathematics*. Reston, VA: Author.

National Council of Teachers of Mathematics. (1991). *Professional standards for teaching mathematics*. Reston, VA: Author.

National Research Council. (1989). *Everybody counts: A report to the nation on the future of mathematics education*. Washington, DC: National Academy Press.

Neilsen, A. R. (1989). *Critical thinking and reading*. Bloomington, IN: ERIC Clearing House on Reading and Communication Skills.

Woodward, A., Borasi, R., & Packman, D. (1991). Supporting Middle School Learning Disabled Students in the Mainstream Mathematics Classroom. Grant proposal submitted to the National Science Foundation (Award TPE-9153812).

CHAPTER 5

Can Computer Technology
Transform Mathematics Instruction?

The emergence of the current movement to reform mathematics education co-incides with the widespread introduction of computer technology into the schools. The two narratives that follow attest to the intersection of these developments. But the computer is only the most seductive of a number of promising instructional tools, media, and techniques in increasing use in the mathematics classroom—sometimes in association with the reform effort. Thus, many of the stories told in earlier chapters contain references to work with manipulatives or calculators, cooperative small group formats, or journal keeping. However, in framing those narratives as interpretations of key motifs of the rhetoric of reform, the nature of that association was not itself raised to the level of reflection.

That is the point of this chapter—computer technology serving as a kind of test case—and for this reason: The greatest danger to the success of the current reform effort is not that it will be ignored but that one or another of these techniques and tools will be hailed as *the* "solution to the crisis of mathematics education." Out of a serious re-examination of the nature of learning, of mathematics, and of the organization of mathematics instruction have come ideas like "the student-centered classroom," "activity-based learning," and "instruction responsive to student thinking." But if their meaning is reduced to "put students into small groups and see what they come up with," "substitute work with manipulatives for paper-and-pencil exercises," or "set kids in front of computer screens—the interactive software will take care of the rest," we can add the current reform effort to the long list of failures.

Can computer technology transform mathematics instruction? In their narratives, Nina Koch and Susan Smith certainly show how the computer's ability to display different forms of representation—changes in one instantaneously affecting changes in another—offers unprecedented opportunities for responsive, individualized exploration. When Koch describes how a graphing project using the computer software Green Globs (distributed by Sunburst, Inc.) challenges her learning disabled student to confront some basic arithmetic notions that had eluded him in earlier grades, or Susan Smith traces how her sixth graders use Logo to investigate the properties of triangles, it seems that computer technology has *already* transformed their mathematics instruction. But, as teacher educator Daniel Chazan argues in his essay, these programs—examples of what he calls "inquiry tools"—are "laconic and nonjudgmental": They cannot set the context in which they are used or interpret the meaning of what they display.

Perhaps the issue raised by the title is a semantic one: What counts as "really transforming" mathematics instruction? On the other hand, teachers should not assume that because their students are exercising the Logo turtle or blasting Green Globs out of cyberspace, they are necessarily learning important mathematics. They may just be learning how to use the machine. And this distinction is more than merely semantic.

Nina Koch teaches high school in a college town, and Susan Smith teaches sixth graders in a rural district.

ONE LAST STAB: HIGH SCHOOL KIDS AND ARITHMETIC

Nina Koch

Lots of kids in high school have missed out on some of the most basic ideas in arithmetic. They don't know the difference between additive and multiplicative relationships. They fail to grasp the structure of our number system. Thus, it's not unusual for a student to add $5 when he intended to add 5%, or to be unable to tell you that ¹⁰⁄₃ is a number that's a little more than 3. Most high school teachers have a full portfolio of anecdotes about students who are amazingly uninformed about numbers.

It can be particularly difficult to address these concerns in the high school setting. Students recognize the arithmetic as a topic from elementary school and feel embarrassed or insulted to have to "go back" to it. Also, many mistake familiarity for comprehension. They have done these problems so many times, they *think* they understand the material. To review arithmetic, they believe, they simply need to be reminded of previously memorized techniques: "I already know this," they insist, "I just forget it." These students do not see a need to consider the concepts in any depth and will resist strongly a teacher's efforts to get them to think about what they are doing.

Furthermore, most high school students are enrolled in algebra or geometry courses, with overpacked curricula that do not allow time for exploration of arithmetic. It would seem, then, that one way to get high school students

to reconsider the arithmetic they've missed is to sneak it into their study of
more advanced topics. This allows them to continue along with the material
that should be learned in high school and also provides a new context for problems. Students working in unfamiliar territory are less likely to give knee-jerk,
mechanical responses.

The study of graphing in a coordinate plane provides a splendid opportunity for sneaking in arithmetic. I am especially interested in emphasizing a geometric approach to graphing, because it allows so much room for students to
explore math on their own. To approach graphing geometrically, they look at
a family of functions, perhaps a family of lines or a family of parabolas. For
example, in Figure 5.1, we see a particular family of parabolas described by
equations of the form $y = x^2 + k$. The "family resemblance" is clear: All of
the parabolas have the same steepness and the same axis of symmetry. They
differ only in their vertical location. This height is controlled by the value of
the number inserted for k. Thus, the graph of $y = x^2 + 5$ is located directly
above the graph of $y = x^2 + 1$. We refer to k as a *parameter* of the equation
$y = x^2 + k$. The parameter can assume any numerical value.

Setting the parameters of an equation acts to fix the attributes of the cor-
responding graph. Changing the value of a parameter will change something
about the way the graph looks, such as its steepness or location on the plane.
For linear equations, we use the two-parameter equation $y = mx + b$. Choosing values for m and b fully determines the line, and any particular line can
be identified uniquely by just those two parameter values.

FIGURE 5.1. A Family of Parabolas of the Form $y = x^2 + k$

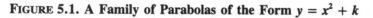

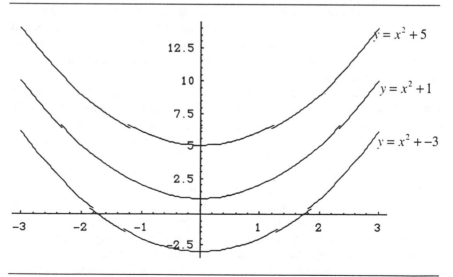

To describe all possible parabolas, three parameters are required: one to control the width of the parabola (A), one for horizontal location (H), and one for vertical location (K). We use $y = A(x - H)^2 + K$ as the geometric form of a quadratic equation (as contrasted with the standard form $y = ax^2 + bx + c$). For graphing, the advantage of the geometric form is that each of the numbers has a *direct physical meaning*. This allows students to learn by experiment, as they attempt to figure out which parameter controls which attribute of the graph and to develop some mastery in "steering" the graph by changing parameter values.

To explore parabolas (or any other family of functions), students can use one of the graphing packages widely available for classroom computers. The "Green Globs" program works very well. It displays the equations on the screen with clear notation and does not require much familiarity with the computer itself. After a brief introduction, the students can just jump in and try things.

At the start of Green Globs, the computer sets up a coordinate grid on the screen with x and y axes. It scatters a total of 13 globs at random integer locations on the grid. The object of the game is to take a "shot" by writing an equation and then see how many globs the graph of the equation hits. Rather than being a distraction, the globs serve to give some focus to students' exploration of graphing. As targets, the globs establish conditions that the graphs must satisfy. The students are not just tossing up different parabolas and seeing what the curves look like; they are trying to make a parabola that goes through particular points. They must gain control over the parameters in order to do this.

I have tried the Green Globs program with a wide variety of students, many of whom are participating in a remedial math program at the high school. Jason (a composite character) is a bright, likable kid with some significant language-based learning disabilities. Enrolled in Algebra I as a tenth grader, he is very aware that most of his friends finished that course last year in ninth grade. Still, he maintains a good attitude and works hard, especially when he feels intellectually engaged. The following narrative is an account of the interactions that might go on in the computer lab when a student like Jason works on an exploration of parameters in graphing.

"Miss Koch," Jason called me over. "Scott's not helping and I don't see how I can finish this."

"Oh, I don't expect you to finish the whole thing today," I reassured Jason. "But I do expect you to be working on it the entire period. And I do want you to work together. That's what your classwork grade will be based on."

Scott wheeled around in his swivel chair at the mention of the word "grade." "So get going already, dirt bag." He gave Jason a light shove.

"I am," said Jason. "I'm going to type something in." Jason is usually overanxious about completing assignments, especially when any reading is required. His difficulties with written language make him very concerned about being "behind" the rest of the class.

A few of the other students in the class work very quickly, so I had included a lot of problems on the worksheet to keep them challenged. I knew that most of the kids would not finish the sheet. Overall, I was hoping they'd get far enough on the worksheet to know what a parameter is and so have some degree of control over each of the parabola's three parameters.

I also was planning for the worksheet to raise some issues in arithmetic for the students. Fine-tuning a shot in Green Globs demands the application of number sense. Although he is largely unfamiliar with traditional notation and vocabulary, Jason does have very good number sense. He thinks proportionally and estimates well, which is especially important for him since he often makes errors in computation. I thought that the Green Globs activity, with its visual impact, would help Jason to make some connections about arithmetic on the basis of his cognitive strengths.

At the beginning of the worksheet, I had given the class the general form for their equations, as shown in Figure 5.2. This particular style highlights the idea that each parameter is like a slot into which the student inserts a numerical value. To convey the general idea of a parameter, I wrote, "Each parameter is like a control knob on a TV. If you turn the knob up or down, you will change something about the way the graph looks. Conduct some experiments to figure out how each knob works."

"I hate it when she says 'experiment,'" Scott groaned. Jason and Scott frequently beg to work together as a pair, although they argue with each other most of the time they're working. "We're supposed to be using these stupid equations with freaking exponents, which we haven't really learned yet. We haven't even done these equations. I hate it when she makes us do things we haven't done yet."

"Well, so, we figure it out, okay?" Jason began typing with a heavy stroke on the keyboard. "Okay, we go y equals, right? Then we have to choose a number for A. What should we put?"

"How do I know what to put? She never said. She just expects us to get it by looking at the screen. I wish she would teach."

"Well, I kinda get it," Jason ventured slowly. "Like she said about the

FIGURE 5.2. Students Worked with Equations of this General Form

$$y = \underset{A}{\underline{\quad}} (x - \underset{H}{\underline{\quad}})^2 + \underset{K}{\underline{\quad}}$$

TV control knob. You know, you turn it and you see what it does. So we'll put in numbers in the slots; then we'll change them and see what happens.''

"Well, I just don't see why they're paying her when she doesn't teach. We end up learning it ourselves. You just sit there and figure things out. That's so lame!''

"Yeah, okay, but look what I tried. I did $y = 1(x - 1)^2 + 1$. You know? Just all 1s in there. And we got a curve on the screen, that bottom one there. So then I did the same equation but with a 2 at the end, and then I did it again with a 3.'' Jason pointed at a stack of parabolas on the screen.

"But that only changes the last number. We have to do all of them for this sheet.''

"We're going to do all of them, but one at a time. See what changing the last number did to the graph? So now we know what K is. It's height. Changing K changes the height. So we can move the curve up or down.''

"She never said we had to change the height. You're just doing extra work, dork-nerd.'' Scott turned away from the screen and started crumpling up pieces of scrap paper to practice shooting baskets into the trash can.

"Yes, up there at the top, it says we should find out what each parameter's job is. We know that K's job is to control the height. Now we have to figure out A and H, what they control. I'm pretty sure one of them makes it go sideways.'' Jason cleared the screen and began typing a new equation.

"Well, you can do it. You know, the other Algebra I class is just doing lines. Our class has to do curves. And we're still on question one, and you haven't even told me yet what to write on my sheet for the answer.''

Jason made an attempt to get Scott to stay with him. "Wait. Look down at number four.'' The fourth question on the worksheet asked the students to compare the curves of $y = 2(x - 1)^2 + 4$ and $y = 3(x - 1)^2 + 4$. "Let's go ahead and work on number four, okay? 'Cause that'll tell us what A does. You know? See how it's only the first number that changes? We'll change A and see what it does to the graph.''

"I don't see why we have to have A, H, and K when there's already x and y. It's too many letters.''

"Yeah, I know,'' said Jason. "But see, the x and the y, you just leave them in the same place all the time. Then the A, H, and K—that's what we're experimenting with. So now I'm going to see if changing A makes the curve go sideways.'' He typed in the two equations with different values for A. The computer screen displayed two parabolas with the same vertex (see Figure 5.3).

"You're busted! It didn't do it. Sideways. Right. Like you would know.'' Scott kicked the wheels on Jason's swivel chair.

"No, okay, it didn't work. But anyway, we still know something. 'Cause, see, it got thinner.''

"Thinner?''

FIGURE 5.3. Two Graphs with Different Values for A

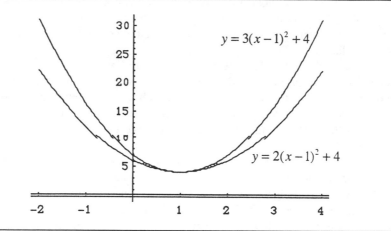

"Yeah, closer together. See, it's not as wide. So changing A makes the curve get steeper. So we can use that." Jason made some notes on his worksheet.

"Okay, do it with 4. Put a 4 instead of a 3. See if it gets steeper again."

"Um, okay. We could do that." Jason went along with Scott's suggestion, although he already felt fairly certain of the results.

"See—I told you. Look, it's almost straight up and down. All right, now do it with 5. It'll be super steep."

Jason indulged Scott's penchant for repetition a few more times and then nudged him on to question three on the worksheet. I had designed the worksheet to begin with a very general, open-ended question about the parameters and then to move on to a series of short, focused questions like, "What is the difference between $y = 2(x - 1)^2 + 4$ and $y = 2(x - 3)^2 + 4$?"

For students who can structure their own learning, the open-ended question serves as a jumping-off place. It presents them with the problem to be investigated; they proceed to design and conduct their own experiments. These students spend quite a bit of time on that first question and write long, detailed responses to it with full sentences. The rules they generalize during their experiments then allow them to breeze through the short, focused questions. For them, a question like the one above is simply a specific application of their general knowledge about parameter H.

Students like Scott, however, typically give highly superficial responses to open-ended questions. They write a phrase or two, just to have something on paper. Scott considers it his teacher's job to tell him exactly how to proceed and he resists any effort to get him to draw his own conclusions. His favorite math activity is a set of 25 drill-and-practice exercises, each one a facsimile of the sample problem done by the teacher on the board. He pulls out a clean sheet of notebook paper and immediately writes the numbers 1–25 down the left-hand edge of the paper, with one line of the paper allotted for each problem. My computer lab activities don't fit very well into Scott's notebook-paper picture of what math should be. He pleads, "Why can't we just do *regular* math?"

No amount of cajoling will get Scott to provide a satisfactory response on an open-ended question. For students like him, actual exploration does not even start until they get to the series of short, focused questions. They need those questions to direct their exploration. This was especially important on the Green Globs activity, because on their own several of the students never came up with the idea of controlled experimentation (changing only one parameter at a time).

As Scott worked through the short questions and began to find what he considered "right answers," he became more engaged in the activity. "Okay, try a 7 for *H*," Scott told Jason. "I bet it moves even further to the right."

"Yeah, you're right. You know what? I was thinking maybe we could try to get those globs over there. See how they're kinda lined up in a curve shape? I think we could get three or four in a row, all in the same shot. We just need to move it over there and make it flatter."

"But we don't know how to make it flatter. We only know how to make it steeper."

"Well, I was thinking we could still use *A*—change *A* to make the curve flatter." Jason motioned with his hands across the screen.

"No, *A* is the one that makes it steeper. You said that before. I already wrote that on my sheet." Scott started to scratch out a response on his worksheet. "Okay, fine, I'll take it out."

"Wait, Scott, don't cross it out. It's not wrong. *A* does make it steeper, 'cause remember? We saw that happen. Like when you said change it to a 4 and change it to a 5. It got steeper. You were right."

"Yeah, I rocked on that one. So why you'd tell me to change my answer on the worksheet if I was right before? Now my paper's messy."

"Well, maybe we could just say more. We could say *A* makes the curve get steeper when you use a higher number and it makes the curve get flatter when . . ."

" . . . when you use a lower number," Scott broke in. "Hey, I get it now."

"Yeah, it really is like the TV knob."

"Okay, I see how. 'Cause you could turn the knob up or down, and that's like steeper or flatter." Scott picked up his worksheet again. "Of course, she couldn't just say that to begin with."

"So anyway, let's try a 1 for *A*, since that's lower than what we tried before."

"Okay, I'll do it. I type better than you." Scott put in $y = 1(x - 1)^2 + 3$. "Yep, it's flatter like I said. Now what were we going to try to do with it?"

"Well, I was going to try getting those three globs in a row, using the curve. We just need to move it up and over a little."

"But wait, let's just do what's on the sheet. I don't want to do anything extra."

"Yeah, well, number seven says to see if you can hit three globs on a single shot. So we can just skip down to that." The boys worked on changing the horizontal and vertical location of their parabola, getting it closer to the globs they were trying to hit. I walked over to their machine and saw that they had typed in $y = 1(x - 2.2)^2 + 3.6$.

"Hey, Miss Koch, we're rocking now." Scott pointed to the equation on the screen. "Look, we put decimals in there and now we're hitting three of those puppies. Blip-blip-blip."

"The decimals made a difference?" I asked.

"Oh, yeah, we had to. Like with the height. First we used a 3 but that was too low. Then we did a 4. It was high enough to get two of the globs, but too high for the third. We needed something in between. So the little guy here," Scott pointed at Jason, "he thought of using something like 3 ½ for the height. Only he thought 3 ½ was 3 point 2! *I* had to tell him it's 3 point 5."

"After that we raised it to 3 point 6," Jason continued, "because 3 point 5 was just a little too low."

"Yep, we got decimals here. They look raggedy, but they work."

"Hey, Scott, look at that fourth glob there. We're so close to it. If we made the curve just a little flatter, we'd have all four in the same shot."

"But we're already down to a one for A. How are we going to get lower than that?" Scott paused. "Unless—oh, I know. Do minus. Minus one. That's lower than one. Use minus."

Jason hesitated but typed in $y = -1(x - 2.2)^2 + 3.6$. The computer drew a downward-pointing parabola, a reflection of the one they'd drawn before. "Oh, it's just opposite," he said.

"Well, that's cheap. It shouldn't have done that. We're trying to get it flatter and we used a lower number like we're supposed to, but it doesn't work. That's not fair. We didn't do anything wrong." Scott elbowed me to lodge his complaint. "A minus number is supposed to make it flatter, but it's going upside-down."

Jason turned to me. "Miss Koch, there's something really weird here with these negatives. See, I thought I understood them already, and it made sense before when we were working on height. You know, you just decrease the number for K and the height drops. You go 2, 1, 0, minus 1, minus 2 and the height drops each time. I just think about the curve moving down the screen and K is the thing that's pulling it down. It's so logical. When you need to get lower than 1, you go to 0 and after that you go to minus 1 and so on. It just follows in a row.''

"Yeah, I think it makes sense, too, Jason,'' I told him. "So what was it that made it seem weird?''

"Well, when we started decreasing A, we'd go 4, 3, 2, 1, and the thing would get flatter. But then we decreased it even more, down to negative 1, thinking it would just get even flatter, but it didn't. It turned upside-down. I can see how to make some use of the upside-down curves, but still—it just doesn't go how I thought it would. The negatives on A work so different than the negatives on K.''

"It does seem inconsistent, doesn't it?'' I agreed with Jason. "Now what about H? Does H work more like A or more like K when you do negatives?''

"Oh, H is like K,'' Jason answered quickly. "They're really the same. They both move the curve. It's just that K moves it up and down, and H moves it sideways. They still work the same way. Oh wait,'' he turned back to the keyboard, "I have to try something.''

Scott had tuned out while Jason conversed with me, and was busily trying to communicate by lip-reading with a friend out in the hall. "Scott, what's Jason doing?'' I asked as I waved good-bye to his friend.

"Oh, I know, I know. We're trying to get it flatter. We're doing problem seven.'' He turned to look at the screen. Jason had typed in $y = 0(x - 1)^2 + 1$, which made a horizontal line at $y = 1$. "Hoo boy, that's *really* flat. Nice try.''

"It's a line. Now, how could it be a line and not a curve? See, Miss Koch, it's happening again. That same problem I had before with the negatives. I decided to check out what zero would do. I put in a zero for A. And look, it destroyed the curve.''

"So how's that the same problem you had before?''

"Well, because, A doesn't act like K. You can put a zero in for K and it doesn't wreck the curve or anything. It just fits right in, just a place between positive one and negative one. But with A—I don't know—it's like zero isn't even the same kind of number. I don't get it.''

Jason was struggling with a basic issue in arithmetic: the difference between addition and multiplication. Parameter A is a multiplier in the equation $y = A(x - H)^2 + K$, while parameters H and K are addends. In general, additive parameters control location of a graph, while multiplicative parameters influence shape. One can think about adding (or subtracting) as a shifting motion, and multiplying (or dividing) as a shrinking or swelling.

Jason's right, actually, that zero isn't "the same kind of number" when used for parameter A. As an addend, zero is completely harmless; it doesn't change the value of the sum at all. As a multiplier, however, zero is an annihilator. This is what destroyed Jason's curve. He's right, also, that his confusion about zero was the same trouble that he had with negatives. As addends, negative numbers are decreasers. As multipliers, negative numbers are reflectors—not shrinkers.

Many of my students overgeneralize and attempt to apply additive rules in multiplicative situations. When asked to find a value for n such that $8n = 2$, they try negative numbers for n because they believe that a negative multiplier will shrink the 8 down to a 2. It can take quite a bit of pushing to get them to realize that they need to use a fraction for n. Fractional multipliers (proper fractions, that is) are the shrinkers. And even after students learn to solve correctly equations like $8n = 2$, they might still walk over to the computer lab and make exactly the same mistake when trying to flatten a parabola on Green Globs. Parameter A needs to be decreased. They need a number less than one, and negatives are the first thing to come to mind.

I could see that Jason was in the process of discovering that basic distinction between addition and multiplication when he was describing how parameter A does not work the same as parameter K. But I was also fairly sure he would not attribute the difference to the arithmetic operations themselves. In fact, I suspected that he was not even aware that the number sitting next to the parentheses indicated multiplication. Jason was acting on a physical classification scheme. That's how he knew that H belonged in the same category as K. Both H and K are locating parameters, while A is a shaping parameter.

I decided not to press the issue of operations for the time being. That was more my agenda, not Jason's, and his scheme worked very well for him for the time being. Sometimes I have to restrain myself not to push students in a certain direction just because I think it's such a neat idea in mathematics. (This restraint is especially difficult when I've recently discovered the idea, myself.)

Meanwhile, both Scott and Jason were interested in what they saw when they used zero for parameter A. "It does it every time," Scott reported. "You put a zero in there and you get a line. No curve at all. Just completely flat."

"So zero makes it too flat?" I asked.

"Yeah, and one makes it too steep, you know, for the globs we're trying to hit," Jason said.

"Could you just trace out with your finger what you'd like the curve to look like?" I asked, looking at Scott.

"Oh, okay. It would go right here. It's under this one, but not way down flat like the line is. Just somewhere between." The word "between" seemed to cue an idea for Scott. "Oh, hey, Jace, we can do that. We can get between. You know, with your raggedy-looking decimals, like before. Do half. Put a half in there."

Jason typed in $y = 1.5(x - 2.2)^2 + 3.6$. "Well, that's not flatter," he said slowly. "Maybe decimals won't work the same on A as they do on K."

"Hey, it might help if you put in half like I said. You did 1 and a half. Here," he grabbed the keyboard. "I'll do it with point 5 like it should be." Scott typed in $y = .5(x - 2.2)^2 + 3.6$, which made a fairly flat curve.

"Yes!" he made a triumphant fist. "Scott rules! The math stud! See? I told you it would work."

"Yeah, and it's almost perfect for getting all those globs. Let's go just a little steeper, maybe point 6 instead of point 5," Jason said.

I left the two of them to continue fine-tuning their shot, now that they realized they needed to use numbers between 0 and 1 for parameter A. Several other students in the class had run into the same trouble. I thought about how I might revise the worksheet next time to help them figure out multiplicative decrease. For Jason and Scott, it had been an important step to try out zero for parameter A. I should include a question about that. Also, that word "between" was so critical for Scott. I should work that in somehow, too, I noted to myself.

Jason and Scott worked fairly well together for the remainder of the class period. At this point, they both had the same goal—to hit as many globs in one shot as they could. They continued to make use of decimals for their parameters and also experimented with inverted parabolas by putting in a negative number for parameter A. For this particular task, their different learning styles complemented each other well. Jason was good at eyeballing which globs could be lined up in a curve and seeing how the curve needed to be shaped. Scott provided attention to detail in the writing of the equations.

"You guys make a good team," I told them when I passed by again.

"Are you kidding? We're awesome!" Scott looked as pleased as he does when he's solved a sheet of 25 equations correctly, and he didn't even realize he was improving his class participation grade. "Miss Koch, we just got five in a row on that last shot." He looked at Meg and Kristin working a few seats away. "Hmm, they're doing the same thing we are. I wonder if the ladies might require some assistance."

Actually, Meg and Kristin were working on one of the more challenging questions at the end of the worksheet. It asked if they thought that *any* three globs could be connected by some parabola. Scott sauntered over to the girls, but when he overheard one of them say the word "noncollinear," he wheeled around and went back to his seat.

The next day, Scott missed class for a golf match, and Jason elected to work alone at the computer. He started with question eight on the worksheet, which asked him to type in the equation $y = .8(x - 5)^2 + {}^-1$ and then design another parabola that would be slightly flatter than that but still centered at the same location. Jason typed in $y = .8(x - 5)^2 + {}^-2$, which caused the curve to shift down. "No wait," he said to himself. "That's not right."

I walked over to check in with Jason to be sure that he really did want to work alone for the day. "What are you trying?" I asked him.

"Oh, I'm on number eight, but I did it wrong. I forgot which was which. I changed the wrong number." I started to get more concerned about Jason working alone. He often forgets "which is which." He switches word pairs like vertical and horizontal or parallel and perpendicular. He needs someone like Scott, who has a good memory, to help him keep things straight.

"You know, Karen doesn't have a partner today, Jason. Maybe the two of you . . . "

"No, Miss Koch, I can't." His Irish complexion got redder. "She goes too fast."

I started to launch into my "You're a smart kid, too" speech, but held back when I remembered how angry that had made him in the past. "Well, you do have a good eye for this stuff. You guys made a lot of progress yesterday." I was careful not to be too effusive in praise.

"So, why do you think I can't handle it by myself?" Jason is a perceptive and sensitive kid. Clearly, I'd already blown it with him.

I tried to cut my losses. "Okay, I'll see if someone else wants to work with Karen."

"Anyway, I know what I did wrong, now. I just switched A and K. I'll do it right, now," Jason said without looking at me.

I stood back from Jason's machine but kept an eye on him while I went to help another pair nearby. I was just going to have to let him be mad for a while. I reminded myself that, overall, Jason really did like being in this class and fared well here. It was the first time since seventh grade that he'd gotten better than a D− in math. Last year he'd been in Mr. Robbins's pre-algebra class, along with Scott, doing "regular" math. Jason would take that assignment of 25 identical problems, misapply some rule, and do it consistently down the page, so that every single problem was wrong. In my class, he was still making mistakes in mechanics, but at least he had more opportunities to demonstrate the strength of his ideas.

After his initial mistake, Jason now knew that he needed to lower the value of parameter A in order to flatten the curve. It was exactly what he and Scott had been working on the day before; he knew what to do. Still, he called me over to his machine for assistance. "A needs to be lower," he told me. "What should I use?"

"Well, what's it at now?"

"Um, 8. No wait, it's point 8."

"So what are you thinking?"

"I don't know. Maybe negative point 8."

I didn't flinch. "Try it. See what happens."

"I knew you'd say that!" He turned back to the keyboard.

I tried not to look disappointed as I watched him type in the negative value for parameter A. He *had* to know that wouldn't work. He had known it yesterday. I had *seen* him know it. He and Scott were maneuvering those parabolas all over the screen with a great deal of sophistication.

"Hey, it's upside-down," he reacted when the graph went across the screen. "Oh, yeah. That's right. The minus sign did that. A minus sign will make it go upside-down. Okay, I don't want that." I started to feel relieved that Jason was back on track until he added, "I guess I should have made A be higher than point 8, not lower." He looked over at me for confirmation, which he knew he would not get. "I know, I know, try it and see what happens. The Koch method."

This time, I had to conceal horror as well as disappointment. I was watching him regress in understanding. His conclusion was completely wrong. How could he think that? I hated to see him fumbling like this, but I had to let him find out that this idea wasn't going to work, either. He put in a series of equations, each with a higher value for parameter A. Of course, as he increased the value, the parabola got steeper—the opposite of what he was trying to do.

He stopped typing and folded his arms. "That didn't help. It's just getting worse. This is stupid. When I increase A, the curve gets steeper, but when I lowered A—you know, with the negative—it didn't get flatter. That's dumb. It should run like an opposite. You know, increase makes it steeper and decrease makes it flatter. That would be logical."

"I see what you mean about running like an opposite. Makes sense to me." I knew this was little comfort.

"But it doesn't work! All it does is go upside-down!"

At this point, I was scrambling to try to figure out how to intervene. I certainly wasn't going to leave him this frustrated. I also knew I shouldn't just come out and tell him what the trouble was. He knows I rarely do that. It might make him feel like I thought he was stupid, and I couldn't risk that.

"When does it go upside-down?" I asked him.

"When I use the minus sign. I don't really want to use the minus sign, but I have to do something to get the number lower."

"I noticed you tried point 9 without a minus sign," I pointed out.

"Yeah, because point 9 would be one notch higher than point 8. But that just makes it steeper, and I don't want it to be steeper."

"It got steeper when you went one notch higher?"

"Oh wait—you're right. It shouldn't be one notch higher. It should be one notch lower." Jason looked at the screen.

We had cleared the hurdle. He would be fine now. I had deliberately echoed his use of "one notch higher" because I wanted him to realize that he could work down from eight-tenths in the same way he had worked up. He had known all along that he wanted to decrease that number; it was just a question of *how* to decrease it.

"So, how will you make it one notch lower?" I asked.

"Oh, that's easy." He was already typing. "Just go the other way. Do point 7 instead of point 9. That's gotta work. No, I'm not even going to ask you if that's right." He turned and smiled a bit. "I'm just going to try it and see what happens."

I advised Jason to make some notes for himself on his worksheet, in case he got mixed up again on another day. He jotted down some complicated cartoon-style sketches with arrows and symbols of his own making, along with the word "opsit" as a reminder for himself. I left to go help two kids who had once again managed to crash their machine.

I thought more about the interaction between Jason and me. I was lucky, really, that it had turned out all right. I still wondered how he could have gotten so bollixed up. Then I remembered that it was actually Scott who had suggested using a fraction in order to decrease parameter A, when the boys were working together the day before. Jason had accepted Scott's suggestion and worked with it, but he hadn't come up with the idea himself. Maybe he needed to go through that on his own—to make the progression from the additive to the multiplicative sense of decrease. And, I warned myself, he may even need to go through it again a few more times. Additive relationships are the ones learned first, after all, and that set of conceptions can take a powerful hold in the student's mind.

Now that Jason had made his breakthrough on using decimals to make the curve flatter, he was happily focused on fine-tuning a shot to hit several globs in a row. After a while, he called me over for some advice. "Okay, Miss Koch, I've got it down to somewhere around point 3 or point 4. But here's the thing—point 3 is too flat and point 4 is just a little too steep. See, look. It needs to be in between these two," he motioned at the graphs. "But there aren't any numbers to use."

"You need a number between point 3 and point 4?"

"Right. But there aren't any. I wish I could use halfs or something." Jason had gotten skillful in using the tenths place in his equation, but he was not identifying those numbers as fractions with a denominator of 10. To him, it was just "point this" or "point that" and he knew which ones were higher and which ones were lower. He was not aware that hundredths were available as parts of tenths, because he'd never had a working understanding of those fractions.

Most students do have a working understanding of half, if of no other fraction, so I decided to pursue that with him. "How would you use the half?" I asked.

"Well, you know. Like $3\frac{1}{2}$ is halfway between 3 and 4. I need something like that. But they're not going to let me use point $3\frac{1}{2}$."

"You couldn't write it that way?"

"No, look. I even tried it already because I knew you'd make me." He gave a sly smile. "Watch what it does." Jason typed in ".31/2" as the value of parameter A. The computer interpreted this as $.31 \div 2$, which is .155. "It comes out way too wide," he reported. "It's like even lower than .2, which makes no sense at all. It doesn't even look right after I type it in there. The typing makes it look like 31 over 2, not 3½.'' He was right about that. The computer could take improper fractions, but not mixed numbers.

"What else did you try?" I asked.

"Oh, I don't know. I was thinking I could do point 3 point 5. You know, because 3½ is the same as 3 point 5, like Scott said."

"So you typed that in—point 3 point 5?"

"Yeah, I did and look, the computer won't even do it at all." Jason typed ".3.5" as the value for parameter A, and the computer typed back, "I don't understand." "See, you can't use two decimal points on the computer," he said. "It doesn't understand."

I was surprised that the computer wouldn't accept Jason's number with two decimal points. I had seen kids put in numbers like that on a calculator, which simply ignores the second decimal point and displays the number with its correct place value. "You're right, Jason. That's not going to work on the computer. Did you try it on your calculator? Just to see what the number looks like?"

"Oh, I guess I could try that. Just to see." Jason entered ".3.5" on the calculator, and saw ".35" on the display. "Well, the calculator's really messed up. It does point 35."

"Why is that messed up?"

"Well, because. Come on, no way. Point 35? That's way high. I want something between 3 and 4. Not all the way up to 35."

"Have you tried something like that on the computer?" I asked.

"No. Why should I? I know it's not what I want. It's way too steep. I'll have to think of something else." At this point, Jason was operating on a primitive understanding of place value. He was taking a rule that works for whole numbers—the more digits you have, the greater the value of the number—and applying it to fractional numbers. Many students make this overgeneralization; it is certainly not unreasonable. Thirty-five things *is* more than four things, as long as you're talking about the same size thing. With whole numbers, the things are always ones, so we compare them without explicit reference to the unit of comparison. But, to the right of the decimal point, "four" could mean four-tenths or four-hundredths or four-thousandths, and so on; it certainly makes a difference. And yet, students in their speech don't acknowledge the size of the number. They say "point four" which allows them to escape noticing that it's actually four-tenths.

Of course, it's not only students who say "point four" instead of "fourtenths." Most adults do also. I had been doing that in my conversation with Jason. Now I began to feel complicit in his incomplete understanding of place value. I hesitated quite a while before I responded to his strongly stated conviction that point 35 is much larger than point 4. I was trying to decide what tack to take. I knew he was good at drawing diagrams. I could remind him of the names of the tenths and hundredths places, and then have him use his diagrams to compare the numbers in size. It might work, but we'd already done those diagrams so many times. He understood them by themselves, but he didn't seem to be transferring that comprehension to this new situation. Anyway, it felt like I'd have to do too much telling.

Luckily, Jason himself came up with another approach. He had picked up his calculator again. "Hey, Miss Koch, look at this. I was thinking about how to do point 3½, right? So anyway, I know that 3½ is half of 7. I can do halfs with regular numbers. So then I figured, well, point 3½, wouldn't that just be half of point 7? I mean, it makes sense. It's a comparison. You just cut the point numbers in half like you would with regular numbers."

"Okay, how are you going to cut point 7 in half?" I asked.

"Oh, that's got to be dividing by two. And I can do that on the calculator. So I punched in point 7 divided by 2. And look, I get that point 35 answer again. That is so weird. I mean, 7 divided by 2 is 35? I don't know. But decimals are weird anyway, so I guess you could get an answer like that. At first I thought I punched it in wrong, like maybe I did 70 instead of 7. But I tried it a few more times real careful and that's what you get. It's point 35."

I wanted to tell him that he *had* done 70 divided by 2, that .7 is the same as seventy-hundredths. Still, I knew he could get through this on his own. He was so close, and he seemed eager. I paused and asked, "Okay, that point 35 you're getting—is there a way to check that? Any other computations you could do on the calculator that might make you believe it more?"

"Well, the only thing I can think of is to do point 8 divided by 2, you know, to see what half of point 8 is." He punched it in. "And look, it's point 4, which it ought to be. And now I'll see if half of point 6 is point 3. And it is. So the calculator must be working. It's taking those decimals and cutting them in half. My idea about dividing by two, that must be right. I guess I could go ahead and try it on the computer."

"And see what happens to the curve?"

"Yeah, before I was thinking it would be really steep with point 35, but now I think it might be okay. Because of the calculator and everything, you know. So I'll see how it looks." Jason typed in a value of .35 for parameter *A*. The curve was not at all steep, but rather went in between the curves with values of .3 and .4. "Sweet!" he said at the sight of the curve.

I was sorry that Scott was not there to declare Jason a math stud. I said something mildly congratulatory, while thinking to myself, "God, this kid is smart."

Jason didn't even hear me. Now that he'd seen that .35 would help him get between .3 and .4, he was busy trying .37 and .38 to fine-tune his shot. I decided to leave him alone for a while. After all, his goal was to hit globs, not learn decimal numeration. As I started to walk away, he called over his shoulder as he continued to type, "Hey, Miss Koch, you know what else? Let's say I needed to get it between point 37 and point 38. Well, I already know what I'm going to use. I could do point 375. That would be between. I already know it will work. You just keep moving further out with the decimal places. You can tune it as fine as you want; you just use more places. That's how the decimals work."

"Good idea," I told him. "Use it. And write it down somewhere, will ya?" We still had a lot of work to do on Jason's understanding of place value. Yet, I was satisfied that he had given up one of his misconceptions about decimals. No longer did he believe that the more digits in a number, the greater its value. He was able to give this up because he had something to replace it with. Now he associated the number of digits with the precision of the number: the more digits, the finer the tuning. I knew we had a good foundation that we could build on later.

After class, I walked up toward the mailroom and thought some more about Jason and his fine-tuning. The kids in this algebra class had widely varying levels of understanding about decimals. A couple of them were still very confused and would do things like writing two-thirds as "2.3." Others could do computations and use the system flawlessly, but had never thought much about its structure. I needed to accommodate all of the kids and also to frame the activity in the context of an algebra lesson. Next week, I decided, I would bring in a classroom set of scientific calculators. We could start our unit on exponents by investigating powers of 10, and eventually generalize to powers of x.

I could already imagine some of the misconceptions that would start flying around while we worked on exponents. Scott would be quoting half-baked rules that he thought he remembered from ninth grade. Jason had never understood those rules well enough to remember them at all. He would be starting from scratch. Actually, he's better off that way, I thought. I won't have to undo anything. We'd only look at what we could motivate, and we'd derive our rules from noticing patterns. I could even see him coming up with the idea of negative exponents on his own, because it's "just logical, you know." He could do this stuff, I was convinced, even if he still didn't know all of his multiplication tables. And his newfound appreciation of exponents would improve his understanding of decimals.

Jason is one of those kids who's missed out on arithmetic. But just because he's in high school now, doesn't mean I have to give up on teaching him those fundamentals. We can do algebra *and* arithmetic, and do it in a meaningful way. Now if I could just figure out what to do with Scott . . .

$$+ \quad - \quad \times \quad \div$$

LOGO: A TOOL FOR EXPLORING MATHEMATICS

Susan B. Smith

"Is it Wednesday? That means Logo. Right, Mrs. Smith?" asked Jane one morning, early in the fall.

"What do you think?" I replied with a smile.

"Oh, good!" She grinned and continued to her seat.

Jane's reactions to Logo mirror those of most of the 16 kids in my sixth-grade class. Every Wednesday, as part of my math program, I bring the school's seven computers into our room for a 90-minute Logo lab. The class thoroughly enjoys the experience and, like Jane, looks forward to it. Interestingly, she likes Logo, although she seems to have more difficulty than some others. Somehow she doesn't allow herself to become totally frustrated. Instead her confusion seems to push her on. There's a desire to "try just one more way."

ABOUT LOGO

Logo is a computer programming language whose simple commands make it available to very young children. However, it is powerful enough also to be used by high school and college students. One component of the program allows the user to draw geometric shapes and pictures, or create complex designs: a "turtle" on the screen (often represented by a small triangle) traces a line as it moves in response to the user's commands. Logo fosters "playing around" since, as commands are executed, the resulting lines on the screen provide immediate feedback. Through this feedback, students can experiment and explore ideas.

A few simple commands allow the user to create complex shapes and designs. The following are a few of the commands Logo understands:

FD An abbreviation for FORWARD. The user must type a number (or input) to tell the turtle how far forward to go. FD 40 or FD 130 will make the turtle go forward 40 or 130 "steps," respectively.

BK BACK. BK is like FD and needs an input to tell the turtle how far to go.

RT RIGHT, turns the turtle to the right. The user has to tell it how much to turn, e.g., RT 30 turns the turtle 30 degrees to the right.

LT LEFT, is used in the same way as RT. LT 50 results in a 50-degree left turn.

Using these simple commands, the user can make the turtle draw a square: FD 100 RT 90 FD 100 RT 90 FD 100 RT 90 FD 100 RT 90 (RETURN) (see Figure 5.4).

FIGURE 5.4. Logo Commands for Drawing a Square

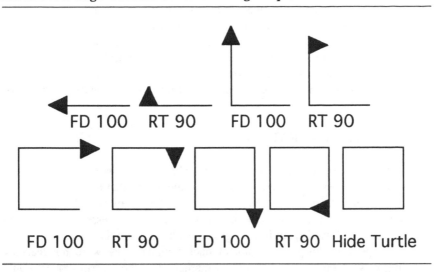

FD 100   RT 90   FD 100   RT 90

FD 100   RT 90   FD 100   RT 90   Hide Turtle

This is the first year that Logo has been such an important feature of my class. I am a first-year, sixth-grade mathematics teacher, but have used Logo on a limited basis over the past three years with third and fourth graders. Based on the positive reactions of my younger students, I decided to make it a weekly component of my sixth-grade math program.

In the years since I discovered Logo, I have thought about why children enjoy using it so much. Its open-endedness and the sense of control given to the children are very powerful features. After six weeks, Jane, one of my sixth graders, wrote in her math journal, "My partner and I are in charge of whatever it does." Carin wrote, "I'm glad Jane and I messed up so many times, because sometimes you can learn from your mistakes." She felt that being wrong in Logo wasn't the same as being wrong some other times, since errors could be corrected easily and privately. Also, errors in Logo often give clues to the solution, so they are not just mistakes. As Eric and Jane wrote in their journals, "I like experimenting with Logo."

My own understanding of the possibilities that Logo presents is still growing. While taking a computer course several years ago, I learned about Seymour Papert, the creator of Logo (Papert, 1980). He feels that the computer is a tool with which to think. When I see Logo providing the children with many opportunities to develop problem-solving skills, I agree with Papert. They formulate theories as they analyze a problem, work out solutions, and test those theories. For example, earlier in the year Jane and Carin worked on a task that required them to take the turtle on a backward walk around the screen while also making 10 left and 10 right turns. As they planned their moves, they visualized where they wanted the turtle to go and estimated how many degrees it would have to turn, as well as the number of steps it would need to take. Since I added the constraint that the turtle could not leave the screen, the girls were forced to make their moves carefully—mistakes meant starting over. In order to be successful, they needed to think.

Perhaps Maureen put it best when she wrote in her journal, "Logo is for using your mind."

A SERIES OF EXPLORATIONS

After several sessions of weekly Logo labs this fall, as I watched and listened to what my students were doing, I became aware that although the activities I had been planning were helping them learn to draw with Logo, that focus was not helping them explore any new mathematics—especially the eight students who had used Logo in fifth grade. Although now happily creating extensive, repetitive designs on colorful backgrounds, they were not learning anything new. I wondered what serious mathematics these sixth graders could be learning.

All of a sudden, it occurred to me that I had not seen any students making triangles, and I realized this could be a whole new area for them to explore. As a new and unfamiliar topic in Logo, it meant that the entire class could work together on the same ideas. Thus, I determined that, for the next six weeks, we would use our weekly Logo sessions to explore the properties of triangles.

Equilateral triangles: Week One

The first problem I gave the students was to create a triangle with sides 40 steps long. I was somewhat surprised by the amount of difficulty most of the pairs experienced. I was also surprised by what the various pairs learned from the activity. Each took different things away from their explorations.

One pair, Mike and Dane, both of whom had used Logo in fifth grade, experimented for an hour on the size of each of the angles as they tried to draw the triangle. Their first commands were: FD 40 RT 60 FD 40 RT 60 FD 40 RT 60. The results, shown in Figure 5.5(a), surprised them. They had used what they knew about making squares—the command RT 90—and decided that since the internal angle of an equilateral triangle is smaller than that of a square, they should turn right less than 90. They assumed, as did the rest of the class, that what they were prescribing were the interior angles of the triangle. But what they hadn't realized from their previous experience, was that they were turning the turtle around the outside of their figures. Therefore, in Logo they were actually prescribing the exterior angles. Since both the interior and exterior angles of a square are 90 degrees, it wasn't until this explora-

FIGURE 5.5. Several of Mike and Dane's Attempts at Creating the Triangle

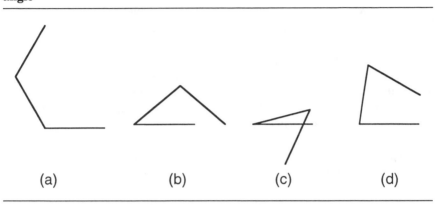

(a)   (b)   (c)   (d)

tion of triangles that the students were able to discover the difference between these types of angles.

After a few more attempts using estimation and trial-and-error, the boys realized they had to rethink what they were doing when they programmed the turtle to turn. They saw that they had to turn more, but were not sure why. As they drew each of their attempts on the screen, they worked on each angle independently of the others. (See Figure 5.5 (b)–(d) for a few of the figures these two boys drew.) Mike and Dane continued increasing and decreasing the individual angles until close to the end of class. Throughout their exploration, they didn't seem to notice that what they did to the size of one angle would affect the shape of their figure. After they had been working hard at the task for about an hour, a neighboring group told them the angles had to be the same. With that information they quickly found a "rough average" of their last angle measurements: 120 degrees. They used that amount and were very happy when they finally drew their triangle. They were amazed that they had been "so close and hadn't gotten it" on their own.

A second pair, Carin and Jane, also worked hard during the class period. They began as Mike and Dane had: Using what they knew about squares, the girls also first thought that the angle would be smaller than 90 degrees. After discovering their error, they pursued a similar strategy, increasing the size of the angle to between 100 and 135 degrees for the different angles in the triangle. However, through their investigations, the girls began to see a relationship between sides and angles, which Mike and Dane had missed.

> *Carin:* Oh, I know. Jane, look. We came up with this and we tried all
> these things and we didn't think they were right because we didn't

have the same degrees [in each of the angles]. They [the angles]
all need to be the same!

Jane: Why didn't we think of that? It would have to be the same.
Wouldn't it? It makes sense that it would be the same thing.

This was a powerful idea: that equal angles went with equal sides. Carin
had come close to solving their problem. However, it took them still longer
to see that the measurement was 120 degrees on those exterior angles. Now,
thinking that the angles should be all the same size, the girls experimented
with different numbers of degrees.

Jane: Okay, now (narrating as she types) FD 40 RT 115 FD 40 RT
115 FD 40. (She presses Return and Figure 5.6(a) appears on the
screen.)

Carin: It's not there. So it's more than 115. So it's 117 degrees.

Carin erased the previous figure and typed in: FD 40 RT 117 FD 40 RT 117
FD 40. The resulting figure was closer, but it still wasn't closed to form a
triangle. There was silence as the girls stared at the screen and then at each
other. They smiled wryly.

By this time, the girls had been working for more than 45 minutes, and
as I joined them, I felt their frustration.

Carin: We did it this way and we were this far away. (She points to
the small space between the last two sides of their triangle.) We
tried 115-degree angles and then 117, but it didn't work.

Mrs. Smith: Was 115, or was 117, closer to the triangle you are looking for?

Jane: 117.

Mrs. Smith: What might you want to try next then?

Carin: Something bigger than 117, 'cause that should get us closer.

FIGURE 5.6. Carin and Jane's Drawings

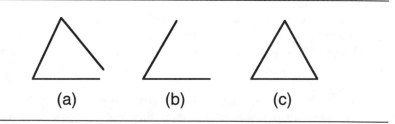

(a)   (b)   (c)

Jane: Let's try 120 degrees. (Narrating as she types.) FD 40 RT 120 FD 40.

She pushed Return and watched as the base line and the left side were drawn on the screen (see Figure 5.6(b)).

Jane: Then RT 120 again, right? (She asks Carin.)
Carin: Yeah, that looks right.

I wondered why Carin thought that, so I asked them to explain why it "looked right."

Jane: 'Cause it's the same. It [the top of the triangle] is right in the middle kind of, so it [the top angle] would be the same.

Jane pointed at the middle of the base line and then at the location of the other side angle.

Mrs. Smith: What do you mean, it's right in the middle, so it would be the same?

I realized that Jane was talking about symmetry and was using that idea to visualize what their triangle would look like, but I wanted to hear the language she used to explain it.

Jane: That [side] would be like that [side].

She pointed first to the left side and then to where she thought the right side would be drawn. Then she pressed Return and we saw the turtle turn 120 to point in the direction the third side would be drawn.

Carin: Yeah, it looks like the same thing.
Mrs. Smith: Oh, so it looks like the top is right above the middle of the bottom line?
Jane: Yeah.
Mrs. Smith: So why does that mean that this angle would be the same as this one?
Carin: Because if it [the top of the triangle] is in the middle, this side will look the same as the other side.
Jane: Because that's half of the middle, so they'd be the same.
Carin: (points to where the third side would be drawn) And that will be the other half.
Jane: And we want the sides to be equal.

Jane typed in the final command, FD 40, and pressed Return. The turtle traced the last side to form the equilateral triangle (Figure 5.6(c)). The girls looked at each other wide-eyed and smiled. Carin giggled.

> *Mrs. Smith*: Well?
> *Carin*: We did it!

The girls patted each other on the back.

Exterior angles and much more: Week Two

For our next Logo class the following week, I wanted to bring the class together to discuss their various discoveries from the first triangle exploration. I also wanted to discuss angle measurement so they could articulate what they had learned about interior and exterior angles. The individual groups knew a great deal about angles, but it was time to share their findings with their classmates.

Discussion began with my request that the students review for the class what they had done the previous week. Several groups shared the steps they had gone through to create the triangle with sides of 40 steps. Using an overhead, I drew a 40-step square and a 40-step triangle. I asked what they knew about the sizes of the angles on these figures. The class labeled them 90 and 120 degrees, respectively, as shown in Figure 5.7(a).

Next I wanted to see if they knew that they were measuring the exterior angles, so I extended the sides of the square, as shown in Figure 5.7(b), and asked a student to describe what the turtle was doing as it went around the square. At this point Eric's hand shot up. He said the reason the turtle needed 120 degrees for the triangle's angles was that it needed to turn more than it did on a square, since we were measuring around the outside of the triangle. I drew this as in Figure 5.7(c).

FIGURE 5.7. Overhead Displays During Group Discussion

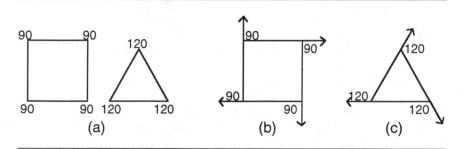

(a)   (b)   (c)

I asked if anyone had any other ideas to share. Carin and Jane suggested that a triangle with equal sides had equal angles. The class agreed that was true for this triangle and Helen then introduced the term "equilateral triangle." Jane added that both sides of this triangle were the same, or symmetrical.

Now Brian stated that he had just noticed that the turtle made a complete trip around the triangle, and he saw that since there were three 120-degree angles, the trip around the triangle described 360 degrees, which was a circle. This fact was exciting to many in the class. I asked if anyone thought that it was an important piece of information. Several agreed. Then Mary, who had been quiet so far, put her hand up slowly. She smiled with confidence and said she had noticed something. She speculated that we could create a figure of any shape if we divided the 360 degrees by the number of sides in the figure, but she wondered if it would work only when all the sides were equal in length. She said she was looking forward to investigating her ideas. I was as excited as Mary about her conjecture, but at this point the rest of the class was not following her. Later, I would set up an activity so the other students could explore Mary's generalization.

Isosceles triangles: Weeks Three and Four

In the meantime, I wanted the students to use what they had already learned from their investigations of equilateral triangles to explore the relationship between the angles and sides of triangles. I also wanted them to explore the implications of a fact they had already established—namely, that the exterior angles add up to 360 degrees. I asked the students to create some triangles with two equal sides at least 10 steps longer or shorter than the base. Then I asked them to see if they could come up with a rule they could use to draw this type of triangle.

Just as Carin and Jane had noticed the symmetry of the equilateral triangle, Mary and Helen realized that the top of this triangle would be over the midpoint of the base, too. Therefore, they speculated, if the two base angles are equal, when they drew an imaginary line up through the middle of the base the sides would meet there. The following dialogue shows how they made use of this symmetry, as well as their knowledge that the turtle trip around the figure added up to 360 degrees:

> *Helen:* We'll draw the base first. How long should it be? 50 steps, okay?
> *Mary:* Yeah, and then turn RT 100 degrees.

The girls had already decided that they could probably use any number greater than 90 degrees (a right angle) for the two base angles.

Helen: Okay. RT 100, then FD 100. (She types in the commands and hits Return. The figure shows a 50-step base and a 100-step side.) Not quite. It's not right in the middle yet.

Mary: No, it has to be more.

Helen: We'll go FD 40 more. (They watch as the side lengthens. They want to get it up to just above the midpoint of the base line.) A little more. FD 10.

Mary: Let's try that. (The result of the last command is shown in Figure 5.8(a).)

Helen: I think that's perfect.

Next they moved on to thinking about the measurement of the last angle of this triangle.

Mary: If we have 100-degree angles on both sides, we'd have 160 degrees left.

Since the girls knew that the two base angles would be equal on this triangle, they had subtracted their sum from 360 degrees, the total number of degrees in the triangle's exterior angles. The difference, 160, would give them the number of degrees of the remaining angle.

Helen: So, RT 160.

Mary: Now, how much forward did we go before [on the other side of their triangle]?

FIGURE 5.8. Helen and Mary's Drawings

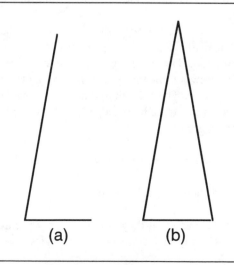

(a)   (b)

Helen: We went FD 100, FD 40, FD 10, so that's 150 steps. (She
   types in the command. See Figure 5.8(b) for the result.) YES!
Mary: Holy Smokes!
Helen: All right! All right!

They wrote their commands in their journal and also drew a picture of their
triangle. Then they erased their work on the screen and tried it again in order
to check it.

Mary: I think this is like too amazing, to do this the first time.
Helen: But maybe this is all we have to do. Find the middle, and then
   . . . All we have to do is go up in what you think is the middle!

At this point the girls called me over. They were very excited. During their
discussion with me they often interrupted each other, finishing each other's
thoughts.

Mrs. Smith: Do you think you can write a rule that will always work to
   draw these triangles?
Helen: No.
Mary: Well, yes we can! Because the sides . . .
Helen: (interrupting) Like you gotta make them go to . . .
Mrs. Smith: Then write a rule for triangles that have two sides the
   same length and try to prove it.
Mary: Try to prove it? Well, if you make a line up the middle . . .
Helen: (To the teacher) For a triangle with two equal sides, you make
   the bottom, go up until you get to the middle . . .
Mrs. Smith: Can you write it down?

At this point the girls began discussing their "rule." Their conversation again
reflects how they both really were thinking the same way about their work.

Helen: Okay. If you make your base, then you turn any number you
   want [at a base angle], then go up the side until you get to the mid-
   dle of the base.
Mary: Both turns [angles] on each side of the base have to be the same.
   So the top one is the difference. And all turns . . .
Helen: (Interrupting again) All turns have to equal 360!
Mary: I think that works! We have to write it down.

Here is the statement Mary and Helen came up with to share with the class.

Isosceles Triangle: The angles on either side of the base have to be the
same. The top angle added with both of the bottom ones has to equal

360 degrees. The sides have to meet an imaginary line going up from the middle of the base. The two bottom angles can be any number more than 90.

They decided they were not yet ready to call it a rule since they felt there might be more information needed.

The following week, Mary and Helen presented their statement to their classmates, who then used it to create their own isosceles triangles. Later, other students made revisions to the statement.

Interior angles: Week Five

I began the next Logo class with a discussion about interior angles. It seemed to me that most of the groups really had not yet thought much about them. I was interested in whether they could see any relationship between the measurement of interior and exterior angles. In addition, individual students had learned a variety of different facts about the angles of squares and triangles.

In the discussion, Dan volunteered that the interior angles of an equilateral triangle have to be 60 degrees since the degrees of the interior and exterior angles need to add up to 180 at each angle. Drawing the diagram in Figure 5.9 on the overhead, he was able to show the class what he meant. The class agreed that his idea made sense. Then he showed us that the sum of the three interior angles of an equilateral triangle was also 180 degrees.

Brian said that the interior angles of any triangle would equal 180 degrees. Students looked at their journals to check the triangles from their earlier explorations: All supported this idea.

Next I asked the class what they thought the sum of the interior angles of a square was. Ted said it would be 360 degrees since all the angles are 90

FIGURE 5.9. Dan's Drawing Illustrating that Interior Angles Are Each 60 Degrees

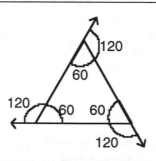

degrees and there are four angles in a square. He also volunteered that there were two isosceles triangles in each square. This was challenged by a few kids, but as Ted re-explained his thoughts, there was growing agreement. Eric stated that they had to be isosceles since all four sides of the square were equal and the diagonal through the middle of the square was longer than the sides. Others said that when a rectangle was divided diagonally, each half would be a triangle. Various students drew differently shaped rectangles and divided them in two.

ASSESSING STUDENTS' UNDERSTANDING

After the first two weeks of their triangle explorations, I wanted to know what each student was thinking about triangles. I also wanted to have a record of how their understanding of triangles grew during their investigations. Therefore, I asked the students to each make a chart in their Logo journal. On one side they listed everything they knew about triangles at that time. On the other side they listed anything they thought might be true, or ideas or questions they had about triangles.

The variety of ideas on their charts revealed to me the wide span of understanding in the class at that time. Some students, Carin, for example, wrote only that triangles had three sides and three corners. Others had more to say. For example, Mary described equilaterals and Mike wrote that exterior angles equal 360 degrees. Since students' experience up to that point had been primarily with equilateral triangles, the students' charts also showed that some overgeneralizations were being made on that basis. For example, several students wrote that triangles were symmetrical.

Although some statements were not correct as written, I wanted to give the students the opportunity to discover this for themselves. After writing the lists in their journals, the students began their investigations with isosceles triangles. Through this additional experience, they would be able to catch some of their overgeneralizations and inaccuracies.

Two weeks later, I gave each student a copy of a chart that listed all their ideas about triangles. In order to start a discussion, I asked them for comments. Again, this was an opportunity for the students to learn from each other. As I expected, various students brought up different items for discussion. They saw immediately that the chart contained several overgeneralizations, pointing out that "the statements were not always true." For example, Eric said triangles were not always symmetrical.

Their revisions to the list indicated to me the class' increased understanding of triangles. However, since this was a group discussion and revision process, it didn't reflect what individual students understood about triangles. Since I wanted to find out what each child knew, at the start of the next Logo class, in the sixth week of their triangle investigations, I asked them to make new charts in their journals, listing what they knew about triangles at that time.

Figure 5.10 provides evidence of the increased understanding of triangles that was gained from our explorations. It shows the lists of three of the students mentioned earlier. While Mike's second list shows increased knowledge, the gains in Carin's and Mary's knowledge are more obvious. At the start, Carin had been very insecure and hesitant about working with the computers and Logo. As time progressed, her confidence grew and she became quite willing to take risks. These girls also put a great deal of effort into their work. The types of ideas they explored were quite different from Mike's. The girls' lists also reflect the variety of ideas that the class had explored. Only three weekly Logo sessions had passed since they wrote their first individual lists.

These lists only sample the class' ideas about triangles. As they illustrate, student understanding of triangles had grown. Also, the variety of learning that

FIGURE 5.10. "What I Know About Triangles"

Mike's first list
1. Triangles are shapes.
2. Triangles have 3 sides and 3 angles.
3. The angles all have to equal 360 degrees.

Mike's second list
1. Triangles have 3 sides and 3 angles.
2. The sum of the outer angles equals 360 degrees.
3. Equilateral triangles have the same angles.
4. Triangles are usually symmetrical.

Carin's first list
1. Triangles have 3 sides and 3 corners

Carin's second list
1. Triangles equal 360 degrees on the outside angles.
2. Equilateral triangles have equal sides and angles.
3. Isosceles triangles have different sides and angles.
4. Inside angles equal 180 degrees.
5. The taller a triangle is, the less degrees there will be in the top angle, the more on the bottom ones.

Mary's first list
1. Triangles have 3 sides and angles.
2. Equilaterals have equal angles.

Mary's second list
1. Triangles have 3 sides and 3 angles.
2. Isosceles triangles have two sides the same and the bottom different (see our statement).
3. Equilaterals have all the same angles and the same length of sides.
4. Any triangle can be made by dividing 360 degrees 3 ways with any number in each group.

took place is significant. Since they began their explorations from different levels of comprehension and then made different choices as they went along, the students often constructed different understandings out of the same tasks. Depending on their interests and efforts, they explored different ideas and developed different degrees of understanding. Yet, almost two months worth of weekly sessions had grown out of only two problems: draw an equilateral triangle and draw an isosceles triangle.

AND NEXT?

As the children extend their accumulated knowledge through new explorations, I see them working with other geometric concepts. For example, they are now using Logo to investigate other polygons. Mary is already at work on her conjecture about creating a figure of any shape by dividing 360 degrees by the number of its sides. Others are thinking about ways to create circles. What will come after these, I don't yet know. But I do know that there is no end to the mathematics this class can uncover when we "do Logo."

REFERENCE

Papert, S. (1980). *Mindstorms: Children, computers and powerful ideas*. New York: Basic Books.

$$+ \quad - \quad \times \quad \div$$

TEACHING WITH TERSE TOOLS

Daniel Chazan

One perspective on the two stories we have just read is to view them as cases of teaching mathematics with computer tools—in Susan Smith's case, Logo, and in Nina Koch's case, Green Globs. To explore how these tools support learning, I have found it useful to anthropomorphize the software and to think about each program's interaction style. In contrast to garrulous and judgmental tutors or drill-and-practice programs, these two programs are not conversationalists. They speak tersely to the initiated, and perhaps cryptically to the uninitiated. Interestingly, other inquiry tools—microworld software (various geometry-conjecturing environments such as The Geometric SuperSupposer, The Geometer's Sketchpad®, and Cabri Geometre™), calculators, or manipulatives—share this characteristic; they are also laconic and nonjudgmental characters.

When presented with a command it cannot recognize, Logo's chattiest response is, "I don't know how to . . . " Otherwise, Logo carries out whatever command the user types. In the turtle geometry mode, the turtle acts; it either moves, draws, or picks up a new pen. Logo doesn't make any independent judgments. It does not know what the user intends and does not evaluate whether a command brings the user closer to his or her goal. The user must decide whether the turtle acted as intended.

Similarly, when Green Globs cannot parse the symbols a user types, it responds with, "I don't understand." Otherwise, it makes a graph that corresponds to the string of symbols entered by the user. If the graph goes through (or near enough to) a glob, the glob "explodes." Again, Green Globs doesn't decide whether this graph was the intended one; the user must make that decision. Frequently, users will miss globs they aim at and hit unintended targets. Green Globs has no way of knowing when this is the case.

These kinds of terse tools can be useful when one seeks a classroom in which students have the authority to decide what is true. These tools bring another source of evidence into the classroom, evidence that students can use to support their claims. Thus, rather than go to the teacher or to a text's answer key to find out whether an answer is right or wrong, students can go to the tool to test their ideas. The terse, nonjudgmental feedback indicates to a discerning student whether his or her idea is correct or not. However, the decision rests with the student; the student must decide how to interpret the feedback.

Susan Smith's and Nina Koch's stories illustrate some of the power and challenges of bringing such tools into the learning environment. Specifically, I raise three issues for consideration.

Use of the tool does not guarantee that students will be working on the teacher's mathematical agenda.

In addition to being terse and cryptic in their feedback to students, these programs are not directive; they do not forcefully promote a particular agenda. They are pliable and open to whatever uses students put them to. Thus, when teachers introduce such tools into their classrooms, they must structure activities in which their pedagogical goals are embedded. In addition, when students pursue explorations that stray from the teacher's initial focus, the teacher must assess the value of those explorations and, at times, flexibly adapt their goals to the students' pursuits.

For example, Smith points out that while her students were initially learning to draw with Logo, she felt that, although they were having fun, they were not exploring new mathematics. She had to structure their activity by asking them to create triangles. Only then did they begin to examine angles and the properties of geometric shapes, and only then did Smith begin to feel that her students were learning mathematics.

In Koch's case, Jason and Scott did not focus solely on the activity's agenda of exploring the ways in which the coefficients of a quadratic equation affect its graph. In order to get the program to do what they wanted, they had to figure out how to generate numbers between 1 and the negative numbers, which, in turn, led to questions about decimals. Koch is quite clear that she valued this exploration and considered it an important opportunity for her students to engage with arithmetic ideas that they had not yet mastered.

These tools can challenge students' ideas, but they don't suggest alternatives or help students reflect on their experiences.

These two tools are not pedagogues. They respond to questions, but do not offer their own points of view. There is much that can be learned from them, but learners are required to use any prior knowledge they have and to be active participants. A teacher can then use the results of students' interactions with the tools to help the students reflect on and develop their mathematical conceptions.

When Smith introduced the challenge of creating an equilateral triangle, she found that most students thought that repeating FD 40 RT 60 three times would create the desired shape. That is, they thought of the angles in Logo as interior, rather than exterior, angles. The students were surprised when the turtle did not draw the figure they expected. Logo left it to them to decide that it didn't work, and they had to figure out what was mistaken about their conception. Through trial and error (and a hint from some classmates), Mike and Dane, for example, eventually figured out that an input of 120 degrees results in the triangle they were after, but that still did not mean that they understood why their initial try didn't work. Here was an opportunity for a rich discussion.

Similarly, Jason and Scott in Koch's class were looking for a number between 1 and the negative numbers in order to create a graph that was slightly wider than the one on the screen. When they tried 0 and saw the resulting horizontal line, they concluded that they needed a number between 0 and 1. However, the software did not provide suggestions. They needed to bring their prior knowledge to bear. Koch played an important role by asking questions that challenged the boys to articulate what they already knew or believed about the coefficient they were looking for. Her questions eventually elicited the word "between," which, according to Koch, seemed to cue Scott to try a "raggedy-looking decimal." Once the students came up with that idea, they were ready to turn back to the computer to explore graphs with coefficients of .5, .7, and so on.

Terse can be cryptic or even enigmatic.

Finally, with this type of tool, teachers must decide how much they are going to help students understand the tool's feedback. One danger is that if students do not understand enough about the program and the mathematics that one needs to speak to it, then they will not be able to understand or appreciate the feedback given by the computer. On the other hand, if we insist that students know everything about the mathematics used by the tool, then it is no longer a tool for learning mathematics, but rather a tool for those who already know mathematics.

On a purely syntactical level, in order to use these tools effectively, students need to learn to speak to the program. In Logo, they must learn the elementary turtle commands (FD, BK, LT, RT, etc.). In Green Globs, they must learn that the program expects expressions written only in certain forms: As Jason says, "y equals . . . "

Beyond these syntactical issues, students must be able to interpret the feedback they are given and figure out why the program did what it did. For example, Smith's students were initially surprised that they didn't get a triangle from the commands FD 40 RT 60 FD 40 RT 60 FD 40. Yet, they were able to interpret the results and, thus, did not get derailed. They looked at the drawing resulting from their commands and concluded that RT needed a larger input.

One can imagine other situations where students might get derailed by feedback that they find mysterious or cryptic. For example, Jason starts with $y = 1(x - 1)^2 + 1$. His choice of 1s for A, H, and K is a fortuitous one. Had he chosen 100, 0, 0, he might have thought that no graph appeared on the screen (because that graph is indistinguishable from the y-axis). This feedback might be very confusing to someone who did not really know about scaling in graphs and how graphs represent expressions (see Goldenberg, 1988, for further examples).

Thus, it is important for the teacher to figure out what sorts of knowledge are necessary for students before they use a "terse" tool, lest students find their interactions unsatisfactory.

For further reading, see suggested reading listed below.

REFERENCE

Goldenberg, P. (1988). Mathematical, technical, and pedagogical challenges in the graphical representation of function. *Journal of Mathematical Behavior, 7*(2), 135–173.

SUGGESTED READING

Abelson, H., & diSessa, A. (1981). *Turtle geometry*. Cambridge, MA: MIT Press.
Chazan, D., & Houde, R. (1989). *How to use conjecturing and microcomputers to teach high school mathematics*. Reston, VA: National Council of Teachers of Mathematics. [Geometric Supposer]

Cuoco, A. (1990). *Investigations in algebra*. Cambridge, MA: MIT Press.

Dugdale, S., & Kibbey, D. (1990). Beyond the evident content goals. *The Journal of Mathematical Behavior, 9*(3), 199–288. [Green Globs and others]

Feurzig, W. (1988). Apprentice tools. In R. Nickerson & P. Zodhiates (Eds.), *Technology in education* (pp. 97–120). Hillsdale, NJ: Lawrence Erlbaum.

Harvard Educational Review. (1989). *Visions for the use of computers in classroom instruction*. Cambridge, MA: Author. (Reprinted from *HER* (1989), Issues 1 and 2)

Nesher, P. (1989). Microworlds in mathematics education. In L. Resnick (Ed.), *Knowing, learning and instruction* (pp. 187–215). Hillsdale, NJ: Lawrence Erlbaum.

Nickerson, R., & Zodhiates, P. (Eds.). (1988). *Technology in education: Looking toward 2020*. Hillsdale, NJ: Lawrence Erlbaum.

Papert, S. (1980). *Mindstorms: Children, computers and powerful ideas*. New York: Basic Books. [Logo]

Pea, R., & Sheingold, K. (Eds.). (1987). *Mirror of minds: Patterns of experience in educational computing*. Norwood, NJ: Ablex.

Schwartz, J. (1986). The power and peril of the particular. *Machine-Mediated Learning, 1*(4), 345–354.

Wah, A., & Piciotto, H. (1993). A new algebra: Tools, themes, concepts. *Journal of Mathematical Behavior, 12*(1), 19–42.

Starting the Conversation

Deborah Schifter

By 1989, when the project that produced this book was conceived, Summer-Math for Teachers had been working for six years at helping teachers in western Massachusetts construct a new mathematics pedagogy. Although founded well before publication of the *NCTM Standards*, the program has been guided by a similar vision of mathematics education reform.

Historically, program activities have fallen into three main categories, but the premise that continues to underlie them all is that teachers must identify and examine their enacted assumptions about mathematics and how it is learned and, in the light of new and evolving understandings in these large areas, reconsider their own teaching. Thus, one set of activities involves project staff teaching teachers mathematics, in-service lessons functioning as laboratories in which one's own experiences as a mathematics learner can be studied. A second set of activities concentrates on student thinking—teachers conducting one-on-one interviews of children, analyzing videotapes of researchers conducting such interviews, and studying videotapes of children solving problems together. The third set focuses on discussion of the structure and goals of the mathematics curriculum. Throughout, teachers and staff engage in extended reflection, oral—in large groups, small groups, and one-on-one settings—and written.

To staff making weekly follow-up visits to participating teachers' classrooms, it was evident that, as a result of engaging in such activities, some teachers *were* dramatically transforming their practice: Student thinking and mathematical discourse had moved to the center of their mathematics programs.

However, many others were failing to make changes. The reasons given were varied: "I don't see how my third graders are going to learn multiplication unless I tell them what they need to know." "Sure, you can arrange a classroom like that with a group of adults, but you can't do it with a roomful of ten-year-olds." More troubling still were those teachers who were convinced that in introducing manipulatives or inaugurating a once-a-week problem-solving session they had successfully transformed their practice and had no more changing to do.

As I considered the variation in how project activities were being interpreted, I concluded that if the only pictures teachers had of grade school mathematics instruction were derived from their own histories as mathematics students and teachers, it would be beyond the powers of most to imagine a roomful of children involved in discourse about, say, different ways to solve a missing-addend problem or whether multiplication is commutative. What was happening in different classrooms needed to be brought into the open. I knew my own sense of possibility was greatly enriched by observing, in a variety of classroom settings, different groups of children with their teachers. In effect, I was being shown how the reform agenda my colleagues and I were interpreting in our courses and institutes was being interpreted in turn, and put into play, in the classrooms I was visiting. In the same way, I felt, making detailed descriptions of classroom events available to teachers could expand their limited stock of images of possibility.

TEACHERS WRITE PAST THE JARGON

My first idea was to invite researchers to spend time in individual teachers' classrooms, recording instructional process and capturing student dialogue. The researchers would be asked to trace the development of a mathematical theme or idea over a period of weeks or even months—third graders' conceptions of multiplication, say, or high school students' thoughts about irrational numbers. Their purpose would be not so much to contribute to cognitive research on children's understanding of multiplication or irrational numbers, as to provide accurate, vivid, believable narratives showing real students in real classrooms enacting a process most teachers could not otherwise picture.

As I let this idea steep, the conviction grew that, if there was merit to this idea of narratives of classroom process, then there were also good reasons why the teachers themselves, rather than visiting researchers, ought to do the writing. Three were particularly compelling: First, I thought it important that these narratives convey in as much detail as possible the thought processes—the instructional intentions, the observations and analyses, and the decision making—of their authors; second, I knew that teacher-readers would feel a more immediate connection to a narrative voice conveying the texture of unfamiliar classroom process from the perspective of a fellow teacher; and third, writing about their own instruction would, I believed, extend and deepen teacher-authors' understanding of their changing practice.

As the Mathematics Process Writing Project (MPWP) began to crystallize around these convictions, the next order of business was to devise a structure that would support the writing. I began to canvass writing teachers, hunting down books and articles about process writing and about teaching writing, and I thought back on my own experiences as a writing student and writer. The result was a design for a course in which teacher-participants would write for weekly meetings at which they would share and discuss their work; in addition, they would receive regular feedback from me (their course instructor) and they would be asked to read published papers for both style and content.

When the teachers finally set to work, some actually wrote in ways that fit quite closely my original conception—following over time the development of a particular mathematical issue or theme. But others chose to explore central pedagogical concerns less tied to specific mathematics content—for example, addressing in a mixed-ability setting the needs of "math stars" accustomed to pull-out programs, or supporting high school students who have missed out on the fundamentals of arithmetic. Still others wrote frankly about confronting their histories of failure at mathematics or described experiencing the challenges they faced working to transform their instruction. (These latter essays appear in Schifter, *What's Happening in Math Class?, Volume 2: Reconstructing Professional Identities*, 1996.)

As teachers' writings expanded the scope of the project, they also sharpened my sense of what would be required for them to be effective. Through the weekly assignments and the feedback I offered, I contributed to shaping their work. My "interventions" had two principal purposes—to push teachers to think more deeply about their own teaching, and to help them create narratives that would be useful to other readers. With both objectives in mind, I tried to steer teachers away from using abstractions, like "constructivist teaching" or "the student-centered classroom," that convey little or no meaning on their face.

For many, the task of characterizing their practice without recourse to the shorthand of educational jargon proved a difficult challenge. However, it had early-on become apparent to me that this was perhaps the major contribution these teachers could make—offering interpretations of the rhetoric through specific and detailed descriptions of classroom process.

There was much evidence that using the rhetoric of reform could retard, rather than advance, the *goal* of reform. In previous in-service courses, I had seen that teachers wanted a name for what they had learned. Some used the word "constructivism," others talked about "doing SummerMath for Teachers," and still others talked about "IT." All these teachers appeared to believe that there was some single method or approach that "it" was, that "it" had been taught in the course, and that everyone else had learned the same "it." But for some, "it" meant using manipulatives or other alternative representations, or students working in groups, or emphasizing word problems; to others, "it" meant encouraging students to look for patterns, offer conjectures, entertain alternative solution methods; to still others, "it" meant de-emphasizing "the right answer" or "placing student thinking at the center of instruction." Nonetheless, most had carried on as if they were talking about the same thing, which, they agreed, it was regrettably impossible to describe in common English.

To be honest, it was not only SummerMath for Teachers participants who had this problem. In 1986 when staff met to design project assessment procedures, we faced a similar challenge. We agreed that a teacher's fluency in constructivist jargon did not necessarily reflect what we were trying to teach. We also agreed that new instructional strategies or tools—for example, small groups, manipulatives, and computers, all of which we used in our work with teachers—could be adopted without what we regarded as significant change in practice. On the other hand, we each could identify teachers who, we felt, *had* transformed their practice significantly and *were* moving along a trajectory we supported. However, it took a year of discussion to characterize stages of that trajectory and then to begin to design an assessment instrument to capture the distance traveled along it (Schifter & Simon, 1992). Presenting to one another episodes we had witnessed in individual classrooms or recounting our one-on-one conversations with teachers proved the most important component of the process.

Similar problems were—and still are—evident at conferences of teacher educators, researchers, and policy makers, where everyone is fluent in the rhetoric, but it is far from obvious that we share the same meanings. For example, although any number of things might be meant by the phrase, "the *NCTM Standards*," educators frequently invoke *it* the way SummerMath for Teachers participants invoke "it."

When the first set of papers was completed, I shared some with colleagues, anxious to hear how they would be received. In one of the first responses I got, a preservice teacher educator reported, "All semester long we'd been talking about 'discovery' and 'discourse,' but the students didn't really get what we meant until they read Virginia Brown's paper. After that, they kept referring to her paper in every discussion we had."

Readers of this anthology will decide for themselves how useful Brown's and her colleagues' interpretations will prove for them as they grapple with the challenge of making sense, in their classrooms, of the rhetoric of reform. But as these authors describe in detail episodes from their own teaching, as they articulate their instructional intentions, their analyses of student thinking, and their pedagogical decisions, they move us past the jargon to reflect on how basic principles might be realized in specific courses of action. By making their stories public, these teachers provide grounding for much-needed discussion of the possible meanings of phrases like "discovery" and "discourse."

FROM IMAGES TO PRINCIPLES AND BACK: SOME WAYS TO READ THIS BOOK

Although Mathematics Process Writing Project participants wrote with an audience of teachers in mind, their narratives speak to the concerns of other constituencies within the education community. The papers intersect a range of issues relevant to the work of education policy makers, school administrators and supervisors, and teacher educators, among others. With their particular professional responsibilities in mind, members of these constituencies can read and discuss both the teachers' stories and the accompanying essays—moving from image to principle and back as questions are raised and thinking is stimulated.

Where teacher narratives represent enacted interpretations of basic principles, the essays by teacher educators are intended to address explicitly those principles. The narratives are rooted in the specific; the essays extend the narratives back to the general and the theoretical. Martin Simon draws on teachers' stories to suggest how they might be read to think through the implications for classroom practice of constructivist views of learning; Joan Ferrini-Mundy calls attention to what they tell us about how adopting new goals for student understanding affects other aspects of mathematics instruction; Virginia Stimpson alerts us to what they have to say about issues that arise during the shift to new and dramatically different patterns of classroom interaction; Raffaella Borasi considers what they can contribute to discussions about issues of diversity and inclusion; and, finally, Daniel Chazan examines what they suggest about how employing popular instructional tools—in this case, computer technology—can support or constrain a transformed mathematics instruction.

Each essayist starts from an assigned set of narratives to illustrate the principle he or she was asked to discuss. Whereas these teacher educators help us take some first steps toward reading the narratives in the light of general principles, readers are invited to return to the specific and, breaking through the chapter boundaries that confined the essayists, further reflect on and refine those principles. For example, in Chapter 1 Simon refers to Elizabeth Clark's narrative as he explicates the idea that "learning happens in response to challenges. It may be necessary for students to explore some alternative conceptions before returning to the more appropriate one, this time with a firmer understanding of why it is appropriate." And then, commenting, "In several of the episodes, there seems to be an expectation established that learning can be derived from incorrect solutions," he recalls, as further illustration, an event described in Virginia Brown's narrative. Just as Simon does here, readers, once having encountered a principle, are able to return to the stories to identify still other interpretations that may advance the development of the new pedagogy.

Many teachers include accounts of students' "alternative conceptions," that is, constructions that, in a conventional mathematics class, simply would be dismissed as "wrong." For example, most of Joanne Moynahan's students' responses are "Division" when asked, "Which of the four basic operations could replace 'of' in the statement '⅓ of 15 = 5'?" Nina Koch's student, Jason, looking for a number between .3 and .4, tested ".3.5" and ".31/2."

Many of Donna Scanlon's students, asked to calculate the perimeter of "9 pentagons in a row," came up with the same answer, "33."

No one will be surprised that as students impose their own interpretations and create their own theories, much of what they construct is, if viewed conventionally, just wrong. The division sign does not replace "of" in " ⅓ of 15 = 5"; according to convention, ".3.5" does not represent a number between .3 and .4; and the answer to the question Scanlon posed to her students was 29, not 33. However, the authors of these papers show us that, more important than these answers being wrong, is that they are not *merely* wrong. They issue from a process containing elements of logic, which, when identified as such, can be mobilized to help students work through the illogic in their constructions.

Inviting students to voice their partially formed thoughts can be a scary prospect for teachers, especially those who worry whether their students are taking mistaken ideas away from a lesson. Listening to all that confusion can be overwhelming. Readers may recall an example from Chapter 2, where Virginia Bastable represents this dilemma through the story of Alice:

> Right now I'm feeling like my classroom is a confused mess. . . . I was having trouble keeping the whole group going in a linear fashion. James was bugged that his calculator wasn't good enough. I was wondering if my students' understanding of decimals was strong enough that they knew which of the answers *was* closer to 5. On top of all that I kept thinking that I shouldn't have let that statement about zero go by without comment. . . . How do you deal with a class discussion when so many issues are brought up?

Using the literary device of a correspondence between two teachers, Bastable answers the question by interpreting the same classroom events differently.

> Do I have days like that? Oh yes, and when I do, I feel good about them. To me it sounds like your students are engaged, are sorting out their ideas, and are working hard! . . . Your students are giving voice to their mathematical ideas. Sometimes they are right, sometimes wrong, but they are talking about what they are thinking. Since each student has his or her own way of thinking, the variety of comments and approaches can contribute to a sense of confusion. Yet in this confusion, sometimes through it, they can sort out their thoughts.

Bastable then turns the tables, offering a counterinterpretation of the more traditional classroom in which the voicing of mathematical ideas is more carefully controlled.

I am thinking about your classroom experiences and how they compare with the scenario you related about Karl and the $\sqrt{10}$. That was an orderly classroom. Students were quiet, watching your work. You didn't have the sense that it was confusing. But look what happened. Even while they were quiet, and, you thought, attentive, students were forming their own ideas. Again, some of these were right and some were wrong, but *you* didn't get to hear them. It just wasn't part of class to discuss them. Whatever ideas they had were left unchallenged.

By sharing with us this fictional conversation between two teachers (which, she has shared privately, is an actual conversation that has taken place in her own head), Bastable alerts readers to the need for teachers to redefine their responsibilities as they transform their practice—including, in this case, their criteria for judging the success of a lesson.

Perhaps more disconcerting to teachers than being overwhelmed by a babel of student ideas is being greeted by deep and prolonged silence in response to the question one is counting on to unlock a lesson. This is an issue raised in Virginia Stimpson's essay in Chapter 3, where, referring to Jill Lester's description of a first day of school, she suggests that a teacher's willingness to tolerate silence can make space available for students to discover their own mathematical voices. Looking beyond the confines of that chapter for other instances of silence, we find one at the start of Anne Hendry's unit on measurement, when her would-be Pilgrims are told, "This ship cannot sail until you tell me how big it is."

"Well, what should we do? Who has an idea?" I asked. Thus our discussion on measurement began . . . or I thought it would begin. But there was a period of silence—a long period of silence.

Here is another instance, from Virginia Brown's class:

I decided to continue with this line of thinking and asked if there are any more combinations that equal 36. . . . The children were quiet as mice for the next few minutes.

Teachers frequently are exhorted to provide "wait time" to allow students to think about the questions posed. Brown's description of her third graders "intently studying the board, foreheads in a frown, faces fixed in intense concentration" likely represents the image that first springs to mind on hearing it.

But Hendry's and Lester's detailed descriptions of the uncomfortable silences they endure in their classrooms expand our repertoire of understandings of what wait time may entail. Lester waits, and waits, until finally one child musters the courage to do something (anything?), starting the children on the road to figuring out how to be in this strange, new kind of classroom. Hendry, too, waits, until one of her students, however tentatively, ventures an idea that unfreezes discussion. These stories make the issue of wait time more complex—not only is it a matter of giving students time for obviously productive thinking, but also, on occasion, it may mean allowing students to sit with their confusions, making everyone in the room, teacher and students alike, uncomfortable. How can one judge whether this apparently barren time is, in fact, productive? How does a teacher learn to endure such discomfort? As Stimpson ponders the implications of Signet's weeks-long wait, so do we.

Readers not only are invited to revisit the narratives to test further the meanings of the principles articulated in the essays—as I have done in the preceding paragraphs—but are, in addition, urged to explore other issues only implicitly addressed in this volume. The rhetorical motifs around which this volume is organized—the themes instanced by teacher narratives and reflected upon by teacher educators—are not uniquely determined by the papers themselves, but result from editorial choice. Other thematic assignments would group the narratives differently. For example, for interpretations of the principle, "Ongoing assessment of student understanding should guide teachers' instructional decisions," one might look to Moynahan, Bastable, and Koch. Their narratives, in particular, present opportunities for reflection on the kind of listening required for such "ongoing assessment." Other readers, intrigued by the possibilities writing assignments promise for such assessment, can turn to Riddle and Smith.

It is not uncommon for supervisors and administrators who believe themselves committed to the new pedagogy to interpret it in terms of past reform movements whose premises are in conflict with this one. For example, they may encourage their teachers to enact the *NCTM Standards*, but when visiting classrooms for purposes of evaluation, look for goal-directedness, coverage, and closure—criteria generally inappropriate for an instructional practice centered on problem-generated mathematical exploration. Through the kind of detailed and specific accounts of classroom process provided by teacher narratives and the discussion of principles offered by teacher educators, those who have authority over teachers can come to appreciate that learning may be going on when they observe a class engaged in debate about a question whose answer seems trivial to adults (for example, when Brown's students wondered whether multiplication is commutative); or they can be led to see that productive teaching can be consistent with a classroom in which students appear to be milling about chaotically (as when Hendry's students decided to measure each other, the classroom, their desks, and the rug using "Zeb's foot"); or they can allow that teachers will sometimes be confused (like Bastable's "Alice," after the class discussion that brought up "so many mathematical issues''). As novel classroom processes and structures become familiar and understood in terms of principles of learning, the ability to judge both student and teacher performance in terms appropriate for the vision of the *Standards* will develop apace.

The narratives by Sheinbach, Gagnon, and Riddle and the essay by Borasi included in Chapter 4, thematizing the implications of policy decisions concerned with heterogeneous grouping, "inclusion," and mainstreaming, should be of particular interest to policy makers and administrators. And as they think through and discuss the complexities of the issues, other narratives can offer additional insights. For example, Bastable's story is based on "mixed-group" mathematics classes within a tracked high school system; Scanlon writes about both her basic-level and college prep classes; Signet works with children in a pull-out program; and Koch teaches high school students in a remedial class.

Where matters pertinent to their work are not sufficiently addressed in the essays, administrators may draw their own lessons from the teachers' stories. Scanlon's and Riddle's discussions of the concerns of the families of unhappy students are a case in point. Their narratives, which set this issue in the context of theoretical and practical commitments to student learning, can be helpful to administrators devising policies for communicating with students' families or preparing for their own meetings with concerned parents or guardians.

As mathematics instruction undergoes the dramatic transformation envisioned by reformers, pre- and in-service teacher education efforts must undergo concomitant and analogous shifts. Teacher educators and those who shape teacher education policy can find in the narratives bases for programmatically oriented discussions of important indicators of teachers' educational needs, many of which are specifically identified in the essays.

Thus, where Ferrini-Mundy is "intrigued" by the challenge Bastable and Scanlon take on of charting a mathematical course and of building powerful mathematical connections, the issue for teacher development policy becomes, "How can teacher education programs begin to prepare teachers to take on such challenges?" Simon observes that Hendry, Clark, Brown, and Moynahan have made their students' mathematical knowledge central considerations in their instructional decision making, but the programmatic question raised is, "What sorts of teacher development activities can help teachers learn to assess their students' mathematical knowledge in order to make their decisions?" And while Chazan reads Koch's and Smith's stories to analyze the characteristics of computer software used to support mathematical inquiry, the concern for teacher education programs is, "How can teachers learn to employ such tools to meet the goals of a reformed mathematics pedagogy?"

REFERENCES

Schifter, D. (Ed.). (1996). *What's happening in math class?, Volume 2: Reconstructing professional identities*. New York: Teachers College Press.

Schifter, D., & Simon, M. A. (1992). Assessing teachers' development of a constructivist view of mathematics learning. *Teaching and Teacher Education, 8*(2), 187–197.

About the Contributors

Virginia Bastable spent more than 20 years as a mathematics teacher in a public secondary school. She entered SummerMath for Teachers as a participant in 1986 and is currently directing the program, continuing to pursue her interest in mathematics education.

Raffaella Borasi received her Ph. D. in Mathematics Education from SUNY at Buffalo. She is an associate professor in the Warner Graduate School of Education and Human Development of the University of Rochester. Her research has focused on developing the implications of an inquiry approach to mathematics education and studying what happens when such an approach is implemented in a variety of instructional contexts.

Virginia M. Brown began her teaching career in 1970 and has taught third grade at Westhampton, MA Elementary School since that time. She became involved with the SummerMath for Teachers Program in 1987 and continues to participate in SummerMath courses.

Daniel Chazan is a Dow-Corning clinical assistant professor at Michigan State University and a senior researcher at the National Center for Research on Teacher Learning. To research mathematics teaching and learning, he has taught algebra at a local public high school. His interests include teaching mathematics by examining student ideas, using computers to support student exploration, and the potential of philosophy of mathematics for informing teaching that emphasizes such exploration.

Elizabeth Clark worked in special education during the time her children were growing up. After receiving an M. Ed. from Smith College, she began teaching second grade in Southampton, MA in 1988. She has taken advantage of many opportunities for involvement in SummerMath for Teachers projects since 1989.

Joan Ferrini-Mundy is a professor of Mathematics at the University of New Hampshire. She has been involved in a wide range of mathematics teacher education activities, including the SummerMath for Teachers program. She is interested in finding ways of portraying evidence of change and reform in mathematics education, and in understanding how students learn calculus.

Allen Gagnon has taught mathematics in Holyoke, MA public schools for

26 years. In the past few years, he has studied alternative teaching strategies. He is currently a staff member in the SummerMath for Teachers Program.

Anne M. Hendry began teaching in 1969. She has taught in Chicopee and Sudbury, MA and is presently teaching in a combination first- and second-grade class in Goshen, MA, where she has taught for the past 13 years. She has participated in SummerMath for Teachers since 1987.

Nina Koch teaches mathematics at the public high school in Amherst, MA. She is currently writing a piece of computer software, "TRANZ," which uses the context of transformational geometry to encourage high school students to think about arithmetic.

Jill Bodner Lester began her career as a teacher in 1969, left for seven years to raise her daughters, and returned to the classroom in 1978. She has taught first to sixth grades. Ms. Lester has been involved with SummerMath for Teachers since 1986, as a participant, as a staff member, and now as the program's assistant director. She is pursuing a doctorate in Mathematics Education.

Joanne Moynahan has taught sixth grade in Westhampton, MA public schools for 18 years. She received a B. S. Ed. from Westfield State College in 1963 and an M. Ed. from Lesley College in 1991. She has been a participant in SummerMath for Teachers since 1987.

Margaret Riddle began teaching in a remote community in northern Michigan after a brief career as a newspaper reporter. Since then she has taught students from age two through eighth grade in public and private schools. She recently completed a CAGS degree in Mathematics and Science Education, and she is a staff member with SummerMath for Teachers.

Donna Babski Scanlon has taught mathematics in Holyoke, MA public schools for 20 years. For the past two years she has been a teacher-leader in a statewide initiative to improve mathematics and science education. She is also an instructor in the SummerMath for Teachers Program.

Alissa Sheinbach taught elementary school for seven years, most recently in Shutesbury, MA. She is currently working part-time and staying at home with her two-year-old son. She was a participant in two SummerMath for Teachers courses.

Mary Signet has been an elementary teacher for more than 30 years. In 1969, after a five-year hiatus, she returned to teach in the Holyoke public schools, spending the next 20 years in first grade. In 1988, she became involved with SummerMath for Teachers and has worked as a mentor teacher for others participating in SummerMath.

Martin A. Simon is an associate professor of Mathematics Education at Penn State University. His research is on the development of prospective and current teachers of mathematics as they move from traditional to reform-oriented views of mathematics, learning, and teaching. He is a mathematics teacher educator, educational consultant, and former classroom teacher. From 1985 to 1988, he directed SummerMath for Teachers.

Susan B. Smith began teaching in 1972, later leaving for nine years to be home with her three children. In 1987 she returned to the classroom full-time. Susan first participated in SummerMath for Teachers in 1989. She is currently working on the four-year project, "Teaching to the Big Ideas," along with 35 other Massachusetts teachers who are researching the teaching and learning of mathematics.

Virginia Stimpson is a high school mathematics teacher and mathematics curriculum lead teacher in the Mercer Island School District. She has assisted districts in the Seattle area in gathering data on current practices. She has worked in the SummerMath and SummerMath for Teachers Programs and co-taught, with Dr. G. S. Monk, an NSF-funded program, "Teaching Mathematics for Conceptual Understanding," at the University of Washington. She has been co-researcher, with Dr. Jim Minstrell, on grants from NSF, NIE, and the McDonnell Foundation related to the teaching and learning of physics and mathematics.

ABOUT THE EDITOR

Deborah Schifter works with the Center for the Development of Teaching at the Education Development Center in Newton, MA and is currently directing a project called "Teaching to the Big Ideas." She began working with the SummerMath and SummerMath for Teachers Programs at Mount Holyoke College at their inception in 1982 and served as the director of SummerMath for Teachers from 1988 to 1993. She has also worked as an applied mathematician and has taught elementary-, secondary-, and college-level mathematics. She co-authored, with Catherine Twomey Fosnot, *Reconstructing Mathematics Education: Stories of Teachers Meeting the Challenge of Reform.*

Index